EDDIE REGORY

Wallace Park

THE COMPELLING COMING OF AGE STORY
OF LOVE, HOPE & FRIENDSHIP

Wallace Park

Eddie Regory

A division of Portland Dream Publishing
Wallace Park
Copyright 2012 by Eddie Regory

Cover Photo and Design © by Eddie Regory

Author Photo by Doyle McCranie

A special thanks to Ali McCart and Kristen Hall-Geisler
at Indigo Editing & Publications for doing an amazing job

This is a work of creative nonfiction. These are my
memories; I am the teller of my own story. Characters
have been combined and events have been condensed.
Certain episodes are imaginative recreations. To protect
the privacy of others, some names have been changed and
characters conflated.

Contact email: wallaceparkmemoir@yahoo.com
Follow Eddie Regory on Twitter: @superwriterboy

To my wife, Hazel,
daughter, Eliana,
son, Edmond,
and my family,
with love.

Wallace Park

Preface

Acknowledgments

I am more than grateful to everyone who supported me in the endeavor to bring this story out. They are my in-laws, Gladys and Doyle McCranie; my brothers, Joseph and Michael; and my sister, Anna Regory. I thank Betty Buffington and family for allowing me to express myself about her son and my best friend, Edmond Jerome. I thank Gerard Regory for giving me the brotherly advice and reasoning to continue my dream. And, finally, to my wife, Hazel; you are the light and love of my life; may you always know that every word and story I think up comes because of you.

Preface

Alberto rushed at me in the school hallway, pushing me and then punching me square in the face. I cried and ran down Essex Street to Uncle Carlito's and told him what had happened. He was furious, so he put a razor blade in his leather jacket, grabbed my hand, and said, "I'm gonna go kill me a bully! C'mon!"

Carlito pulled me briskly down the street back to the school. It was hard for me to keep up with Carlito's stride, but I was determined to see the look on Alberto's face. Uncle Carlito pushed open the classroom door. The teacher took a step back, and her voice cracked when she asked him to leave, but Carlito was determined to find the bully. I pointed him out.

These were everyday occurrences. The screams, shootings, noise, and bizarre behavior were part of everyday life in the projects. It infected us all, but our strength as a family kept us together.

Even though we were living on welfare in a roach-infested apartment, my mother believed in the future—someday we would live in a better place. But times were tough. More than once, my father took the meat from free lunches that kids threw away to provide us with a meal. My brother was once stabbed while saving my life.

My parents finally scraped together enough money to send us to a place called Portland, Oregon. It was a desperate attempt at a safe new life, but our sudden escape from the ghetto actually meant the beginning of the struggles I faced growing up in Portland.

Here, I write about failures, triumphs, and the changes we went through every day. I write how the loss of my mother at an early age and, years later, the loss of my father were put into perspective by the love and support of a childhood friend who would later become my wife.

6

This is a story of my internal fight to see my mother's dream for me come true; it details the stark contrast between surviving the ghetto and facing the challenge of starting a new life in an unknown place. It shows that, like a recovering alcoholic, a person who has lived with violence must forever fight to channel that violence into new tools for survival, and it chronicles the passion and frustration born of such a beginning. It shows that the dream for a better life can come true. I'm an average person, and my story is everybody's story.

Part One

Chapter 1

New York City—Lower East Manhattan

The horrifying scream became louder as I groggily awakened. I didn't know what was happening and was terrified to discover what these screams were. *Maybe it was a dream*, I thought, glancing over to my twin brother, Joey, who was still sleeping. I froze as the blanket covered my frightened body. The spineless hesitation I felt about climbing from my mattress, however, would soon diminish as I gradually slipped off the edge of the bed. I made my way toward the bedroom doorknob. As I inched closer, the screams reverberated off the apartment walls and grew disturbingly louder. I slowly creaked open the door and heard my mother begging, "No, Michael, no!"

I looked down at the floor and saw a line of blood drops leading toward the kitchen. Barely awake, I followed the puddled drops and saw my mother's little body moving from side to side as she extended her arms to block the front door so my brother Michael wouldn't get out.

"No, Michael! No. You don't need to do this."

"Mom, just move. Please!"

Mom begged in her accented English, "No, Michael! My God! Please, Michael, God, please!"

"Mom, please!"

Michael's forehead was masked with blood dripping profusely over his eyes and face. I had never witnessed this much blood and could not understand why it was happening.

"Please, Michael! Sit down. I'll clean your head, and it will all be forgotten."

"No, Mom. I can't!"

"You can, baby. You can," Mom said. "Please, sit down!"

"No, Mom! I'm gonna kill 'im!" Michael yelled before he dashed toward the kitchen drawer and grabbed a butcher knife, scattering the roaches off the utensils.

He yanked the kitchen window open, leaped out, and disappeared through the next window over, into the building hallway five stories up. Mom tried to stop him, but he was too strong.

I started to cry, mostly for my mom.

She prayed to God, "*Ay! Dios mío, Dios, por favor salva a mi hijo!*"

"Mom!" I cried, running toward her. "Mom! What happened?"

"Oh! *Dios mío!*" Mom prayed aloud.

"Mom? Where'd Michael go? What happened to Michael?"

"Oh, *Dios!* My baby!"

I pulled Mom's apron, even though it was spotted with blood, and said, "Mom, Mom, it's okay, it's okay—Michael will come back."

Mom's eyes were bloodshot as tears streamed down her cheeks, her body exhausted from worrying about Michael's fate. She struggled toward the kitchen table and sat there quietly. Confused, I stood beside her trying to soothe the pain she felt in her heart, stroking her long black hair with my shaky hand.

She rocked herself back and forth like you would a baby in your arms, and with her hands over her face, she uttered, "God will be with my Michael. God will watch him."

I later found out that a junkie in the hallway had stabbed Michael because he wouldn't give him the money in his pocket. I felt an angel was with us that dark morning; it took notice of our prayers, and Michael never found the junkie he was going to kill.

***

I was eleven years old when this happened, and I was the youngest of five, with Joey a few minutes older, and then it was Anna, Gerard, and Michael being the oldest. Fighting was all I seemed to learn in the ghetto. The idea of having a better life seemed like it was only true in those stories you read in magazines.

My mother prayed for a special place where someday she would free us of all this torment; she hoped to give us a life away from the projects. But that was a hope for a future I couldn't understand. This upbringing was my normal.

It was the year 1977, when owning a pair of black bell-bottom polyester pants and a pair of white-and-royal-blue, low-profile Pro-Keds sneakers would fit you in with the other kids. But designer clothing wasn't for Joey and me. Instead, Dad only got us what he could afford and would last the longest, including the second-hand shoes the kids called skippies and always made fun of.

It was a time when the New York City blackout happened and people were breaking into store windows and apartments. A time when Jack LaLanne was a television staple, as was using a 45 adapter with a worn-out disco single to play the Bee Gees or Captain & Tennille. The music echoed through the project hallways.

I recall taking long walks with Michael down to the Pickle Guys, passing my favorite toy store and wishing I had that new G.I. Joe in the window, or watching the neighborhood Pigeon Man feed the birds. Our favorite places to go was Coney Island or the World Trade Center. It was like Disneyland in the 'hood.

Parked Cadillacs rang out to the sound of "Another Star" by Stevie Wonder, and the indistinct noise of tapping heels and snapping thumbs resonated over the neighborhood benches. It was a time when homeboys sat on the benches playing congas and drinking Miller beer buried in brown paper sacks, making catcalls to the Spanish girls who passed by dressed in tight-fitting jeans and revealing shirts. A time when the seven of us would sit in front of the colorless TV in our two-bedroom apartment to watch *Kolchak: The Night Stalker*, *Welcome Back Kotter*, or my favorite, *The Six Million Dollar Man*, never missing an episode.

In my neighborhood, people thought of the projects as home. I thought of it as a sewer for criminals who lingered in unlit hallways, looking for someone to rob. It was common to catch a junkie shooting up heroin in the stench of his own piss, sitting on the stairwell with no hope for any future. A prostitute, or almost anyone, could be having sex anywhere. But in the midst of all this, for us, the projects were home.

It was a melting pot of people on welfare, including us, and simple existence was based on your survival instincts. Neighborhood winos, prostitutes, and junkies infested every crack of this jungle, and our trusted men in blue would simply drive by, making fun of their misfortune.

The night mornings were the worst. That was when we were asleep, and it was early enough in the morning to still be dark, and gunshots would echo between the buildings. We wouldn't know if a bullet would go through a wall and hit any of us. I would lie in bed frightened until daylight.

The Hell's Angels, who lived across the street, would keep that side of the block calm. It was like watching a mafia movie from my fifth-floor window, where the big guys would protect their turf and no one would mess with them, gaining respect by fear alone.

Where we lived at Twenty Avenue D, Apartment 5e, there were Hispanics, blacks, Jews, and even Italians. You might call it the United Nations Building, where everyone was on equal ground and no one had more than the other.

We never knew where our next meal might come from, and our apartment was crammed, but that didn't stop us from relying on the one trait that kept us together—love.

***

I dreaded school—you never knew what might happen. In the classrooms or the hallways, there would be a fight. Sometimes I'd cower away from it all so that I wouldn't get hurt, but pain always seemed to find me. It was particularly hard in the schoolyard. It was as if kids waited for recess just to go out and fight. The teachers had no control over this epidemic.

My disease, however, seemed to be with a young boy named Rocheet, a black skinny kid who often had pieces of leftover lunch poking out from between his crooked yellow teeth and a hair pick wedged into his baby afro. He loved to pick a fight with me. Rocheet hated me, people, and even birds because they were free.

Yet, I had a distorted respect for him, maybe because he would not quit a fight. Even if I mangled his face, Rocheet would still come back for more. I would rank him up with some of the greatest fighters, like Rocky

Marciano or Muhammad Ali, except he didn't fight fair and rather enjoyed using me as his punching bag.

Rocheet looked over with a smile as if he was happy to see me, but I knew he was only delighted about the hate that flowed through his veins toward me and the idea of gearing up for another fight.

"Eddie?" he said.

"Whatta you want?"

He gave a crazy snarl and said, "I feel like fighting."

"Rocheet, leave me alone."

"You got lucky last time, Eddie. This time, I'm gonna get lucky. C'mon!" he challenged, motioning me to come closer. "Let's dance."

"What's to prove today?" I said.

"No proof, Eddie. You just scared?"

My smile faded as I sensed the hatred in his voice, shaking my head in disbelief. "Rocheet, if you don't stop, I'm gonna kill you."

"Bring it, Spam boy!" he said, slumped down and awkwardly threw his fists up.

I glared with fury in my eyes, and then I danced toward him, grabbing his skinny neck and using my weight to force him to the ground.

"Ah!" Rocheet yelled.

"Had enough?" I shouted, squeezing the air from his body with my right arm wrapped tightly around his scrawny neck. "You had enough!"

"Let go! Let go," he pleaded. "Okay! I had enough! I had enough!"

As soon as I let go, he jumped to his feet and declared, "C'mon! Let's fight!"

"You gotta be kidding me," I replied, exasperated.

"C'mon!" he shouted, motioning me to come closer. "C'mon, white boy!"

Most Hispanics in our neighborhood were Puerto Ricans with dark complexions. I seemed to have the lightest skin of anyone, which gave reason for the neighborhood bullies to harass me.

I made a grumbling sound and lunged at him, grabbing his neck and pinning him to the ground like a wrestler. He plunged his fingers into my eyes as I repeatedly punched him in the face. I reached up and tore his hand down and out of my eyes before biting his fingers.

He squirmed out from under me and jumped into a Bruce Lee stance, brushing his thumb over his nose. He brought his head down and charged at me like a raging bull, knocking me backward into the ground.

"Ah! You bit my arm!" I yelled, knowing if I didn't do something to stop him, he would fight even dirtier. I leveraged my hands under his chest, and then with all my might, pushed him over, jamming my fingers into his eyes.

He begged me to stop, but I wouldn't. Now I was going to teach him a lesson. Then he got loose again. I tackled him to the ground and pounded his face. As Rocheet lay there protecting himself, an evil grin formed from his face.

Rocheet pleaded, "I quit! I quit!"

"You promise? Say you promise."

"I promise! I promise!"

I jumped off him once again, hoping it was over.

"I'm gonna kick your ass, Eddie."

I shouted, "Don't you ever give up?"

I rushed toward him as anger bubbled up from my stomach. He looked at me, eyes wide with shock. I tackled him to the ground as we fought like animals. A teacher rushed over and shouted, "Stop it! Stop it!" forcing her skinny arms between us as the blood from my arm trickled over her hands. I jumped to my feet, ready to go another round and moving in to hit him when the teacher snatched me by my arm and pulled me aside. "That's enough, Eddie."

"He started it!"

"I don't care who started what. I'm sick of you two fighting! Both of you, come with me."

Half running to keep up with her long strides, we followed the teacher into the principal's office. Bruised up, scraped, and tired from fighting, we sat there waiting for him to talk. My eyes peered intently at the gaunt solitary figure sitting in his stitched woven chair.

The principal hovered over his desk, flicking his pen, and finally said, "What is it with you boys?" The principal thought for a moment and then said, calmly, "Almost every day, Rocheet, you feel this need to fight Eddie. And Eddie, almost every day, instead of reporting him to one of the teachers, you indulge him in a fight. What am I supposed to do? I could expel you, but I don't think that would do any good. I tell you what I'm gonna do. I'm gonna suspend both of you for a day and speak with your parents."

"He started it!" I exclaimed, glaring at Rocheet, pointing my finger at him. "He always starts it!"

Rocheet snickered an evil laugh.

"Settle down!" the principal interjected. "I don't care who started it. You're both going home to cool off. Next time I see you, maybe you can get along. Now I want both of you to shake hands and promise you won't fight again."

At first Rocheet seemed hesitant, but he reached his arm out to me with his head partially down. Then, behind his black veil of silence, he smirked before extending his hand for me to shake. "Sorry," Rocheet said.

I was shocked but cautious. "Me too," I responded.

But Rocheet's peace gesture wasn't about repentance; it was just a stall until the next time we met on the playground.

Upon leaving the principal's office, I looked intently at Rocheet, noticing the holes in his shoes and the ragged secondhand clothes he wore. I began to feel sorry for the enemy who annoyed me every day of my life. I believed that somewhere in his heart, there was good, and maybe fighting was the one way he thought people would respect him.

Chapter 2

Crazy Lady

Entertainment came cheap in the neighborhood. If there wasn't a couple of wild Puerto Ricans climbing the outside window ledges to see who could reach the fourteenth floor first, somebody was throwing a mannequin from the rooftop and then yelling down into the crowd.

These were dysfunctional, idle-handed pastimes that people found positive. But my favorite entertainment was playing by the living room window with my Star Trek and Evel Knievel action figures or watching the show *Baretta*. Mom didn't like Joey and me playing outside much because she was constantly worried about what could happen.

It wasn't long before the circus act would bellow a horrid sound outside the living room window. I hurried over, gaping down into the street where a crowd of people gathered and the Hell's Angels kept their motorcycles. I spotted a heavy black lady who must've weighed at least three hundred pounds dancing half-naked through the crowd of heckling passersby in the middle of the street. She was singing and flailing her big flabby arms as if she were in the privacy of her own home.

A couple of guys sitting on the neighborhood bench were shouting profanity at her, laughing and

17

taunting to see more. I waited for the police to show and take her away, but it seemed like an eternity. Then I heard a deafening sound of sirens echo through the Lower Manhattan streets, screeching to a complete stop as cops rushed out of their cars in disbelief, quickly making their way through the barrage of people and grabbing the lady's flabby arms.

Our corpulent lady dancer then screamed, "Ah! Let me go! Rape! Rape! Somebody, help me! I'm a virgin! Please don't take me away!"

One cop exclaimed, "Lady, shut up! No one's gonna rape you."

"Please don't take my virginity away," she pleaded.

The cop had a disgusted look on his face and became impatient, forcefully saying, "Lady, I'm just going to cuff you, then take you in." Then to the other officers, "Damn, I can't cuff her from behind! Her arms are too big."

"Just put her in the car," another cop suggested.

They forced her in, but she kept pulling herself back out by grabbing the doorjamb.

The lady yelled, "Don't you put me in this hot box!" She screamed, "Diana! Diana! Diana!" referring to the singer Diana Ross.

"You crazy bitch!" the cop yelled, pulling his billy club out and pushing it into her rolls of fat to force her back into the police car.

"Police brutality!" the lady shouted. "Police brutality! Police brutality!"

People watched from their windows as the lady made a run for it. At least six cops tackled her. Kids in the area were laughing and rolling on the ground in tears. That's when a police van pulled beside the fat lady.

"I'll count to three," the cop said. "Then we're gonna have to inch her in."

The fat lady yelled, "Ain't there no justice? You hurtin' me! Ah! You piece o' white bread honky!"

"Lady, shut up! We haven't even moved you yet," the cop said. "Here we go, guys. On three. One, two, three. Li-ift!" They heaved, but progress was slow. "Hurry! Put her in the van!" he insisted with a strained look on his face.

"Why don't you make her get up and walk?" a bystander shouted with a sickened look.

The cops successfully shoved her into the police van, and the crowd cheered and clapped. The show was soon over, and as they drove away, the fat lady kept yelling and banging on the windows. I knew that in a few weeks, however, she would be back in the streets singing another tune by her favorite artist, Diana Ross.

To get away from this craziness, our family would gather around the sofa, a badly torn, overused centerpiece that brought us together near an antique Yamaha piano. I couldn't think of a better way to marry a family but with music. We would embrace my sister's voice singing while my brother Gerard played my favorite song, "Let It Be" by the Beatles. Joey and I would be playing Connect Four or Rock 'em Sock 'em Robots nearby.

Gerard's ability to play music brought a joy to the family that lifted us away from the daily grind, but these moments were cut short when he left. At first I thought he was going on a Christian tour to play music, but a few days turned into weeks, and then months. My sister, Anna, left to meet up with him, and I still didn't know why he left or when he'd come back. The idea of not seeing my siblings come back home didn't occur to me at first—we were family, and we were supposed to be together.

We often stood around the dining table draped with a flowery, heavy plastic cover, eating fried Spam, Spanish rice, and black beans. If it was live theater we wanted, then Michael could slip a sock over his hand and turn the evening into a Muppets show. In some way, we all possessed a special talent. We even tap danced randomly in the middle of the living room to the Dean Martin records Mom enjoyed.

My mother was the glue that held the family together and showed us the importance of love, always making certain that our stomachs were full, even if it meant she didn't eat. Despite her love, she was a temperamental woman, not to be messed with. Her authoritative, Catholic background and strong will commanded the respect that she so deserved.

Of course, like any brother with siblings, I had a favorite: Michael. I would mimic the way he'd lifted weights, grunting to the scratchy soundtrack of *West Side Story*, or running men's Brylcreem through my hair to recreate Michael's famous curl over my forehead.

Michael showed me how to be strong and unafraid. He told me not to walk away from a fight because if I did, I could find a knife plunged into the back of my spine. He wasn't part of any gang, nor was he a follower, yet he was respected as someone who believed in honor and who would confront the neighborhood trash with a baseball bat if they harmed anyone in our family.

I believe Michael's power came mostly from my father, a man who had many stories about the Korean War. Dad was also the hardest on Michael. Regardless of how difficult and sad my dad's life might've been, however, unlike other fathers in the neighborhood, my father never abandoned us.

***

I hated nothing more than being so scared of a bully that death became an option. Alberto was the evil I tried hard to avoid, but he looked like Godzilla with his rough face, short Brillo hair, and pitch-black damaged skin. He brought fear wherever he went.

I would always be alert and ready for a fight with anyone else, but with Alberto, I would try to get to class before he could see me. I've never seen a kid as mean and vicious as this one. His chin was tucked into his broad, muscular shoulders, and his gruesome face was a sight that not even a mother would admit to loving. Most kids at that school felt the same fear of Alberto as I did.

My efforts to conceal myself from him were to no avail when he saw me walking to class one day, though. He rushed toward me, raised his right hand, and pushed me backward by my face. The back of my head slammed against the school wall as all the other kids watched in terror. My books fell to the ground, and another kid kicked them down the hallway. I looked around, but there was no teacher I could call for help. Afterward, I was too embarrassed to go to class, so I rushed out of the school and ran to my Uncle Carlito's house on Essex Street.

When I got there, I hurried into the elevator, anxiously pressing the button to the fourteenth floor. "Carlito! Carlito!" I cried out, banging on his front door.

"What is it, Eddie? Whatta you doing outta school?"

"Alberto pushed me in the face!"

"Alberto? Who the hell is Alberto? Whatta you mean he pushed you in the face? Where is this kid?"

I replied, breathing with difficulty, "I was heading to class, and he just pushed my face against the wall!"

Carlito threw his leather jacket on, snatched a razor blade from the bathroom cabinet, and grabbed my hand. "C'mon. Let's go! I'm gonna go kill me a bully." Then he briskly walked me back to school.

When we arrived, Carlito walked in that school like he owned the building and everything in it. Carlito looked down at me and asked, "Where's Alberto's class?"

"This way," I anxiously said, guiding him down the hallway, targeting my finger at the classroom door.

Without hesitation, Carlito kicked it open and exclaimed, "Where the fuck is Alberto?" Then he carefully removed the sharp razor blade from the inside of his jacket and looked intently at every kid in the classroom.

The teacher, with a crack in her voice, politely said, "S-sir, you're going to have to leave."

He ignored her and focused his attention on the older kids. I could see Alberto's face swollen with fear and his body paralyzed at the back of the classroom, knowing there was little hope for his future.

I cringed but said, "There he is."

Alberto's eyes grew wide as Carlito approached him. Now he felt like I felt when he bullied me. As the other kids watched my uncle's massive frame slowly move past them, he kicked aside a chair and walked over to Alberto.

Carlito rested a heavy palm over Alberto's desk, bent over, gazed straight into Alberto's fearful eyes, and angrily said, "If you ever fuck with my nephew again, I'll kill you," holding the blade close to his rough face. "The next time, you die."

The teacher didn't say another word while this happened. Alberto, with his mouth partially open and his eyes wide, could barely nod.

Carlito walked back to me and said, "Let's go."

I grabbed his hand as we walked down the hall.

"Where's your classroom?"

"That way," I replied, pointing into the far distant hallway.

He walked me to the door, squatted to my level, and said, "Listen, if this Alberto kid messes with you again, you let me know. But I doubt he will."

Carlito was right. After that day, Alberto didn't even look at me in the school hallways—he had a new respect for my presence. When rumor got around about how he got scared straight, other kids started telling Alberto that if he bullied them, Carlito would find out.

***

The best times I recall were with my crazy friends Louie and Nanny. They lived beneath me and had the same street view, where we could clearly see the big black lady dance or the older kids hopping a ride on the back bumper of the city bus.

Louie was a skinny, toothless kid who had black, curly hair, a narrow face, and who laughed like a hyena. He was extremely entertaining. A total nutcase, some might say, who would do the craziest stunts. His favorite was to pee out his fourth-floor window over the bushes below. As I watched him do this, I could see Nanny riding his banana seat bicycle and cheering Louie on. Louie would then look up at me laughing and waiting for an expression of approval. He would even throw his toys out the window just to see them fall. Nanny was a pudgy, giggly kid who lived on the second floor and would often stop by our apartment for a free meal. He looked as if he came straight out of the funny papers.

My best friend, however, was named Carlton. He was undoubtedly the biggest eleven-year-old black kid I knew. He could eat almost a whole Big Mac in two bites, drink a milkshake like taking a shot of tequila, eat a side of extra-salted fries, and when he was all done, ask for seconds. Carlton was out of his element in the ghetto because he was kindhearted and giving, and he never used his size over anyone.

When we were bored, Louie, Nanny, and I would go spy on the flirtatious, husky Spanish lady on the fourth floor. Everyone said she was schizophrenic, but I didn't believe it. We'd often spy on her through her keyhole,

23

imagining she enjoyed the idea of us watching, spread out on her sofa with her top off. We racked up enough images for any kid to soak in for those late-night pastimes.

Louie had a talent for staying out of trouble, or maybe I should say he could talk his way out of a fight—defending himself wasn't his strong suit. Sometimes he would simply scream like a girl and run away.

Our dysfunctional friendship kept the three of us together. Nothing could hold us back from being who we were because doing risky pranks was considered a normal part of our lives on the Lower East Side.

One day we decided to pay a visit to our Spanish friend. I glanced over and whispered, "Hey, Louie, Nanny—look! Her door is cracked open."

"Let's go check it out," Nanny suggested.

We sneakily inched our way toward her front door.

I peeped through the keyhole and quietly said, "Damn! Look at those."

"Let me see!" Nanny whispered. "I wanna see."

She was slouched on a torn-up leather chair, watching television without even a bra. Louie chuckled and whispered, "Breasts," drawing the word out. "Push the door open, Eddie."

I was too scared. "You open it." I stepped away from the door.

"I'll do it," Nanny volunteered, giggling the whole time.

"Okay, do it!" Louie demanded.

Nanny hit the door open. We backed up, and the lady, with a shocked look on her face, covered her breasts and gave chase through the hallway after us. We laughed so hard we could barely breathe.

She ran after us as I swiftly pushed open the steel door to the fifth floor. Then Nanny jumped on her back and started to squeeze her breasts. I couldn't believe what he was doing as she yelled, "Pig! *Puerco! Estúpido! No me toques! No me toques!*" She spat and tried to get him off.

Nanny shouted, "Eddie! Run!"

As the lady struggled up the stairwell, I said, "Nanny! Get off her!"

"I can't," he stressed. "She's pulling my hair."

Finally Nanny let go and ran back down the stairs. With a piece of Nanny's hair in her hand, the Spanish lady chased after him. We followed behind as she frantically yelled, *"Puerco! Puerco!"*

Louie and I ran back up the stairs to the fifth floor, rolling on the dirty hallway floor laughing.

"Man, did you see her face?" Louie asked, still laughing.

"Yeah, I can't believe what Nanny did." I looked outside the hallway window to see if I could find him. Then we heard a door bang shut from the other side of the hallway. We headed over to find Nanny.

"Nanny? Where'd you go?" I asked. "How'd you get away?"

"Did you see me? Did you see what I did?"

"Yeah, I can't believe it," Louie said. "You're lucky she didn't get you."

I looked over to Louie and asked, "You think she'll tell my mom and dad?"

We went quiet for a moment before Nanny said, "Nah, she won't say nothin'."

"Man, if your dad finds out, he's gonna hit you hard," Louie simpered.

"Shut up, Louie!" I exclaimed. "Your dad's gonna beat you too."

"He's not gonna beat me like your dad does."

"You better take it back," I said, stepping toward him.

"Come on, guys, she won't say anything," Nanny said. "She's crazy. Everyone knows that. We can just say it never happened."

Louie looked over to Nanny and asked the one question that every eleven-year-old, perverted boy would die to know: "Hey, Nanny? How did it feel to touch them?"

Nanny stood up straight like a proud father holding his newborn and smugly replied, "Like a big Twinkie."

What better way to describe such a celebrated moment between friends? Louie and I could have only imagined it, but Nanny lived it for all the boys who dreamed of this moment.

Chapter 3

Welfare Sucks

I hated being poor and would lie that I was sick to get out of going to the welfare office. I'd even say I got food poisoning from Mom's cooking. That was fairly credible since we had to scrape together whatever we could for a meal.

But we had to be on welfare because there were seven of us on Dad's limited income. I once asked him why he took me to the welfare office with him, and he said it was because he wanted me to see how hard life was and to never take any opportunity for granted.

There were some people who went crazy with eagerness when it was time to pick up their checks, as if they would devour anyone who even thought of cutting in line. I wondered how so many people were out of work. In the summer, the welfare office would be so hot that you could even see the sweat drip off people's faces to the ground.

One day Dad and I waited in line and noticed an old lady bracing her body on her walker. Then she slowly fainted, her body falling toward the ground. Somewhere a black man exclaimed, "See what y'all did to this poor ol' lady? She fainted 'cause y'all take so long to give her a check."

Dad bent over and held the lady's arm. "Lady, you need some water?"

"I'm hot," she answered. "I need me my check."

"Hey!" Dad shouted, to a welfare clerk. "Can't you see the lady fainted here? It's too hot in this place, and you make us wait all day long. Why don't you just give her the check so she can go home?"

A manager came kneeling down to the lady's level. "Lady? Are you okay?"

Dad frowned. "Hey, bozo, of course she's not okay. You think she'd be laying on the ground because she's in good health?"

The manager glanced up at Dad with resentment. "Hey, buddy, I'm trying, okay?"

Shortly afterward, the ambulance came and the manager handed the lady her check. The same black man blurted, "Shit! If all I had to do was faint to get my check…. Shit."

Dad would say there was no dishonor in being poor but there was no honor in it either. The poor gave more because they shared what they didn't have, whereas the rich gave money because they had plenty.

He always tried to help those who had less. Sometimes he would bring food to Salvador—a quirky but close friend of the family. He was a quick-minded, amusing, and witty man. He had some extraordinary talents and a very strong, slender body. I used to think he worked in a circus because he could do a handstand and stay there for more than ten minutes. Salvador had a photographic memory, but he never took advantage of his talents. Like most people around the projects, he hung around the neighborhood benches drinking beer and talking shit.

What better way to pass time than to watch baseball? It was like a religion in our neighborhood, and if

I had a glove and bat in my hand, that was all I needed to feel like the next Reggie Jackson. Yet there was nothing more exhilarating than to watch Abraham, a sixteen-year-old who had a Babe Ruth swing like nobody's business. He was the only Jewish kid I knew in our building, and playing baseball was like breathing for him. Everyone in the neighborhood loved to watch him play. If anyone could make it out of the ghetto and into the pros, it would be Abraham. People would wait around the park benches with their beers in hand, egging for him to show up and hit a few out the park and over the PS-188 school roof.

If you couldn't afford a glove, then stickball or handball was the next game in line. All you needed was a good long stick and a Spalding ball, and most people had that. Or if not, a hard black handball would work. The handball was a favorite for people who simply wanted to play against a wall, but after a while, your hands would become numb from the constant slapping of that tiny black rock.

Summer was the best time for cool waters. That's when I'd grab a tin can from the cupboard and split open both sides so Nanny, Louie, and I could place it over the fire hydrant's stream of water rushing out from its opening. When you're a kid and it's hot out, that fire hydrant was heaven. Someone would open it wide enough for the spray to umbrella over every kid in the street. Ah yes…and then there was Hilia from the fourth floor. She was beautiful and would walk through the waters like an angel. The first time I fell in love was underneath one of those hydrants.

I'd guide the can over the hydrant outlet where the water pressure rushed out, creating a broad, heavy stream directed at the cars or crowd of kids running through the water. Kids would be wearing tank tops, no shoes, and jean shorts shredded at the ends. Some of them would be sitting inside the trunk of an old Chevrolet Impala, licking away at a Funny Face or Snowball ice cream.

In those moments, the neighborhood camaraderie grew as people had fun and left all their problems behind while listening to "Saturday in the Park" by Chicago blaring out an apartment window. Even dogs with no nametags ran into the water, barking and lapping their tongues into the spray. All the while, the beautiful Latin natives would dance with their friends and families. There was an old Dodge near the curbside lifted on steel box crates, where several guys would be working on a transmission while moving their feet to the music.

But the summer wouldn't be complete without the famous neighborhood *helado* stand. If you owned a snow cone cart, then that would gain you respect. This was the mark of a true businessman. Every kid, parent, and passerby would stop just to buy a snow cone. Even the Hell's Angels would stop by to slurp a cold, frosty, flavored icy. I was the proudest son in the projects because Dad had built a stand out of scraps. He would walk that cart everywhere. It didn't matter.

He knew what hard work and a hard life were about, and he had the scars to show for it, including an old bullet wound in his stomach from the war. But Dad had poor health due to years of smoking up to four packs of cigarettes a day and taking an occasional swig of religious liquor, as he called it. Despite these shortcomings, he was my giant, and I loved him.

One time Dad and Salvador were so consumed with making a sale, I snuck away to a nearby park to play on some swings. I saw a guy who looked about twenty years old. He crimped his eyebrows, walked up to me, and just out of nowhere demanded, "Get off the swing!"

I replied, "No."

Puffing his chest out, he clenched his hands into fists and punched me directly in the face.

I fell off the swing and blurted, "You asshole!" as I ran back to Dad's cart. Out of breath, my face in pain, I said, "Dad, Dad. This guy hit me."

"What?"

"Some guy hit me," I said, covering the hurt left side of my face.

Dad was surprised. He hadn't realized I'd left.

"Sal, go find this guy for me," he said in an authoritative voice. "I can't chase anyone down."

The guy who hit me started to walk in our direction.

"That's him!" I cringed but pointed him out.

"Hey! C'mere!" Salvador yelled at my attacker. "Hey! C'mere!"

"What?" the guy answered with an attitude. "Fuck you want?"

"Did you hit him?" Salvador motioned to me.

"What you wanna know for?" he answered, scowling and slowly backing away.

Salvador stepped toward the guy.

The guy warned, "Man, you betta step off 'less you wanna get hurt!"

Salvador went closer, and Dad followed.

"I said step off!" the guy shouted as he smashed Salvador dead on the right eye.

I couldn't believe this guy was on a punching spree.

"You punk kid!" Salvador shouted in disbelief.

The guy was quick and swiftly moved out of Salvador's range, dancing like a boxer in a ring.

Dad tried to catch up to both of them, saying, "Just hold the guy for me, Sal. Just grab a hold of him."

The guy yelled, "You losers!" He flipped us the middle finger then kicked Dad's cart over before he ran across the intersection, disappearing into the crowd.

"I can't believe that guy," Salvador said. "He hit me right in the eye."

"Goddamn kid!" Dad said. "Sal, you okay?"

"Yeah."

"I swear if I see him in the streets, I'm gonna run him down."

"Don't worry about it, Al."

"Let me grab some ice," Dad said, lifting his cart back up, scraping ice off the ice block, laying the shavings into a hand towel. "Here, put this over your eye."

Dad turned to me then. "Where'd you go, Eddie?"

"I just went to the park up there."

"How many times I gotta tell you not to take off without me knowing? When we get home, you're gonna be punished."

"It's not his fault, Al," Salvador said sympathetically. "Kid should be able to go to the park without somebody botherin' him."

"He shouldn't have taken off like that."

"Hey, if it ain't botherin' me, it shouldn't bother you. I mean, I'm the one with the black eye here."

Dad looked at me, then at Salvador, and said, "He was a fast son of a bitch, wasn't he?"

Salvador chuckled. "Too fast."

As we pushed the cart away, I asked, "Dad?"

"Yes, Eddie."

"Do you think someday I can own a snow cone cart?"

"You can do anything you put your mind to. Just don't smoke, take drugs, or drink, and always check your pockets when someone says hello to you."

"Why?"

"Because you can't trust anyone. Now let's go home."

Chapter 4

Face Off

Dad kicked his smoking and drinking habit but began eating more, which eventually put him at a high weight, disabling him from work. It put a burden on Michael to do everything for him. Eventually, his weight put him in the veterans hospital, and I only got to see him every other week. Since Gerard and Anna were gone, Michael now became the man of the house. He was prudent with every dollar that came in, and he came up with a so-called brilliant idea of allotting the number of toilet paper sheets we could use to stretch each roll.

I had more important concerns, like holding my own against anyone who'd challenge me to a fight. That's how I would gain the respect I wanted. But bullies like Angel, Frankie, and Edwin roamed the playgrounds like a pack of roaring lions crawling through a field of weeds for the next prey.

Angel and Frankie didn't bother me; they were just wannabes. Nanny's brother Edwin was the real trouble. He was fourteen years old and looked rugged. He sported a flattop haircut, a medium-sized steroid build, and knuckles the size of silver-plated nickels. He was one Puerto Rican demon that nobody dared to mess with.

Edwin always made fun of my weight, clothes, and shoes. I made certain not to make eye contact with

33

him, but one day I was outside playing with a Spalding ball by throwing it up against the building, trying to see if I could reach the fourteenth floor. Edwin was behind the iron bars beneath the second floor spray painting slogans with a can of orange paint on the brick wall.

I walked past the bars, keeping my eyes focused on the park. Suddenly, my legs felt heavy with each step and my breathing got shorter. I had this determined look on my face, like I was a king and was about to overcome my biggest fear: Edwin. A burst of bravery rushed through my veins, and I blurted, "Edwin's got a Juicy Fruit head."

I turned and saw Michael walking home from the gym. This brought another burst of courage, so I turned back in Edwin's direction and taunted, "Edwin's got a Juicy Fruit head, Juicy Fruit head."

This time, he treaded toward me, pushed his face against the inside bars, and vehemently said, "Shut the fuck up, white boy!"

I didn't care if I died or lived that day; I was ready to settle this once and for all. Edwin marched around the bars, focused his enraged eyes on my lesser-weighted body, and just stood there. I felt the Sampson in me could take on ten thousand Edwins, so I brought my arm way back behind my shoulder and dug my small-knuckled fist into his bulletproof face. His face felt like a rock, and my hand felt like melted butter.

"What the fu—?" Edwin exclaimed in disbelief, bleeding from his nose.

Then he pulled his arm back and clenched his fists so tight, I could see the white of his knuckles, and he punched my face until I was in total blackness. Still standing, I woke, looked at Edwin, saw my brother Michael, and almost cried. Yet pride wouldn't allow it because I was fighting for every kid who'd ever been humiliated and frightened by this evil spirit.

I shouted, "You asshole! I ain't scared of you!"

"What'd you say, trash?" Edwin shouted, clenching his fist again.

"You heard me! You won't break me today."

I saw Michael in the crowd that had gathered, and he calmly uttered, "Eddie, you know what you gotta do."

I took in a deep breath and blitzed the Goliath with all I had, seizing his muscular frame with my tiny arms, struggling to wrestle him down. He uttered a laugh and then tossed me like salad into the street. I jump to my feet and circled him. Edwin stood there confused but confident and unworried.

He lifted his right hand to his lips and then slowly licked his knuckles and announced, "You better make this good, white boy."

I continued to circle him like a gladiator in an arena, and then I charged him. He gave me a straight kick to my chest. I tried to get up, but the pain was unbearable. I began to wonder if I had taken on more than I could handle. I jumped to my feet and stood there waiting for Edwin's next move, but he shook his head like this was all a big waste of time.

I glanced at Michael and saw his arms folded. Meanwhile the crowd cheered, so I said, "What are you going to do, Edwin? You gonna come at me or what?"

"Are you serious? You want more of this, chubby boy? Look at you wearin' skippies. They cost a dollar ninety-nine and make your feet smell fine, bitch."

The kids in the crowd laughed.

Edwin snickered an evil laugh and then slowly moved toward me. I backed up several paces, moving from side to side. Michael stepped in and said, "Whoa, Edwin, you're bigger than my little brother."

"Your little brother was calling me names."

Michael gave me a stern look. "Is this true, Eddie?"

I kept silent.

35

"Well, is it?"

I lifted my chest, firmly pressed against Michael's body, and shouted, "Because I'm tired of him messing with me." Then I directed my anger at Edwin. "I'll take you on anywhere, anytime!"

Michael said, "Follow me, both of you," and brought us through a side door of the building. We could smell the urine and saw a wino squatting in the shadows of the stairwell as Michael led us up to the first floor where no one was around.

He paused and, with calmness in his voice, said, "You can both finish the fight here, like men."

I looked at Michael and then at Edwin and felt tears crawl down my sore face. Michael rested his hand on my shoulder and said, "Okay, okay. You don't have to fight, but you're gonna have to make friends."

"Why I gotta make friends?" I said, sniffling and wiping the tears from my eyes. "I'm not the one who messes with him all the time."

Edwin was expressionless as he stared down at me with his deep, shadowy eyes boring into the core of my soul.

Michael said, "Either you make friends, or I let you guys finish it off here."

That's when I reluctantly stretched my hand out. "Sorry I called you a Juicy Fruit head."

"Yeah," Edwin replied smugly.

"Now, Eddie, go upstairs while I talk to Edwin."

Embarrassed for crying, I unwillingly climbed the steps but then stopped on the next floor to listen to what Michael had to say. "I'm only going to say this once. I know Eddie can be stupid, but you're twice his size, so I'm going have to trust this won't happen again. If he messes with you, tell me, but I don't think he will. If my little brother comes home hurt on account of you doin' the pain,

I'll make it a point to get someone your age who will show you the same. Now, do we understand each other?"

"Yeah."

Michael picked up his gym bag and said, "Good."

That day my manhood was tested by courage I never knew I had, allowing me to face my fears in a different way. Michael came to me that night, handed me an early allowance of twenty-five cents, and said I deserved it.

***

After fourteen months in the VA Medical Center in Manhattan, Dad had lost most of his extra weight and was ready to come home. *It's the happiest day of my life*, I thought. *My giant is coming home.* When I stepped through the front entrance, I had this Disneyland feeling inside of me, excited and ready to see him. A man from transportation brought him down, and Joey, Michael, and I embraced him over his wheelchair. He had gone down to his original weight of 250 pounds.

I looked down at what Dad held in his hands and asked, "What's that?"

"It's a Bible, son. You've been saying your prayers?"

"I'm not very good at prayers."

"Push me to that window."

"Okay," I answered, excited about grabbing the handles to the back of his wheelchair as Joey and Michael followed.

Dad had this serene look on his face as we stared out at the patches of brown grass, listening to the muffled city noises.

"You know, Eddie, there was a time when your mom was very sick and almost died."

"She was?"

"None of us knew what was wrong with her."

"Dad," Michael interrupted. "You think you should be telling him that story now?"

Dad paused and continued, "You weren't born yet, and your brother Gerard was five years old. Your brother Michael and I were watching television one night, and Gerard walked into the bedroom where Mom rested. He saw a bright light shine through the window. Do you know what an angel is, Eddie?"

"A good person?"

"It's a gift to you from God, who watches over your every step in life. We couldn't put Mom in a hospital because we couldn't afford it. Well, that day something great happened."

"What?" I asked anxiously.

"An angel appeared and knelt in front of your mother and began to pray for her."

I asked, "For what?"

"For her to get well. He taught Gerard how to pray. The angel asked if he would like to learn and taught him. After that, the angel had Gerard leave and come back. Then the angel was gone."

"What happened next?"

"Well, the next day your mother was well again. Her sickness had passed."

"It did?"

Joey and I looked at Michael for confirmation to the story. He had the same honest look in his eyes.

"Would you like to learn how to pray, Eddie?"

"Yeah, Dad, I would."

We bowed our heads and Dad taught me the Our Father.

That evening we stepped outside into a blue, used '63 Chevy wagon. It was awesome seeing Dad work his new body into the car instead of struggling to get his old overweight body in and out of it. I worked my way toward the back window and thought about what Dad had taught me, as if what he'd said was massaging itself into my heart. For that moment, in some strange, indirect way, I felt changed. I leaned my head against the window and recited the prayer in my thoughts.

Dad pronounced, "I can now ride bikes with you guys. That's going to feel good."

Chapter 5

Payback

Every kid wanted to be a bad-ass Puerto Rican, including this tall, frail, strung-out dope dealer named Papo, who sported a hair pick wedged in his grimy, oversized afro. He wore pointed, tasseled brown shoes that could kick a man to death, a 1970s leather zippered vest, and checkered bell bottoms, and often had a toothpick near the corner of his mouth. Legend even had it that Papo once shot and killed a guy at point blank range.

I stood far from Papo because his body odor alone was foul. It could have been from the drugs or alcohol he consumed, but it didn't matter. I never stuck around long enough to find out. He'd stand in front of the building like a night watchman and barter food stamps for money or alcohol, or push drugs.

One afternoon I came home from school and saw him standing near the doorway of the building. He pulled a switchblade from his inside leather vest, flicked the blade out, and gave me a knife 101 course by brandishing and poising it over my face, where his black knuckles turned white. "See here, son. New York's a jungle, and only the strong survive. Whoever lives here, lives by the rules of this fuckin' hell. You know what this is? This here is power. You feel me, little man?"

I muttered, "I f-feel you," then darted up the five flights of stairs back home.

Papo and his partner, Polo, were constantly fishing for new meat to threaten. Polo had this creepy appearance—about five feet tall with curly, red hair and a long, narrow face with slightly gapped front teeth and a small cleft lip. He would beat on anyone for the sheer pleasure of having power over them.

Carlton and I stayed away from Papo and Polo, but it was like they possessed a check list of names they had to personally pursue. One day in the park in front of my building, we saw them heading in our direction with Polo on crutches. We didn't want to show we were afraid and decided to saunter toward them. We'd barely passed them when Polo stopped, shot Carlton a look of hatred, and blurted, "Whatta you lookin' at, nigger boy?"

Carlton's eyes grew wide, petrified. His body froze, and I knew it wasn't going to get better. Papo stood there laughing, and then he showed us the handle of a knife he had half tucked in his coat pocket.

Carlton submissively answered, "Nothin', Polo, nothin'."

Polo hobbled closer and angrily shouted, "Fuck you ain't, you big, black motherfucker!"

I wanted to strike Polo so hard I could feel his blood splatter over my hand. He suddenly lifted his left crutch above his head and hit Carlton over the face.

Carlton dropped his keys and begged, "Stop it, Polo! Stop!"

"I ain't stoppin' shit!" Polo shouted. "Don't tell me to stop, black boy!"

"Hit him," Papo encouraged. "Hit the nigger in the face again! Look at him go down!"

"Please stop, Polo! Stop! I'm sorry!"

I shook with fear and rage. Polo stopped, picked up Carlton's keys, and flung them over a bench into some bushes. An evil laugh echoed as they exited the park. I kneeled down and held Carlton in my arms, humiliated and disgusted with myself for not protecting my best friend. "Are you okay, Carlton?"

"Yeah, Eddie, I'm okay." He wiped tears from his eyes. "I'm okay."

I walked over to pick up Carlton's keys, and then I paused and held them tightly in my hand. Making my way back to him, I uttered, "We'll get 'em, Carlton. We'll get 'em. I promise you that."

I stood and helped him up, and we quietly sat there. My heart felt black, and all I could think about was vengeance as my blood boiled. What I wanted now was a gun.

***

Days later, the weather turned cold. Mom was in the kitchen cooking Spanish rice and beans with beef patties, my favorite.

"Mom? Can I go outside and play today?"

"No. I don't want you or your brother going out. It's dangerous."

"Please, Mom! I'm just gonna play catch with Nanny, and we'll be close to the building."

Mom could see the hope in my eyes and reluctantly replied, "*Bien*, only for an hour. And grab your coat." She reached into her apron to hand me some change for a soda. "Here, for your Coco Rico. Be careful and play close to the building." Then she leaned over and gave me a warm kiss on my cheek, sending me away.

I walked past the same iron bars where my first encounter with Edwin had been, and I ambled close to the neighborhood benches. I crossed the street, throwing a gum wrapper into the silver metal trashcan that was anchored to the ground near the Spanish Deli Grocery store.

Working my way inside and back to the cooler, I pulled out a can of Coco Rico and brought it to the counter. The clerk asked, "*Algo más?*"

"*No, soy bueno,*" I replied, anxious to step back outside with my soda in hand.

I sat on the back of one of the benches, sipping away, hoping and waiting to see Polo walk by. *This will be the day*, I thought. *I will kill Polo.*

It all became surreal as the minutes ticked by while I sat there knowing I was up against the clock before Mom would call me in. I glanced at the fifth-floor window near the grass side of my building and saw Mom peek out. Nervous, I set my soda down on the bench and shoved my hands into my warm coat pockets. The minutes seemed like hours. This time I didn't care if Polo had Papo with him, or if I got stabbed or even killed. I felt hatred surge through my body, and all I wanted was to taste Polo's blood in my hand, then spit on his body after I had pummeled him to the ground.

Gray clouds crept over the neighborhood, and I suddenly became hazy about the details between Polo and Carlton at the park that day. Maybe it was because I was about to face an unknown future, or maybe I was having fragmented thoughts of cowering back home.

Then I saw Polo's spotty, bright-red hair from the corner of my eye. He was walking with Papo in my direction, and I thought, *Is he going to say something or just walk past me?* My strength now became my fear. I refused to move and sat with fists clenched. I pressed my toes firmly against the seat of the bench, and the bubbling fear in my stomach surged into my throat. Fueled with high-octane hatred, I glared at Polo straight in the eyes as the two almost strutted past me. I could feel the corners of my mouth tighten.

Polo's deep, soulless eyes stared back, and for a moment, I thought I was ready for anything. Instead, I became paralyzed. My eyes dropped to the ground like a victim's, and I began to commit myself to a prayer for strength to face this tribulation. Then the will to kill seething in my heart was exceeded only by the nightmares of the day he'd humiliated Carlton.

"Get off my bench," Polo demanded while Papo laughed at me.

"Hey," Papo smirked. "This kid was with that nigger we jacked up."

That was all I needed to commit. My mind suddenly went blank. Not feeling nervous, I brought my head up above the clouds, fixed my eyes on Polo and Papo, and I confidently stated, "No, Polo. I'm not moving anywhere!"

He was shocked that I had stood up to him. I advanced toward him, bringing my arm past my shoulder and punching him right in the face.

Polo stepped back as blood gushed from his lip. He brought his hand to his wound, coating his fingers with a crimson red. "You're dead!" He lunged at me like a raging elephant protecting his young. We fought our way behind the bench onto the wet grass as a crowd moved toward us from the park, betting to see who would win as if we were roosters in a cockfight. I could hear shouts of "Fight! Fight! Fight!"

"Hey man, look at 'em fight! Goddamn!" one guy said.

"Go, Polo, go!" Polo's followers cheered on.

"Kick some ass!" the crowd shouted.

"I got money on Eddie," a guy in the crowd yelled.

This fight belonged to me, and I didn't want anyone to stop it. I wrapped my right arm tightly around

Polo's neck as we crashed toward the patchy brown grass, rolling over the fecal matter left behind by stray dogs.

"I'm gonna finish you!" I shouted. "I'm gonna kill you for hittin' Carlton. You're fuckin' dead! You hear me? I'm gonna kill you!"

"Ugh," Polo yelled. "Get off me! I'm gonna kill you!"

I was winning, and we both knew it. We separated, and I quickly scanned the crowd. Joey encouraged me, "C'mon, bro. C'mon, Eddie. You can win."

I focused my attention back on Polo in time to see him reach into his pocket. "Oh, God," I whispered.

He pulled out a pocketknife and slowly extended the blade. I then remembered what Dad once said: "If anyone should pull a blade out on you, son, your best defense would be to take off your coat and use that as a guard."

I didn't think it was possible, but I unzipped my coat and brought it in front of me, obstructing Polo's vision to my body. Suddenly, he put his head down and viciously charged into me, plunging his knife arm aggressively back and forth, hoping to stab me somewhere. I lost balance, and my knees buckled. I was terrified and thought, *Where's God?*

Right then, I felt a body struggle into the path of the moving knife. All I could see was the back of this person's childlike legs.

I heard an indescribable scream in a voice all too familiar and looked up to see that it was Joey who had been stabbed.

"Joey!" I shouted. "Joey! Joey!"

Blood streamed from his leg. I was about to help him when suddenly I felt this heavy weight crush onto my back.

"Ugh!" My face crashed face down into the muddy grass. I gasped for air and swiftly raised my head to see that Papo had jumped on me. I tried to get up, but he kicked me several times with his pointed shoes.

"You coward, Papo!" one guy shouted from an apartment window. "I'm gonna come down there and tear your balls out!"

Someone else yelled, "You sonsabitches. I'm gonna come down and jump on your back!" That man came down with a stickball bat, screaming louder, until he was stopped by someone else who said, "Don't do it, man. Cops are coming."

Then I saw an old fat woman waddling and swinging her cane in the air, threatening to strike Papo and Polo with it. I became aware that for once in my life, people in this hell's kitchen had a heart.

Commotion was everywhere and so were the sirens. Suddenly, police officers pushed through the crowd surrounding us, hands poised above their weapons.

"Knock it off!" a cop ordered, breaking up the fight and motioning Polo to retreat to a neutral spot. "You, stand over there."

"Man, I saw it all!" somebody said. "Kid with the red hair did the cuttin'."

I urgently asked, "Is my brother okay?"

"Eddie?" Joey cried.

"Joey," I said running to his side. "Joey, you okay?"

"I'm bleedin'."

"Hey! My brother's bleedin'!" I looked back at Joey. "I love you, Joe."

The cop rushed over. "Let's see," he said to his partner. "Radio an ambulance, then cuff the kid with the red hair."

Minutes later, Mom rushed out with her apron on, and Michael was fighting the crowd to get to Joey. It was total chaos but with an ending I wouldn't have any other way.

Chapter 6

Leaving the Neighborhood

It was a morning in October 1979. The windows were slightly frosted over, and the apartment felt bitterly cold since only one radiator heater was functioning. I could smell my mom's scent as she walked into our bedroom and quietly stepped toward me. She sat down on the edge of the bed and tenderly stroked my head with her soft hand. My eyes squinted as she said, "*Vamos en un viaje.*"

I asked curiously, slowly slipping off the edge of my bed, "A trip? *Donde la mamá?*"

"Where there's no pain, *bebé*. Portland, Oregon."

"What do you mean?" I asked dazedly. "What is Por-Portland, Mom?" I didn't know what she meant, but I was excited about going somewhere.

She stood up and said, "*Donde no hay dolor. Desayuno está en la mesa.*"

I knew when Mom said *breakfast*, she meant there was steaming Spanish farina, a hearty dish made of cream of wheat, sweetened condensed milk, vanilla extract, and—let me not forget—brown sugar and cinnamon.

I rocked Joey's sleepy body almost completely off the bed. "C'mon, Joey! Mom said we're going where there's no pain and she's got *comida* on the table. C'mon!"

We raced off the bed and pulled on the neatly stacked clothes Mom had left on the floor. I reached over to grab my shoes when Joey said, "Eddie, you're tying the shoe wrong."

"I always tie my shoes this way."

Joey said, "Can I wear your shoes today?"

"How come?"

"I just want to."

I untied the stained white laces and jerked the shoes off. "Here."

Joey happily replied, "Thanks."

We headed toward the door and walked into the kitchen just a few feet away. Mom, Dad, and Michael stood near the dining table, where a tall catholic candle was lit in the middle.

They were holding hands and praying—from what I could hear—that God watch over Joey and me and give us a safe trip. Joey and I sat down as Mom kissed us on our foreheads. I was so ready for farina that I began to salivate. Dad called it a poor man's breakfast, but I didn't care as long as it rested on my tongue and trickled down my throat.

After breakfast, Mom embraced us in her small arms and lovingly expressed, "*Te amo, bebé!*"

"I love you too, Mom." Then, "Are you okay, Mom?"

"*Sí, bebé, sí...*"

Mom had two suitcases ready at the front door, and then I saw tears in her eyes. *Why is she crying if we're only going on a trip?*

I reached my hand and softly wiped away the tears from her delicate face. "It's okay, Mom."

She grabbed her black peacoat and wrapped her silk scarf around her neck, finishing by tucking it tightly into her coat.

Dad softly expressed, "It's time to go."

49

Michael also gave Joey and me a long hug and said with a prevailing voice, "Stay tough, Eddie. And Joey, protect your brother. I love both of you very much."

Joey asked, "You coming, Mike?"

Michael's voice choked up. "No, I'm not."

It was the first time I'd ever seen him this vulnerable.

Dad opened the thick steel door that led us out to the hallway as Mom, Joey, and I followed behind toward the elevator. The neighborhood pranksters had taken the elevator door off its hinges again, so we walked down the semi-dark, smelly five flights of stairs, passing an old sleeping drunk on the way down. Mom draped her scarf over her face before she went outside. Then she held our hands and softly spoke, "My babies, I love you."

It was now about eight a.m. and just starting to get light. I noticed no hookers, pimps, or friends outside. The typical late-night drinking, loud disco music, street fighting, and arguing weren't what kept Avenue D awake now. Instead, it was the eerie feeling of the graffiti that ran across the bricks and the misty morning wind that carried the pollution through the streets over the cracked sidewalks. I remembered what Dad once said: "Only people can make a difference in the neighborhood."

Merchants were pulling open their heavy iron gates as we walked across the street to the car parked in front of the grocery store. I glanced at that same old metal garbage can I always passed when I purchased my soda. As soon as Dad unlocked the car, I squeezed my body into the back seat and felt something peaceful in me, as if this was the last time I would ever be afraid.

While Joey and I played in the back seat, I asked, "Dad, where are we going?"

"John F. Kennedy Airport. You're going to meet Gerard and Anna in Portland."

I asked eagerly, "Really Dad? We're gonna go see Gerard and Anna?"

"Yes. Now sit back and play with your brother."

As we neared the airport, Joey put his hands against the car window and animatedly expressed, "Wow, wow! Eddie, look!"

"I see—Mom, Dad? Are we going in one of those today?" I asked, staring at a Boeing 747 roaring through the breaking morning clouds, elevating higher into sky.

"Yes, you kids are," Dad answered, calmly laying his hand on mine.

"What about you?"

"No, just you and Joseph," he replied.

I didn't think about the neighborhood or my friends, about the fighting or drinking, the stabbings, the late-night shootings, the crazy people cursing in welfare lines, or even my last fight with Polo. I just thought about this place Mom and Dad called Portland, Oregon. By the looks of it, Joey was feeling the same. We waited in the lobby until the plane was ready to be boarded. Joey and I walked over to the big window looking out into the tarmac in astonishment, still watching these huge, winged chunks of metal take off into the quiet skies.

Joey whispered, "Man, how do they do that?"

While he was lost in amazement, Dad sat near Mom, comforting her. I stepped away from the window and sat next to her, gently holding her hand. "Are you okay, Mom?"

"*Sí, mí bebé, estoy bien,*" she answered, laying her hand ever so gently at the small of my neck.

We carried on this way for a couple of hours until our plane was ready to board. Mom embraced us with one long, last hug and softly said in Spanish, "My babies are going to begin a new life, thank God."

She cried as Joey and I waved down the corridor.

51

I love you were her last words before we left New York.

***

The stewardess guided us to our seats. I buckled in and set my hand on the window, hoping to see one last glimpse of Mom and Dad. Moments later, the plane started to taxi away from the terminal. It moved faster and faster on this long, stretched-out road in front of us. We were scared but excited too. I pulled my hand away from the window, inched it over to Joey's hand, and tightly held it.

"Are there any roaches where we're going?" Joey asked anxiously.

I knew he was scared of roaches. I couldn't help but smile. "No, flying fat water bugs!"

Joey replied, "No there's not."

"Mm-hmm," I said, in a convincing tone. "There is too."

"How do you know?" he asked.

"'Cause Dad said flying roaches are everywhere," I replied confidently. "Besides, if I see one, I'm gonna smash it with a hammer."

"Yeah, me too."

The plane increased its speed over the tarmac toward the skies, and I could feel my ears clog and my stomach tingling. I looked to Joey with my eyes wide and asked, "Can you feel it?"

"Feel what?"

"Nothing."

My face flush against the window as my breath fogged it up, I ran my finger though it, and watched other ghettos I never knew existed pass below us as the plane flew over the Hudson River, nearing the Statute of Liberty.

Then I felt a deep ache inside of me. *What about Carlton? I'll miss you, Carlton. I'll miss you.*

It was strange leaving our home. Except we weren't sad. We were happy, for something Mom and Dad called better was waiting for us, a promised land that they had worked hard for us to finally walk to.

Part Two

Chapter 7

Arriving in Portland, Oregon

The sooner my family left Avenue D, the better our lives would be. Gerard worked as a gas attendant by day and a baker by night—anything he could do to pay the bills and provide food.

When we stepped off the airplane and into Portland, the first thing I thought was, *If this is paradise, we have arrived.*

I felt like an alien on a new planet. The best part was, nothing reminded me of our neighborhood, except for the blue, junky Ford that Gerard and Anna met us with at the airport. All the green trees, unpolluted areas, and people with blond hair created an image I could not understand. They even said "good morning" and "hi" as if these people cared about us being here. It was surreal and untouchable.

I said curiously, looking at everything I passed as we exited the airport, "Wow! This is beautiful, Gerard. You guys were here waiting for us all this time."

He and Anna smiled at each other. Still in awe, we hurried into the car, and I anxiously rolled down the window.

"Everything is smaller," Joey said. "Is all of Portland like this, Gerard?"

"Pretty much, except for a few buildings downtown."

We drove over bridges and passed quiet, green, grassy neighborhoods. It all seemed like a dream, and after about a twenty-minute drive, they took us to an area called Northwest Portland on 23rd and Lovejoy. I thought, *I have landed in the middle of Mayberry.*

Gerard parked the car by a drugstore that sold comics across from this two-story Victorian building called the Katherine Apartments. After Gerard gave us some change, Joey and I walked into the store. I bought an issue each of *Incredible Hulk* and *Spiderman* and, of course, one soda pop.

We followed Gerard across the street into the Katherine Apartments, and a few feet ahead was a wide stairwell that twisted slightly toward the second floor. We proceeded up the stairs, and my nose inhaled fresh air instead of piss. There was no wino sitting in the stairwell shooting up heroin.

As Gerard led us down the hall to our new home, I noticed the other apartment doors weren't made of two-inch-thick steel like the doors in the projects. He unlocked the front door, and the first thing I saw were hardwood floors, which stretched out into the living room, unlike the old, torn linoleum we were used to.

To my left was a small, white gas stove. Above it was an oak shelf and a small collection of simple spices. We hurried into the living room and noticed four high, white walls and a large paned window with an outside balcony. We rushed toward it and pulled the painted window free, looking down at the other balconies. "Wow!" Joey blurted. "Anna, look! This is cool!"

"Yeah, this is cool!" I touched the balcony. "Gerard, can we go outside on it?"

"Yeah, go ahead."

I followed Joey out to the balcony overlooking a parking lot. There was a small building to our left and houses on our right. Instead of drug deals and fights in the streets, there were kids playing in the lot.

Later that evening, Anna, Joey, and I walked up a hill to a place called Washington Park. As we approached the entrance, there were uniquely shaped, pastel-colored, two-story homes across from each other, staggering toward the park's entrance. Then the road broke off and led into green gardens and a forest-like setting full of trees and assorted flowers. We sat on some nearby swings and gazed out into the city night lights downtown, seeing the tallest building in Portland and smaller ones scattered throughout.

I asked, "Are we on a mountain, Anna?"

She smiled and replied, "We're on the highest mountain in Portland, and we're safe here."

When we got back to the apartment, I stepped out onto the balcony again, and a peaceful mood swathed me. I recalled when Gerard and Anna had sung and played music near the piano. I looked up into the cold, dark sky, stared at the glimmering stars, and then slipped back into the living room to lie on my new bed on the floor.

My thoughts about this new life we were going to start became soothing. I didn't have to worry about getting stabbed while Mom watched out the fifth-floor window, and now Mom can sleep. *Now we can all sleep.*

***

Several days later, Anna took us to enroll at Chapman Junior High School. As we walked to our new school, I saw street signs that read Northwest Lovejoy, Kearney, Northrup, and Pettygrove Streets. We then saw something incredible: a massive field of green grass where kids played this game called soccer. I thought, *Where are the stickball and handball games at?* There were unscathed homes on both sides of the park, and the houses didn't look dirty or broken into. They didn't even have bars on them.

Joey asked, "Anna, what park is this?"

"Wallace," she answered, leading us to the front doors of the school.

There was no vandalism, cussing, smoking, drugs, or hallway fights. Kids were laughing and having fun as if they were happy to go to class. While I was signing up for sixth grade remedial courses at the front desk, people said "hello" and "good morning" to us, and by now I thought for sure I was in a dream. I checked my pockets too.

We didn't become popular overnight, and I was apprehensive about making new friends. I felt my identity was lost because the kids at Chapman looked different, wore different shoes and clothes, and even spoke differently.

The teachers also realized how behind we were in our education, so they kept us in special education courses for longer than I wanted. About the only part I hated was the label used for being in those classes. I really longed to be with the other smart kids and to not feel out of place. So I studied as hard as I could, even though at first, it felt like I wasn't getting anywhere.

English was my hardest subject. I did manage to do extremely well in math and to get into a more difficult science class, but I still felt behind. Not long before, I had been fighting just to stay alive, and now I was fighting to be smarter. I got involved in everything and even attended Outdoor School for one week. We learned how to survive in the woods and about insects, and we all made new friends. It was the best time I ever had. If Nanny, Louie, and Carlton had been there, they would never have believed it.

Chapter 8

My New Kicks

It was 1981 and I was about fourteen years old, entering into the eighth grade. I felt like I could climb a mountain. At the same time, I was relieved to have made it this far. It was the last year before high school, and to the sixth and seventh graders, we were considered gods.

Dad had finally come to Portland, but he had also gained some of his weight back. Gerard put the family up in a new two-bedroom basement apartment on Johnson Street in Northwest Portland, just a few blocks east of the Katherine Apartments.

This was a year after Mount Saint Helen's erupted. I remember that day in 1980—I woke and opened the kitchen window, which led out to a brick walkway up to the street level. There I saw a blanket of volcanic ash on cars, trees, sidewalks, and homes. The gray, flakey snow continued to trickle down from the barely lit sky, and I became frightened thinking that it might be the end of the world.

***

Michael stayed in New York and cared for Mom until it was time to send her. During that time, Joey had become friends with a guy named Jimmy, a white kid who had a thin build, frizzy blond hair, and a heckling laugh that made me laugh. I liked Jimmy because he was funny, outgoing, and poor like us. I soon realized that, unlike my old school in New York, Chapman was divided into two groups, soshies and scum kids.

I could easily tell the poor kids from the rich ones because the rich kids made a big deal about clothes with labels like Brittania jeans, Adidas shoes, and Izod shirts. The poor kids wore the opposite.

When Gerard would let us, Joey, Jimmy, and I would go see one of our favorite double features, *Grease* and *The Warriors* at the Esquire Theatre across from Jimmy's house on Kearney Street.

Joey later started his own club with Jimmy and some friends. They wore nylon shirts, greasy gel through their hair, green silky jackets, and silver letters naming the club *The Lords*. He'd started to branch off from me, which made me sad since our lives were once so close. I thought if I couldn't be a part of the club, then I would visit Jimmy at his house and listen to records whenever possible.

His house was considered affordable housing, but it wasn't like the old dingy project apartment we used to live in back in New York. Instead, it was an astounding two-story home with a second-story balcony made of treated cedar with a railing wrapped around it. Jimmy accepted us into his world as if we were family and because of this, we loved him.

***

No eighth-grade girl was interested in a sixth or seventh-grade boy, but that didn't stop me from trying to impress them. One day a girl with black hair and glittery, deep, dark eyes approached me at my locker. She was cute enough in her own little stuck-up way. I concealed the titles of my books with my arms so she wouldn't know I was taking special ed classes. I had no idea why she was walking toward me, but at the moment, I didn't care.

She gave me a once-over and casually said, "Eddie, if you want to be cool, buy a pair of Nikes."

I looked at my feet and hated the same cheap skippies I'd had when we left New York. Gerard and Anna couldn't afford to buy us shoes, so when the school found out, they set us up with a social worker. She was a nice lady who took me shopping at JC Penney. Joey went another time.

When I got some jeans and shirts, she asked, "Would you also like to glance at the shoes?"

I saw this as a prime opportunity to get the Nikes I'd been wanting. I felt the right shoes would definitely give me the edge I needed to get the girls interested. We went to the shoe department, and a sales lady approached me and asked, "Can I help you, young man?"

The social worker observed.

I politely replied, "Do-do you sell Nikes?"

She gladly answered, "Well, of course we do. Right over here," she pointed to the great wall of shoes, but I simply could not make a decision—nor did I know how to react to all this kindness.

I skimmed over the shoes against the wall and suddenly came across a pair of high-top Nike Blazer basketball shoes in pristine white with a black swoosh. I looked to the sales lady with confidence and declared, "These are the ones."

The social worker stepped over with a questioning look. "Thirty-five dollars?"

"Yeah, thirty-five dollars," I replied, afraid she might say no.

All I could think was how bad I wanted those shoes and that if I didn't get them, my world would be ruin. I was tired of cheap shoes, cheap clothes, and a cheap life, and I wanted, for once, to not look different.

She saw my face filled with hope and said, "Okay. We'll buy them."

"Cool! Thanks! Thanks a lot!"

When I went to school the next day in my new kicks, the same girl came up to me. "Eddie, you got a pair of Nikes."

I replied, in my cool Danny Zucco way, "Oh, yeah, baby, you know. You like 'em?"
When I asked her that question, deep down I was really asking if she liked me.

"Yeah, I do. They look nice," she answered and walked to class.

After that day, my confidence boosted way up above the skies, and I thought I was on the road to stardom.

The school gymnasium is where everyone gathered to have lunch. I would sit at a table with the other kids eating away at my cherry cobbler and chicken whatever, until I noticed the back of a girl's long black, shiny hair. I wondered, *Who is she?* Every day I passed her in the halls and during recess.

I later discovered she was Peruvian, her name was Hazel, and she had a twin sister named Tatiana. She'd walk quietly in her modest clothes and simple shoes to and from the school to where she lived, just blocks away on 27th and Upshur, in the Upshur Apartments complex.

In the middle of our part of town was a neighborhood community center called Friendly House. It was a sanctuary for idle-handed kids or trouble makers who needed a place to keep busy and play a game of foosball. The counselors were always there for us, showing a parental concern for anyone who needed encouragement. The best thing about Friendly House was they didn't see color, race, or the clothes we wore—they just saw potential in anyone who wanted to change. They would set up bike tours, host pool and foosball competitions, and have parties at the center just to bring about camaraderie between the kids in the neighborhood.

As much of an impact as Friendly House had on me, watching movies had a special place in my heart. They say that movies can move the spirit and change one's life. Well, there was no film that had more of an impact on me than *Rocky*. The day I sat in the old Esquire Theatre watching it made me feel like I was there, the underdog, and that nothing was impossible, even falling in love. When I went for a run, I would slip my old pair of cheap shoes on, grab a white towel, and tuck it around my neck into my holey gray sweatshirt just to be like Rocky.

I didn't have weights or a jump rope, so I would pretend and jump in place twisting my wrists for a straight two hours. Afterwards, I would shadowbox in front of a mirror or pretend I was lifting logs, randomly dropping down to the ground to do pushups, anything I could do to get my body in perfect shape.

***

Spring was near, and everyone was excited about soccer season. The Portland Timbers were playing a preseason homecoming game at the Civic Stadium near Burnside Street, across from Fred Meyer Grocery.

I didn't like the game much, but there was one girl I kept my eyes on, and I knew she would be at the game. Her name was Holli, and she was the most popular girl at Chapman. She had streaky brown hair, a light-brown complexion, and bold brown eyes with perfectly spaced freckles on her owl-shaped face. At the time she was dating a guy named Darrel, a skinny soccer player who wore Superstar Original Adidas and Polo shirts. I'd watch her gracefully walk past me in the school halls, but I was always afraid to look at her directly. To a poor kid who once lived in the ghetto, getting a crack at that gem was as unreachable as winning the lottery.

Then the school bell rang, and everyone came running out like the school building had just caught on fire. It was windy, and Holli was playing soccer at Wallace Park. Sitting on the benches behind the baseball chain-link backstop, with my arms resting on my knees, I watched the wind whisk blades of plush green grass as I intermittently looked over to her in the middle of the field. It was then that I saw Holli bloom like the spring flowers that surrounded her. Now I knew how Tony in *West Side Story* felt when he first saw Maria on the dance floor. All I could see was her petite figure gracefully gliding over the ball like a ballerina with wings.

I was taken away, and for the first time in my life, I wanted to be Tony the romantic and just dance with her. After they had finished playing, the team started to walk toward the dugout near their gym bags, close to where I was sitting.

My heart started to pound. Holli didn't stop for her gym bag and instead headed straight for me. I didn't know what to do and almost stood up and walked away, but I had Krazy Glue under my ass and couldn't move. Then words started to come from her mouth, but because I was so absorbed by her ravishing beauty, I didn't hear what she had said. My ears miraculously cleared themselves when I heard her say, "Eddie, if you could take me out, how would you do it?"

I didn't know how to respond—never in my wildest dreams had I thought she would ask that question.

I stammered, "We could...uh-uh-uh go to the...take a walk in the park."

She looked to her friend Mary, smiled and then left giggling. I felt like the park idiot. For the rest of the night, I hated myself for blowing my big chance. Being a romantic was my worst idea.

The next day, Holli's friend Mary approached me and said, "Eddie, Holli would like you to come over to her house."

For a second I felt like I needed a warm blanket and almost didn't have a tongue. I couldn't understand why she would consider the idea, but who was I to disappoint a goddess? As far as I was concerned, I was coming to save the day. If that meant going to Holli's house when she asked, then by God, that's what I was born to do.

I wasn't going to screw this one up, so I replied confidently, "Sure. Sure, no problem. When?"

I listened carefully as she revealed Holli's address. "So, can you remember that?" Mary asked in a snobbish tone.

"Yeah, cool, no problem. I got it. I'll be there."

"You know what time to be there?"

"Yeah, it's all good. Thanks."

The following weekend, I grabbed my new Nikes and the best clothes my money could buy, quickly slipped out the front door of my Johnson Street apartment, and jogged to Holli's house with butterflies in my stomach. I was so excited, the names along the street signs became a blurry vision. Then I got to Chapman School and continued past Friendly House toward the Upshur Apartments. That's where I stumbled across Hazel outside with her sister, talking to friends.

I stopped and said hi.

She replied, "Oh, hi. What are you doing here?"

"Oh, um, I'm just heading up to Holli's house. You know her, right?"

Hazel replied, "Oh, yeah, I know her. Everybody knows her."

"I see. Well, I gotta be going, okay."

Hazel replied, "Okay. Bye."

I jogged past cars and old houses fixed along the streets and then glanced back at Hazel, not reflecting too much on our encounter. After passing the Montgomery Ward store, I turned onto Northwest Vaughn Street and made my way up a long hill. I glanced to my right and saw the gravel driveway leading into a wooded area that Holli's friend Mary had described to me.

My excited feet caught a slide down the gravel hill, but I quickly rebalanced myself. Then I casually headed for her front door, noticing Holli's backyard looked over a picturesque forestry setting. I became nervous, but I was happy that this was actually happening, so I focused my attention on her front door. I took in a deep breath and quietly muttered, "You can do this Eddie," and knocked politely.

"Eddie? Hi!" Holli opened the door and let me in.

I stepped in and noticed her kitchen to the right with pots dangling from a rack over a white tiled bar decorated with Italian olive oil bottles. A small oak table stood to the left with a colorful ceramic bowl of fruit in the center of it.

She asked, "Was it hard to find?"

"Not really. It's kind of a cool place you have here."

"Thanks."

We sat at the table facing each other, and I couldn't help but notice how warm this quaint kitchen made me feel.

She scanned over the bowl of fruit. "Would you like an apple and a Coke?"

"Yeah. That's cool. Thanks."

"Here, it's a Fred Meyer apple." She smiled warmly. Her freckles sparkled like stars in the night, and I couldn't take my eyes away, not even for a moment.

"Looks good. Are Fred Meyer apples better?" I asked, setting it on the table.

"I like 'em." Holli poured Coke into a glass and handed it to me. "Here."

For a moment, we sat there and gazed at each other, not saying a word.

I asked, "So, how do you like Chapman?"

"It's okay. I mean, I can't wait for high school."

"Yeah, me too, being a freshman's gonna be weird."

Holli asked, "Why?"

"I don't know, 'cause it's kind of a big step."

"Do you like records?" she asked.

"Yeah. Whatta you have?"

"Do you like the movie *Fame*?"

"Heard it was good, why?"

"I've got the album. I'll put it on."

"Okay."

She slipped the record over the player and set the needle on the song by Irene Cara, "Out Here on My Own."

That brief conversation over a Coke was the beginning of my first relationship, but in the back of my mind, I wondered, *What about her boyfriend, Darrel?*

***

At school Holli would stop to say hello, and our small talk would be short and lovely. Whenever possible, I'd sit near the sidelines and watch her play soccer with poise and commitment, and I became mesmerized by how she would tuck her hand under her hair and behind her ear. She carried the soccer ball like a swan over still waters.

Word quickly got around that I was dating the most popular girl in the school. *Me*, I thought, *a ghetto boy from the Lower East Side who once had nothing, is now on top of the world.*

For the remainder of the school year, Holli and I grew closer. I had also become good friends with Hazel. One day Holli and I stopped at her house on the way to Wallace Park. I knocked on door number sixteen. When she opened it, she was clearly surprised to see us, but she invited us in. "Hazel, this is Holli."

Soon after, I took out a can of Copenhagen snuff that a Cuban kid named Tom had given me at school. I really didn't know what it was, but he'd explained how to use it. I looked at Holli standing near the kitchen counter as I pulled the lid. She asked curiously, "What's that?"

"I got it from a guy I met at school. It's called chew."

"Chew?" she said, pinching her nose and stepping away theatrically. "Oh, it stinks! I can smell it from here!"

Hazel watched us from the kitchen. I tucked the can back into my pocket when Holli blurted, "Let me try that!"

"Really? Try this?"

"Yeah, try that."

"Okay, but don't get mad if you get sick," I said, pulling the can out from my back pocket, carefully lifting the lid again.

She stepped away, pinched her nose, and exclaimed, "Oh, my God! That stuff does really stink!"

"Well, are you gonna try it?" I asked Holli. Holding the can close to Hazel's nose, I asked her, "Do you think this smells?"

"No, it doesn't smell," she replied quietly.

"See? Hazel doesn't think it smells. Try it!" I insisted in a cool manner.

Holli hesitated but walked toward me. "Well, okay. Just a little, though."

She amateurishly dug her fingers into the can and said, "It feels mushy," but she proceeded to put a pinch in her bottom lip. A look of disgust crossed her face.

"What's up? Is it okay?"

Her eyes went watery as she grabbed her chin and mumbled, "No."

I chuckled, then grabbed the can and said, "Let me show you."

I dug two fingers into it, making it seem like I had years of experience, and placed a large dollop in my bottom lip. I desperately tried not to show my weakness to the dreadful taste of the tobacco. It slushed and circulated in my mouth. Holding my stomach I said, "Oh, man. I think I'm gonna get sick."

Holli said, "Me too." She spit the chew on Hazel's gray carpet, nauseated and announced, "Oh, oh, I feel like throwing up. Gotta go!"

"Wait," I said. "Let's go outside."

She grew woozy, so I held her arm and helped her outside of Hazel's front door and down some chipped concrete steps. As we began to walk away, Holli abruptly bent over and vomited over her shoes on the street.

"Holli," I asked, "you okay?"

"No. Just get me home."

Once again I glanced back at Hazel and saw her quietly standing there. I wondered what she might be thinking about me this time.

Chapter 9

Couch Park

The hot sun was blazing on my exhausted body as I jogged through the streets of Northwest Portland in my new Etonic running shoes. I grabbed the white cotton towel wrapped around my neck and wiped the beads of sweat from my face. My legs drove me to a place called Couch Park on Northwest 19th Avenue and Glisan in the Alphabet District. Since Moving to Portland, I had learned that *Couch* is pronounced not like the piece of furniture but as "cooch," after early Portland developer Captain Couch.

That morning, I hurried to a water fountain adjacent to the bathroom on the east side of the park and drank more than I should have. Still resting, I looked at the play structure in the center of the park. It was made of treated wood, and the higher level had slanted sides with a steep roof made of composite shingles, like a birdhouse. It also had a long metal slide that reached to the bottom of the heavily bedded bark dust. Any time we had the chance Joey, Jimmy and I would go play tag on it and jump off the very highest part of the structure, which was about ten feet up. After those games of tag, we'd go swimming at the Couch school pool adjacent to the basketball court.

The fantastic thing about the school was an old man named Dean, who checked in kids to play in the pool and supervised a weight gym. He was a soft-spoken, fairly tall, heavy-set man who wore thick glasses and had little hair on his head. He was always polite and encouraging to all the kids who came by, as if he believed we could accomplish anything if we put our minds to it. He even had his own achievement board for people who set records for the most sit-ups, chin-ups, push-ups, laps in the pool, or dumbbell curls—anything he could think of to build up our self-esteem.

Nothing was better than being the person who did the most sit-ups, and Jimmy was the all-time champion at that. When I looked at the board and saw "one thousand sit-ups for Jimmy Duncan," I ran over to old man Dean and exclaimed, "Wow! Did he really do this?"

He proudly replied, "He sure did. I sat here and counted every sit-up."

"You think I could do the same?"

"C'mon. I'll hold your feet and count. You can stop any time you want, and this will give you the practice you need to build up to a thousand."

I replied, ready and up to the challenge, "All right!"

I did just three hundred—not even close to Jimmy's record. I had to know how Jimmy was able to do so many. When I asked, he theatrically replied, "Yeah, I did it. But my butt was raw." I decided the glory of the record wasn't enough to have a raw butt, so I stopped trying.

At the park, I finished drinking from the fountain and then ran back up toward the basketball courts when I saw a guy shooting free throws. I approached him and picked up a nearby basketball.

"What's up? My name's Eddie," I said, bouncing the ball.

"My name's Eddie too," he replied, somewhat surprised.

We chuckled.

"Wanna play a game of hoop, Eddie?" I asked.

"Just call me Ed," he insisted politely.

"Okay, c'mon, Ed," I said, dribbling the ball toward the free-throw line. "Hey," I called at two guys playing a game of Horse on the other side. "You wanna play two-on-two?"

They looked at each other and nodded.

Ed asked, "Should I call you Ed?"

"Just call me Eddie," I replied, shooting a layup.

"Okay, Eddie, nice to meet you."

"Yeah! Me too, Ed."

"Yo, winners out, right?" I asked the challengers.

"Yeah, that's cool," challenger one replied.

"Ed, you shoot the die, see who gets the ball first."

"Okay," he replied, dribbling the ball to the free-throw line and taking the shot.

I dashed out for a pass. "Our ball! Ed! Right here, man. I'm open!"

Ed passed it, but the guy behind me stole it, cleared it at the second line, and shot a two-pointer.

"It's all right, man," I reassured Ed. "We'll get 'em."

"Winners out, right?" the guy asked.

"Yeah," Ed answered.

"Let's defend these guys," I said, slapping Ed a low five.

"Ball in," Ed said, handing challenger one back the basketball to resume the game.

Challenger one passed it under his leg to his partner, who shot the ball but missed the rim. Ed rebounded and passed it back to me. I jump shot the ball from the free-throw line—*swish* through the net.

"Yeah!" Ed exclaimed. "That's one for the good guys."

It was two to one, their lead.

"Ball in," I said, passing it to Ed.

Ed quickly worked his way outside the free-throw line. He passed it to me, and I maneuvered between the challengers, faked a shot, and passed to Ed, who jump shot it.

"Good shot," I praised. "That was butta!"

"Two to two, tied," Ed declared, as he proceeded toward the free-throw line for another check.

He passed it in to me, and the guy stole it.

"Damn!" I muttered with my arms extended, defending him as close as I could.

The guy quickly dribbled the ball around me, jumped in the air, and shot a layup, leading the ball with his left hand. We played hard like that for two games. They won one, and we won the other.

After the games, Ed and I headed down the steps toward the shelter and sat down to eat free peanut butter and jelly sandwiches funded by the park. There were also arts and crafts supplies out for the kids. Our favorite thing to make was Gimp, which was made of colored plastic string. We'd braid three color-coded strings at a time to make keychains.

"Man, we could've crushed those guys," I said. "Can you believe that scrappy dude shooting the ball from under his leg? What the hell was that?"

"I don't know," Ed replied, shaking his head. "It was ugly, though."

"Yeah it was," I said. "He wasn't even looking at the rim."

"No way," Ed said, biting into his sandwich.

"You're pretty good," I said. "Where'd you learn how to play?"

"I'm not very good," he replied modestly.

"Man, you were kickin' it out there."

Ed smiled. "You're pretty quick."

"Think so?"

"Yeah, you're quicker than me."

"But you got the outside shot," I said. "Wish I had that."

"That comes with practice," Ed said. "You come here a lot?"

"Not really, just when I get a chance."

Ed asked, "I've never seen you here before. You go to school here?"

"I go to Chapman."

"I go to Lincoln." He asked, "How do you like Chapman?"

"It's cool. Lotta rich kids, though."

"Same at Lincoln," Ed stood up and motioned for me to follow. "Wanna come over to my house?"

"Sure!"

After eating, we walked a few blocks west of the park to a pink apartment building called the Villa Florence on Northwest 22nd and Glisan Street.

"Come on in and meet my mom," Ed insisted in a friendly manner.

I followed and saw a lady about five-feet-six with brownish hair, brown eyes, and a welcoming smile.

She greeted us in a soft-spoken voice, "Well, hello, my name is Betty. We have two Eddies in the house now."

His room was so organized, I wondered if he cleaned it himself or had his mom do it. He had a picture of Clint Eastwood above his bed and a poster of a unicorn beside it.

"That's a cool photo," I said, walking closer to it. "What movie is this from?"

"*The Good, the Bad and the Ugly*," he answered proudly.

"I've never seen a horse like that. What kind is it?"

Ed replied, "It's a unicorn."

"Hmm…what does it mean?"

"Means healing and wisdom, self-knowledge, and eternal life."

"Man, that's a lot of meaning for just one horse."

Ed chuckled. "Yeah, I know, but I like it. I've always liked unicorns."

I asked, "You clean your own room?"

"Nah, man. My mom does it."

"That's cool," I said, "My mom did mine too."

"What do you mean *did*?"

"Oh, she's in New York right now, but she's coming down to Portland."

We stayed in his room and talked for hours about everything: girls, sports, school, and what we were going to do the next day. I soon realized Ed had the same interests and goals as I did, like exercising and going to movies. But we especially loved running. Ed was seventeen years old, three years older than me, but the age difference was no barrier to an evolving friendship I felt was going to last forever. I was thankful to finally have someone I could call a close friend. I hadn't felt this way since I'd left Carlton behind in New York.

***

Before the eighth-grade graduation dance at Chapman, a girl named Debby from our school decided to have a party at her house. Debby had a great personality, and I thought she fit in more with the guys than the girls. She wore All Star Converse shoes and had shimmering blond hair. In fact, I would say she wasn't a stereotypical rich girl but was instead somewhat rugged and real. Debby's mother was on a business trip, so it was a perfect opportunity for a party.

On the day of the party, Ed and I walked up to Debby's expensive-looking home. It was like walking up to a mansion, and her backyard like a forest.

One of Debby's good friends, Sarah, answered the door. "Eddie!" Sarah called. "Debby, Eddie's here," she called inside and then turned back to us. "Who's your friend?"

"Yo, this is my brother," I said. "Ed, this is Sarah."

"Hi, Ed!" Sarah asked, "Is he really your brother?"

"Yeah, he's my brother. Don't we look alike?"

Debby hurried up from the basement and said, "Party's downstairs, guys."

We followed them down a windy stairwell into a recreation room. To the right was a foosball table and a dart board on the wall behind it. I loved foosball and had almost become champion at Friendly House.

"Man, where'd they get all the alcohol?" Ed asked.

"I don't know, man, and I don't care. I'm gonna go crush someone in some foosball, c'mon."

As we played against two girls, Sarah walked downstairs holding a bottle of wine in one hand and a can of beer in the other.

"Sarah," I called. "You think that's enough booze?" I asked sarcastically.

Between sipping the wine and taking gulps of the beer, she slurred, "I'm just get-getting started."

Soon after, people were slurring their words and walking sloppy. Ed and I smiled as we watched everyone drinking and making fools of themselves. After about two hours, the party was out of control, and one guy mistakenly shattered the glass to the liquor cabinet. Some of the party moved upstairs.

Suddenly, Debby darted down the steps. "Eddie, come upstairs, quick!"

"Yo, Debby, what's up?"

She darted toward me and whispered.

I backed up and exclaimed, "What?"

"What's up?" Ed asked, restlessly waiting for an answer.

"Man, you're not going to believe this."

"What? What?"

"C'mon, bro. Follow me!"

We rushed upstairs and noticed some girls surrounding the bathroom door. In the center of the crowd, Holli held her hands to her face and repeated, "Oh, my God! Oh, my God!"

"Holli, I didn't know you were here," I said. "When did you get here?"

"Eddie." She turned toward me. "We tried to help her, but we couldn't get her out of there."

Ed looked at Holli. "Looks like you saw a ghost."

"Worse," she replied, walking away from the bathroom door.

I was forcing my way through the throng of girls when Debby grabbed me. "Just be ready."

"It can't be that bad." I cracked the door open. "Holy crap! What do you expect me to do with that?"

"We don't know," a girl cried.

"What the hell is going on, man?" Ed wanted to know. "Tell me."

"Ed, I'm gonna need your help."

"With what?"

I cracked the door and showed him. "With this!"

"Holy crap!" Ed cried, backing away.

"That's what I'm saying, man," I said, quickly shutting the door.

Sarah had drunk that whole bottle of wine and topped it off with that can of beer. She was sitting on the toilet, holding her stomach as she groaned in pain. We didn't know what to do.

Debby suggested, "She needs air. We'll clean her up, and you guys can take her outside in the backyard."

77

I looked to Ed and said, "Man, I'm glad I don't drink that poison."

"Yeah, me too."

We then heard a loud knock on the front door.

My first thought was, *Maybe a friend of Debby's showed up late*, but then Debby asked, "Who's that?"

She walked briskly to the door, looked through the peephole, and exclaimed, "Oh my God!" Frantically running back to us, she said, "Sarah's mom is here!"

"What?" Holli exclaimed. "No way!"

"Sarah's mom is here. She's at the front door." Debby asked, "What am I going to do?"

She knocked again, and everyone panicked, dashing to find a place to hide or even leave the house.

"What are we going to do?" one girl asked.

"Take Sarah outside, now!" Debby demanded, pacing around, trying to think of a quick fix.

"Okay," I volunteered. "We'll take her out, but you gotta buy us some time."

Before they could pull Sarah out from the bathroom, Ed and I lifted Sarah and hurried for the backyard while Debby hurried to answer the door.

Minutes later, we heard Mrs. Lorish yelling for Sarah. A girl from the party came running outside and shouted, "Sarah's mom is coming!"

Mrs. Lorish didn't believe Debby's story that her mom was at the store and had pushed past Debby to see the empty beer cans littered around the room.

"Damn!" I said. "Ed, help me bring her down the hill."

At the bottom of the hill stood a cyclone fence, which stopped us from going any farther. Sarah was still groaning in pain, so in desperation, I looked over to Ed and said, "Let's throw her over the fence!"

"What? Are you crazy! She'll be torn apart."

"Well, whatta we gonna do?"

"Throw leaves over her," Ed suggested, picking the leaves up off the ground and quickly spreading them over Sarah's body. "C'mon! Help me!"

"Man, you just gonna leave her here?"

"Well, you were gonna throw her over the fence," Ed said. "Don't you think this is a better idea?"

"Okay, okay."

After coating Sarah's body with the wet, dirty leaves, we ran from the scene. Mrs. Lorish made her way across the backyard, still yelling Sarah's name. She then noticed some feet at the bottom of the hill, ran to see whose they were, and frantically brushed the leaves off of Sarah's body.

"Mrs. Lorish, it's not what you think," Debby said. "She just had a little too much to drink."

They helped her to the car before Mrs. Lorish told Debby, "Your mother will hear of this." She rushed Sarah to the hospital.

Chapter 10

Breakup

Weeks after the party, Holli called me to come over to her house. I rushed over on my new ten-speed bike I'd put together with parts I'd purchased from Northwest Bicycles on Glisan Street. I jumped off my bike, dropped it on her porch steps, and hurried to the front door.

She said, "Hi, come in."

I sensed she had something important to say and asked, "Is everything okay?"

"Yes. Everything's okay." She seemed nervous yet relieved that I was there.

I gently reached my hand over to hers. "Is there something you want to tell me?"

"Kind of."

We sat on her sofa listening to the scratchy sounds of old records when she turned to me and whispered, "I want to talk to you, Eddie."

"Okay. I-I'm right here."

She showed me out to the front porch steps. "Sit over here. Eddie, do you love me?"

"Yeah, but why do you ask?"

She whispered softly, "How do you want me?"

"I always want you, Holli. You're in my thoughts, forever."

"Do you love me?" she asked again.

I paused and, with all the affection I could give, vowed, "I love you so much that it kills me inside."

"Eddie, have you ever been with a girl?"

In bewilderment, my mouth dropped partially open. "I-I think so."

"Do you want to try, with…with me?"

My insides warmed, and I replied softly, "I'm not sure what you mean, but I…I think do."

She said, "I know you're the one, the one for me."

"I am?"

She said, "Eddie, I want you to be my first, and I want to be yours. I want you to have me."

"Okay, so, what do we do now?"

"Do you have any protection?"

"Pro-wha'?"

"There called condoms, Eddie."

"No, no I don't. What are they?"

"It's protection, just in case."

"Well, yeah…yeah, I sort of know, but I really don't know how to get them." I hesitantly asked, "How do I get them?"

"Go to Fred Meyer. They have them."

I asked, "How?"

"Just get on your bike and get them," Holli said firmly. "You can do it."

"Man, I don't know. I've never done anything like this before."

"Do you want to just forget it?" she asked, standing up, about to go back into the house.

"No, no! I–I'll try," I said, lifting my bike off her steps. "I'll be back!"

"Okay. I love you!" she said, giving me a look of confidence as I rode my bike down her gravel driveway and into the unknown.

When I arrived at Fred Meyer, I paced toward the pharmaceutical department with no knowledge of what a box of condoms even looked like. I asked a nearby clerk, "Hey, uh…do you know where the condoms are?"

"Um, yeah," he pointed his finger to an aisle and said loudly, "Over there is where we keep all of the prophylactics."

Embarrassed by how loud he announced it, I walked slowly down the aisle, quickly becoming overwhelmed with all the brands and choices. I saw three, twelve, and thirty-six in a box. Not knowing which one to buy, I began to talk to myself.

"Okay, okay, think about this, Eddie. No, I don't want those—not enough. What the heck is a Sheik?" Then I saw a familiar name and triumphantly whispered, "Trojan!"

I felt since this was our first time, I had to do this right, so I grabbed the biggest box I could and grabbed a pack of Wrigley's Spearmint gum, briskly walking back to the nearest open register.

It was just my luck that the only person checking was a woman, and all I could do was move forward. I closed my eyes and muttered, "Holy crap!"

When it was my turn, I hesitantly placed the products on the counter and thought, *Oh man, she's not going to sell them to me.*

Just when I hoped for nothing to go wrong, the lady looked at the products and said with a smile, "Nice combination."

I paid for them and bolted out the store back to Holli's. When I arrived, she led me to her room in the attic and flipped the light switch off. I noticed the self-adhesive stars and moons glowing from her ceiling. Slightly embarrassed and hesitant at first, we both had something magical that day. Even if my mind was cloudy, my heart was clear with love and compassion as we surrendered ourselves to each other.

***

The school was holding the 1981 eighth-grade graduation dance in the gymnasium. I bought my first black long-sleeved rayon shirt, Brittania jeans, and maroon penny loafers at Mario's downtown with the money I'd earned doing side work for Charles Z. Becker hardwood flooring company.

At about eight p.m., people were lined up at the front doors, and I was excited about my first dance. The music vibrated off the hallway walls and out the doors. When I entered the dance floor, the lights were strobing between colorful streamers on beat with music from the late '70s and early '80s. Food and beverages filled a decorated table nearby. A disco ball reflected the lights around the room. Not more than thirty minutes into my groove, my shirt clung to my soaking, sweaty body and my feet were sizzling hot from the dancing. While some kids clapped their hands to the beat of the Police's "Don't Stand so Close to Me" and Toto's "Hold the Line," others drank the cranberry juice and ate finger food by the snack table.

Back in the projects, I'd been used to hearing Tito Puente, Diana Ross, Michael Jackson, and the Temptations. Here it was the Police, Pink Floyd, the Clash, Tears for Fears, and of course U2's "Boy." After several songs, I could no longer lift my exhausted legs to dance and tiredly walked to the table to get a drink.

There, I saw Holli talking with Darrel, her ex-boyfriend, but I pretended it didn't bother me. I nonchalantly stepped outside to gather my thoughts. I was sitting on a concrete ledge shortly after when Holli came out. Toto's "99" echoed through the school hallway.

Holli held my hand in hers and said, "Eddie?"

"Why were you speaking with Darrel? I thought you broke up with him."

"I did. But, but you have understand that this is our last moment together before most of my friends move on to high school. Everything's different now."

"How? I still love you. How is that different?"

"I love you too, but it's not the same anymore."

"Yo, Holli, I gave you my heart."

"And I gave you mine. But I think we should move on."

"Whatta you mean?"

"I mean break up."

I chuckled to hide the sting. "Oh, great. Fine, Holli. If you want to move on, then you move on and so will I—whatever." I stood up. "I gotta go."

"Where are you going?"

"Does it matter?"

"I'm sorry. I'm sorry I broke your heart."

"Sure you are. Have a good life. Maybe you like Darrel because he's rich and I'm not."

Holli brushed her hand over the edge of her ear and sympathetically said, "That's not it, Eddie. You know it's not."

"You know, I don't get you. What was I to you, an experiment? Some guy come down from another planet and you wanted to know what it would be like? Well, guess what, Holli—you didn't have to use me to find out."

She stood there silent.

Deeply hurt and confused, I tore myself away. When Holli broke it off with me, it was like she tore my heart out and melted it in a fire. But I would always love her because, after all, she was my first.

I walked back into the school and showed off every dance step I could. By about nine thirty, the party had wound down, but I was feeling energetic so I walked to the basketball court. That's when I saw Tom, my Cuban friend, near the park shelter.

I cupped my hands around my mouth and yelled, "Tom, Tom!"

"Eddie, what's up, man?"

"Nothing. Whatta you doing here?"

"Just kicking it with Tony."

Tony was the Wallace Park fixture and hung around late nights drinking beer and telling stories about how hard his life was and all the fights he'd won. At times, he was comical. He had long, dark brown hair that reached down to his shoulders; a rough, short, bearded face; a voice that sounded like Wolfman Jack's; and more muscles than a chiseled statue. That was why no one ever questioned him about his stories. I wasn't really afraid of him, though, because he wouldn't even be considered tough where I came from.

Tony gestured a greeting with his thirty-two-ounce bottle of Old English 800.

"Hey, Tony." I pointed my finger at him. "I see you're fuelin' up," I said sarcastically,

"Congratulations, little man," Tony laughed in his raspy voice, referring to my graduation. "What the fuck you gonna do with your life now?"

"I'm gonna move on to bigger and better things, man. You know, talk to women and be a badass," I replied, tucking my hands into my pants pockets. "Maybe I'll write a book."

"Write a book!" Tony laughed. "What the hell you gonna write about, little man?"

"I'll think of something."

"Hey." Tony looked me straight in the eyes, pointed his finger at me, and stated, "You betta make sure I'm in it, you little shit."

"I will, Tony. I'll be sure to let the world know who my man Tony was."

"Good. Yeah, you can't depend on anyone else to be a badass for you," Tony said, taking another gulp of his beer. "Wanna sip?"

"Nah, you drink it." Then, "Hey, Tom, you gonna play football Saturday?"

"I don't know. How 'bout you?"

"I'll play if you play. Man, I graduated. Isn't that great?"

"Man, you're crazy, Eddie. Everybody graduates." Tom said, acting as if I was stupid for saying it. "Ain't that right, Tony?"

"I didn't!"

We laughed.

I said, "Hey, my mom's coming down from New York too."

Tony interjected, "Hey that's great, man. So now you're gonna be a goddamn momma's boy," laughing and taking another gulp of his beer. "Just what we need around here."

"How can you handle that?" I asked with disdain.

"This is a man's beer, eight ball!" Tony declared. "Sure you don't wanna drink, graduate?"

"Nah, man, I'm saving myself. Thanks anyway."

"For what? This will grow hair on your ass!" He laughed.

"Thanks, Tony," I said, briefly waving my hand. "I think the hair on my ass is cool."

"Okay, Rocky," Tony said, giving me a thumb up. "I'll see you running in the streets again."

I stepped back. "Hey, I gotta cruise, but I'll catch up with you later, Tom."

"Okay. Hey, check out my new Converse."

"Those are cool!" I said, leaning over to touch them. "When'd you get 'em?"

"Yesterday. These things were thirty-five bucks. They're the best!"

"They look cool! But I have to split," I said, and scurried past the park shelter when Tom called, "Eddie?"

"Yeah?"

"Congrats, man."

"Thanks, Tom. That means a lot to me."

Tony blurted, "I'm about to get teary here," followed by a fake laugh.

Chapter 11

Mom Comes to Portland

I was fifteen and entering my freshman year at
Lincoln High School. I was excited knowing that before
Mom would come to Portland, we'd move out of our
Northwest Johnson Street apartment and into a two-story
pink house at 4236 North Albina Avenue. It had three
bedrooms, a dining room, a guestroom, one and a half
bathrooms, a basement I used as a bicycle repair shop, and
a huge backyard. I knew this house would be a dream
come true for Mom and couldn't wait for her to see it.
Portland had afforded Dad a small taste of wealth in so
many ways, and renting this house was a step toward a
better life.

The day Mom arrived at the airport, my whole
family anxiously waited for her at the terminal. Michael
and his new wife, Eleanor, were still back in New York,
saving to come next. We could see Mom exit the plane and
walk toward us, and our eyes and hearts opened like a
book waiting to tell her all the stories we had. I was happy
to see her tiny frame and her scarf draped over her neck
and face as she made her way down the corridor. Mom had
this smile I'll never forget. It was like she had been
resurrected now that she could finally see her family alive
and well again.

"Mom!" I yelled with excitement as she extended her arms to hug us all.

I saw Dad wipe the tears of joy from his eyes, "I have a surprise for you."

Joey was on Mom's left side, and I was on her right as she caressed the small of our necks. "Are you okay, *mi bebés?*"

"Yeah, Mom."

She was amazed at the sight of Portland. "Portland's so clean!" she uttered. "I love you all so much. I missed you!"

Dad ushered Mom to the blue, old Ford when Mom remarked with her accented English, "I see we haven't changed our taste in cars."

Everyone laughed.

The airport was about fifteen minutes away from our new home. When we got to the house, Dad parked the car, and Gerard said, "What do you think, Mom?"

She gasped and raised her right hand to her mouth. "What a beautiful home. We live here?"

Gerard helped Mom out of the car, and I hurried to hold her hand on the way into the house.

"This is beautiful!" Mom said. "How did you get this?"

Dad said, "We wanted to give you a real home, honey."

Mom skimmed her hands along the walls over the furniture and said, "This...this is my home?"

Dad answered, "For as long as you want it to be."

Later that night I wanted to explore our new house. To investigate the attic, I walked on the two-by-four beams that crossed the ceiling. I'd brought a pen flashlight with me, but the light stopped working, so I shook it a couple times. When I did this, I lost my balance and my left foot slipped off the beam and onto the dusty, flat sheetrock. Suddenly, my leg crashed through the ceiling into Anna's bedroom.

Anna screamed and frantically ran out of the room yelling, "A burglar's in the attic. A burglar's in the attic!"

No one knew what was going on, and my leg was still stuck between the beams and sheetrock. I struggled to lift myself to safety while the rest of the family ran upstairs to see what had happened. Dad rushed into Anna's room with a stick, Mom hid behind Dad, and Gerard and Joey stood there gaping at the debris and big hole in the ceiling. Everyone waited and watched, including my frantic sister.

I slowly peeped through massive hole that I had singlehandedly created, and Anna saw her burglar. Everyone couldn't stop laughing, and at the dinner table it became our main subject of conversation.

***

On my first day at Lincoln High School, home of the Cardinals, everything seemed much bigger than it had at Chapman. I saw Ed in the hallway heading toward the office to enroll for his senior year classes.

"Ed!" I called. "What's up, bro? Man, isn't this a trip? All these freshmen."

"Yeah, man. Hey, you going—"

I pointed at a girl and said, "Check out that girl."

"What girl?"

"The one over there!" I exclaimed, pointing my finger again at the pink dress on a figure you only saw in the movies. "Can't you see her?"

"Oh, yeah. She's fine!" Ed said, acting like it was no big deal.

"That's it? 'She's fine' is all you can say?"

"Yeah, she's fine," he reiterated. "What do want me to say?"

"A little more than 'she's fine' would be nice." I placed my hand on Ed's shoulder. "Well, you obviously don't care about God's creations walking by, so you wanna go running tonight?"

"Yeah, sure, maybe we can go to Mount Scott."

"What's Mount Scott?"

"It's a place you can go boxing at, out on Southeast 72nd Avenue."

"Box?" I exclaimed. "Why would I want to put boxes away at Mount Scott?"

Ed laughed and did a one-two shadowbox punch. "No, man, not that kind of box. Boxing like in fighting!"

"No way, man," I said. "You mean just like the movie *Rocky*?"

"Yeah. You wanna go check it out?"

"Hell yeah!" I said, standing there ready to go. "When?"

"We'll go tonight," he said. "This guy Andy is showing me the ropes right now. My mom will pick you up."

"Cool." I asked, "Hey, you wanna go see *Rocky* at the theater tonight?"

"Yeah, let's do that too. We can go boxing after school then catch the show."

While catching the number four bus back home, there was always an interesting group of rowdies that would enter the side door and start shouting colorful words of intimidation. It didn't trouble me because I was used to this kind of disorderly conduct. I just didn't like how long it took to get home.

I got dropped off on the corner of Mississippi Avenue, on the same block where there was a bed and breakfast mansion—one home that simply looked like it didn't belong in the neighborhood.

Once home, I anxiously waited for Ed's mom to show. Finally, I heard the horn honk, grabbed an old cassette player, ran toward the car, and practically dived in, I was so excited. After she dropped us in front of the Mount Scott Community Center in her green 1970s AMC Gremlin, we hurried to the boxing gym, eager to get in a hard workout. I set the player against the wall with the *Rocky* cassette already inserted and started the player.

When the *Rocky* theme played, other boxers in the gym became inspired, hitting the speed bag faster and jumping rope harder. The guys at the gym nicknamed me Eddie "Twinkle Toes" Regory for being light on my feet, and Ed's boxing name was Ed "Go Home" Jerome because he would never want to go home.

I got into boxing to feel inspired and stay in shape, but Ed got into it for medals. The first time I saw one of his boxing matches, it lasted four two-minute rounds with a one-minute rest in between. I could see getting hit took more out of him than hitting back did. He never gave up or won a fight, but he had heart and endurance, which earned him respect.

Sports weren't all Ed was good at. If I felt down, Ed was the guy to have around. He often made funny sounds and acted out crazy gestures. While doing this, he would manipulate his face into different shapes. He had a spontaneous, creative, and sometimes unforgettable act that brought out a euphoric feeling in his family and friends. At first it was sort of strange getting used to Ed's eccentric behavior, but he grew on me, and after a while, I tried to emulate him. In fact, an act without the both of us didn't seem right.

Chapter 12

Sudden Changes

I sat near the back of the number fifteen bus heading west on Washington Street as it passed O'Bryant Square park on my right. It was sprinkling, and I couldn't wait to see Ed. I also brought my running shoes just in case he'd want to work out.

Once I was standing outside his place, I cupped my hands around my lips yelled up, "Hey Ed! Hey!" waiting for him to look out his apartment window.

He quickly pulled open the window and yelled down, "When you gonna ring the buzzer, man?"

I laughed. "Come out, man. Come on!"

He rushed down with no shirt on. "Come in!" I followed behind and saw his mom, Betty, watching the morning news.

Ed offered, "You want some cereal?"

"Nah, man. That's all right."

I noticed several cereal boxes on the table: Cap'n Crunch, Cheerios, and Raisin Bran and a jar of his favorite, Adams Peanut Butter. "Dude, why do you have all these opened boxes of cereal?"

"I mix them all in one bowl with peanut butter."

"Serious? Man, that sounds good!"

"It is." Ed motioned. "Follow me. There's something I wanna show you."

We went to his room where he showed me his new black sable pet ferret. It had dark hair and a cream-colored undercoat that barely showed through. His eyes were brown and his nose, ash gray.

"Dude, this is cool! So, where'd you get the ferret?"

"My mom got it for me. Isn't it cool?"

"Yeah, man. Let's take him outside and see what he does on the grass."

We headed for Couch Park with the ferret on Ed's shoulder. When we arrived, we watched the ferret swiftly move on the grass.

"I love it, man!" I said, nudging at the ferret with my fingers.

"Yeah, he's neat, isn't he?" Ed gently lifted the ferret and let it crawl on his chest.

I said, "He looks like he wants to lick you."

"Maybe he does," Ed said, bringing the ferret's nose flush to his own. "His nose is cold."

I smiled and pet it. "Think he's sick?"

"Nah," Ed replied. "He's fine."

After playing with the ferret, we went for a run, making a pit stop at Hazel's place, and then jogged to Fryer's Quality Pie, a business divided into a bakery and a diner. It was great because from outside the window, you could see the doughnuts totally drenched in that shiny, sugary, warm glaze. But the best part about Quality Pie was the people. You never knew who might walk in, especially at midnight. Transvestites from Darcelle XV Showplace, or punk rockers from Club Satyricon.

***

I'd come to appreciate my first few months at Lincoln and our new home on Albina Street. Michael finally came to Portland too, and he and Eleanor got their own place on Southeast Belmont Street across from the Avalon Theatre. Things could not have been better.

In celebration, my family decided to make reservations at a restaurant in the Chinatown district near downtown, by Powell's Books. I don't recall eating in a restaurant with my family in New York, so doing this in Portland was a long time coming. The family sat around the long table, eating a variety of foods including my favorite, chicken chow mein.

Suddenly Gerard stood up and said, "I wanna make a toast."

"Go ahead, Gerard," Michael said. "Make it a good one."

He poured wine into his glass and said, "Mom, Dad, you gave us the gift of life and showed us happiness is attainable even in the worst of times. From all of us, your children, thank you for showing us the meaning of love so we could be here as a family today. We love you."

We cheered and clapped.

That night with my family reminded me of our evenings in New York when we sat near the piano as Gerard played.

The next day I set up a boxing gym in the basement. I used weights, a speed bag, jump rope and bench press, stretching a fifty-foot extension cord from the kitchen down to the basement to connect a radio. I had mastered the skill of jumping rope like a real boxer, doing single and double jumps for an hour straight, and my attempt to consistently hit the speed bag became unfailing.

Then one day was different from all the others before it. That day changed my life forever.

Partway through my training in the basement, I ran up the stairs and noticed Mom was coughing and looking as if she were sick.

"Mom, are you okay?"

"Yes, baby. I'm fine," she replied, still sweeping the dust out the front door, as she always did at the beginning of each day.

I offered, "Do you want some water?"

"No, baby." She asked, "Are you hungry?"

"No. I'm gonna go finish my workout. Are you sure you're okay, Mom?"

"Yes, baby. You finish your exercise."

For days, Mom's cough continued, so Dad decided to take her to the Oregon Health & Science University hospital. When he arrived back home with Mom, he said the doctor had assured him everything was okay and that all she needed was rest. We did everything possible, but her coughing wouldn't stop.

Dad took Mom back up to the hospital and demanded to get answers about what was wrong. I thought it might've been a simple cold or the dust from the floor she swept away every morning. Mom rarely got sick.

Dad finally came back from the hospital, but this time without Mom. We waited in the living room wondering what had happened, and then he pulled his handkerchief from his pants pocket and blew his nose. He had been crying, and I thought, *My giant, crying?*

With a somber face, Dad brought his head up, cleared his throat, and said, "Your mother needs to stay in the hospital for a night. The doctors need to do some tests."

We didn't know how to react, so for a moment we sat there quietly.

Gerard asked, "Why?"

"I'm not sure. We'll have to see tomorrow. They're doing tests and won't know until tomorrow."

Dad had no more words to say and left the room. Later that night, we went to bed confused and scared, missing the one most important person in our lives.

One day turned into a few days before Mom's test results were finally back. This time, Dad sat us all down in the living room. We heard him grasp for words, trying to tell us what had happened. Finally, he struggled to say, "Your...your mother has cancer of the lungs. 'Cancer,' the doctor said. I don't...I don't know how or why. Just know it spread too fast to catch."

He draped his shaking hands over his head. We didn't know what to think, but sadness filled the room. Tears streamed down Joey's face. We waited for Dad to say more, but he never did. We just wanted it to go away.

Dad proceeded to his room, and Gerard followed. We wanted to hear what they were saying, but they wouldn't let us in. I went upstairs and sat on my bed, staring at my *Rocky* poster and wondering, *What would the champ do?*

Joey asked, "Eddie, what's cancer?"

"Don't know."

"Dad was crying," Joey said. "Dad never cries."

"I know."

"I wanna see Mom."

"Me too," I said. "Wonder if Dad's gonna tell us what it means."

"Think Mom will come home?"

"Yeah, she'll come home. She's our mom. Why wouldn't she?"

"What if she doesn't?"

"Don't say that! Don't think that way. She will. She will."

Dad waited for the doctors to say it was okay to bring her home, but they kept saying, "Not today." So he took Joey and me to see her. We sat in the waiting room, and when the doctor came out, his expression looked like hope never existed. He walked to my dad and said in a sympathetic tone, "Mr. Regory, your wife is very sick. At this point, her condition is terminal."

Dad slumped as if he had been drained of all his energy. He looked up at the doctor with his fatigued eyes and anguished face and asked with one last breath of hope, "Is there anything you can do? Anything?"

"I'm sorry. There is nothing we can do."

Dad asked, "Doctor, what if I gave her one of my lungs?"

He sighed and softly expressed, "I'm sorry," then walked away.

Dad dropped his head. We reached out to comfort his pain, but Dad said, "Eddie, Joey, I think it's time to go see your mother." He grabbed us by our hands and guided us to the room.

As we approached the door, my heart pounded, afraid of what Mom would look like. *Is she going to be awake? Is she going to be the same mother I had before this cancer thing came along?*

It seemed as if everything was in slow motion. I saw Gerard waiting at Mom's door. He knelt on one knee and quietly said, "Eddie, Joey—Mom is in there waiting for you, but remember she's sick and…and what you see is only temporary, okay?"

We looked at each other and nodded. Gerard opened the door, guided us to where Mom lay, and slowly pulled away a curtain. I steadily walked in but didn't want to see what I saw. Every inconceivable thought of what Mom might have looked like had come true. Mom lay helpless with tubes connecting her nose and mouth to an oxygen tank to help her breathe. Round, white patches stuck to her chest. I desperately wanted to rip them off. I wanted to believe this was a dream and that I would soon awaken.

I thought, *This isn't Mom. It can't be. None of this is really happening.*

Feeling drained of my own life, I knelt beside her while her eyes barely open. I held her right hand and said, "Mom, I love you, Mom. I love you, I love you."

I forced the tears to stay behind my eyes even though they wanted to flow. Joey didn't stay long because he was so emotional. I stayed there with my head buried by her bedside and began to pray.

Dad was at the hospital every day. He came in early and left late, if he left at all. He prayed day and night hoping for a miracle, holding the Bible in one hand and a handkerchief in the other. On one visit, I noticed a yellow-and-green notepad he had left on the seat of his chair.

"Dad, what's that?"

He said quietly, "Nothing, son. It's nothing."

When Gerard came in, they talked amongst themselves. I guess Dad felt it would be better if we didn't know Mom was going to die.

The doctor arrived. As we looked at him, he said with care in his voice, "Mr. Regory, I feel it would be okay for her to go home."

Dad stood and combed his hair back with his hands. He had prepared for this with a separate bed and an oxygen tank at home.

We sat around Mom's bed daily, taking turns comforting her. Dad wrote and read poems to Mom while she slept. By then, I realized each day was closer to her leaving us. I even wished we could go back in time when we lived in New York when Mom was healthy. It seemed like the dangers we'd faced then were small problems compared to this. It was the only time in my life I ever wanted to go back to the ghetto.

December passed, and on the second day of January 1982, Gerard walked into the room where Mom's bed was. He then came out with a distressed look on his face, closing the door behind him. "She's gone."

I looked over to Joey, who started sobbing so hard that Anna pulled him into her arms. Joey cried, "Why couldn't we have saved her? Is it because we're poor? Why?"

I couldn't cry and didn't know why.

"Gerard," I asked, "can I go see her?"

He looked over to Anna then back to me and quietly said, "Yeah. Go ahead."

I sat by her bedside and held her fragile, pale hand in mine. I looked at Mom's still body and slightly blue face and said, "I'll make you proud, Mom. I promise."

Joey came in and sat beside me, choking on his tears. "Can I hold her too?"

"Yeah," I said, gently setting her hand in his.

"Her hand is soft," Joey said, with tears dripping onto his white shirt. "Did you say anything to her?"

"Yeah," I said firmly, holding back my tears. "I made her a promise."

"What was it?"

"To make her proud of me."

We left the room together. I hugged Joey because I loved him more than anything in the world and wanted him to know I would be by his side forever.

Chapter 13

The Notepad

I later discovered the yellow-and-green notepad Dad had at the hospital was a short diary of Mom's last days. When I read it, only then did I fully realize the pain he must've felt. These are the words he wrote:

December 19, 1981

These first six days were hell. But I prayed and have faith, God made it bearable. She is still with us all. You live all your life, but you don't know how important someone is until something happens to that one. I love my wife! I remember when she came to Oregon, full of life and hope. We all came with hope of a new start. She loved it here. She felt comfortable knowing Edward and Joseph were safe going to school. I thank God for that. I don't understand this cancer. It comes so fast and destroys the person you love, and no one seems to know what to tell you or what to do.

When she got off the plane, she was full of life, hope and so beautiful. When I saw her, I fell in love with her again. She is my right hand! She is my hope! She is my life! She is soft, hoping, loving and gentle. We were happy together. I found that just touching her made me feel good.

December 20, 1981

God gave us another day. That's what we asked
for...one day at a time. She looks so nice! There's
color in her face today. They made her more
comfortable by changing her bed. Mike came....
The doctor and nurse have been so kind to her. She
is still very weak.... The doctor checked her blood
to see if she's getting oxygen.

Lunch

She is eating well. It is good to see her this way.
She couldn't drink the distilled water because it
choked her. The doctor told me the x-ray he took
three days ago showed the same results. But I have
hope! As long as she lives, one day at a time. Anna
just came in, and how happy she is to see her. I
hope Joe and Eddie are okay. Gerard just came in.
He told me Joseph is worried what will happen if
Mom dies. Gerard told Joseph, "God will keep us
together."

December 21, 1981

There is no change. Our hope now rests with God.
Gerard came with me this morning. I see now she
is beginning to understand she has cancer and is
going to die. She's lost lots of weight; she is now
99 lbs. I loved my wife when we first met, but I
find my love is greater now than at first. She is
resting now. The nurse gave her medicine
(codeine). It is hard for her to breathe.

December 22, 1981

She was sitting up when I came in this morning.

December 23, 1981

Anna came in today. She's happy when Anna is here. I sometimes wonder that, when someone you love dies, you ask yourself, did I do everything possible? Did I make the right decisions? Our marriage was long, but not always happy. Not because of her, but because of me.

December 25, 1981

Eddie and Joe came to see her. It made her feel better. She gained a little weight today. I thank God for this day. She seems to be getting better. She said that "Even with oxygen, her chest feels tight."

The oxygen has been lowered to number three. She feels she has not been the kind of mother she would've liked to have been. But that's not true! She was a better mother than I was a father.

I find people are so nice here! Not like most hospitals I've been in. They take their job more than just a job. They love her, and they kiss her when they come in.

December 26, 1981

She looks tired today. I don't know what's happening to her. One day she gains weight, the next day she looks no better.

Eddie and Joe came in with me to see her. They don't understand what's happening.

Today will be a big day for her. All her children will be here. We talked about writing grandma in New York.

I guess it's time I pray for a miracle! I asked God to take me instead of her. The nurses are nice here. Life is hard from birth to death, and yet we fight to live no matter how hard life is.... I look at her and want to lie beside her and die with her. But life is not like the movies. It's real.

I tried to think of our lives together. I can't remember! I don't know why. She says, "How hard it is to breathe."

It must be the cancer taking its toll. She's getting weaker and weaker! I don't understand why they can't give her some medicine to breathe, but there is none. Her lungs are getting worse. Oh God, don't let her be in pain, please!

I feel like I'm in a daze. In the morning I don't want to wake up. I feel afraid of each day. Soon we will take her home to sleep with her family around her.

December 27, 1981

She is eating a little better; she is in pain. The doctor wants to talk to me again. He's letting her come home. There's nothing more they can do.

I read her a poem, and she liked it. Her stitches she got from the operation bother her a lot. She just wants to go to sleep.

December 28, 1981

They talked of her coming home—our only hope is God! Maybe it's best she's coming home. She wants to be with her family.

December 29, 1981

They asked her if she will let the gynecologist look at her. She said, "No!" She looks much better. Gerard...[is] coming over. She did not eat much. Dr. Wolf is looking at her.

January 2, 1982
She is asleep (died).

The following few days, people we didn't know and neighbors we'd never met brought food, cards, and flowers. Dad couldn't believe the kindness that came our way.

Then Holli called me.

"Eddie?"

I was surprised, but happy to hear her voice. "Holli? Hi."

"I heard," she said. "I'm real sorry. Are you going to be okay?"

"I think so, but I don't know about Joey."

"Did they take her to the mortuary?"

I didn't really know what *mortuary* meant, so I answered, "Yeah, they did."

"Well, if you need anything, just call," she said. "Everything will get better, Eddie. It will get better."

"Thank you for that."

When she called, a part of me missed her, but I knew it could never be again. What I would have given to hold her in my arms.

Over the next several days, Dad cleaned out Mom's closet of all her clothes, shoes, and other things she had collected over the course of her life. Then he was inspired to make himself better, so he started exercising to Richard Simmons.

Weeks passed until one early morning I walked outside to the bus stop and suddenly saw a black puppy walking toward me. I reached over to pet it and found myself putting my arm around her neck and pulling her close to me.

I noticed her stomach was bloated, so I picked her up and said, "You wanna come home with me, girl? Sure you do. Come on."

I brought her back to the house and said, "Dad, look! A puppy dog."

He pet it and said, "She looks sick."

"Can we keep her?"

He replied sympathetically, "Yes, Eddie, we can. I'm tired of death. I don't want to see it anymore."

I took the dog to a veterinarian and got her fixed up. We named her Yoko, and she became a part of the family.

After Mom's death, Dad could no longer stay in our dream home, so we moved into a smaller place on the same block. It was divided into two rentals, upstairs and downstairs. Dad, Joey, and I lived downstairs, where there were three small bedrooms and a bathroom. Gerard and Anna lived above us, so at least we were still together.

Chapter 14

September

Michael and Eleanor had a baby girl they named Rachael. Anna later moved out and got her own place and a new job as a bank processor. Ed and his mom also moved out of their Villa Florence building to a small two-bedroom apartment on Southeast 37th Avenue and Powell Street.

Since I'd frequently stay the night with Ed, his mom gave in and bought me a twin-size bed. She could never take the place of my mother, but she was like a mother to me. I was graced with a whole new family—only God would have known I needed this. From then on, I called Betty Mom, and she embraced it, treating me like a son.

The great thing about Ed's new place was the video arcade, Good Times, and DeNicola's pizza place down the street. We spent every last quarter we had playing Donkey Kong and Donkey Kong Jr. When we had no more quarters, the manager at the Thriftee Thriftway store on Northwest Glisan Street would let us stack bottles for money. At the end of the night, we smelled like a brewery, but it didn't matter because those games were waiting for us to come back.

Early one Saturday morning, I went to Ed's house. Betty opened the door and said with her polite, soft voice, "He went running, honey. He should be back soon. Would you like to wait for him?"

"Yeah, Mom. Thanks," I said, walking into their apartment.

"Would you like some cookies, sweetie?"

"Oh, no, thanks."

I went into Ed's room, lay down on my new bed, and waited. I heard a knock on the front door and thought it was Ed, but it was his sister, Cathy. "Hi, Mom," I heard her say.

Cathy was a nice person, but she often seemed troubled. I could hear indistinct words and she yelled, "It's your entire fault for the way I am! It's your fault I can't walk anymore! I hate you! I hate you!"

Betty screamed, "Eddie! Eddie!"

At first I didn't know what to do, so I quickly opened the door and darted to the kitchen, where I saw Cathy trying to hit Betty's face. I barged between them, blocked Cathy's hands, and said, "Cathy, stop! This is your mother."

"It's all her fault for the way I am!" she cried. "I hate you! I hate you!"

"Cathy, what are you talking about?" I asked urgently. "Why are you doing this?"

"Because it's her fault for the way I am. I'll never be able to walk normal again."

I turned to Betty, surprised and somewhat apologetic for Cathy's actions. "Are you okay, Mom?"

"I'm fine," she replied, wiping the tears that had coursed down her swollen cheeks and pale neck.

Cathy limped away to the recliner in the living room to smoke a cigarette. When Ed arrived, Betty told him what happened while I waited in his room. I'm not sure what he said to Cathy, but knowing Ed, he had a way

of making a bad situation good. I heard him joking with
her as she laughed. Then he came into the room and said,
"Hey, Eddie! What's up, buddy?"

"Wanna go to the arcade?" I asked, happy to see
him.

"Yeah. Let me get some money from my mom."

"Okay. How far'd you run?"

"Three miles."

"What was your time?"

"Twenty-three minutes."

After Ed got his money and took a shower, we
played a couple of games at the arcade then caught the
Powell bus into town. We were sitting in the back when I
looked over and asked, "Hey, Ed?"

"Yeah."

"What happened to your sister? Why does she
limp?"

Ed stayed silent for a minute and then answered,
"She tried to commit suicide off the bridge."

"Damn," I said, surprised. "How'd she ever
survive, and why would she want to kill herself?"

He replied solemnly, "I wonder that myself. I
don't know. I really don't know."

"Oh," I responded, dropping the subject.

After transferring to another bus, we got off on
25th and Pettygrove in Northwest. Ed knocked on Tom's
door. "Hey, Cuban!"

I chuckled and added, "What's up, Castro?"

Tom laughed. "Hey, if it isn't the two Ed heads."

I said, "Grab your ball and play some football with
us?"

"Okay," Tom said. "Let me get my cleats."

"Hurry up!" Ed started running toward Wallace
Park.

Tom kept a good distance behind us with his
football in hand and shouted, "Ed, catch!"

"Right here, Ed!" I yelled, running deep. A few minutes into our three-man game, Joey, Jimmy, a couple of other guys, and even a redheaded, stocky girl who loved playing football showed up to play. Tom was probably the fastest running player on the field because of his long bowlegged legs. He could weave his way in and out like a weasel in the woods. We'd often teased him that he was born on a horse.

That day we played hard, including the redheaded girl. No matter how hard we'd hit her, she would just shrug off the pain and get back up. It was as if she was a man disguised as a woman.

We played a lot of football. The mud would cover our faces, hair, and clothes. The love of the game, however, would keep us coming back every weekend with more neighborhood kids joining in.

***

After Ed graduated from the class of 1982, he enlisted in the military for four years to become an Army Ranger. He felt he had a duty to his country and that there was no future for him in Portland. I felt he enlisted because, just like me, he was always broke. Meanwhile, I was excited about my sophomore year at Lincoln.

He wrote letters all the time, but I felt empty inside knowing he wasn't around. One letter made me laugh every time I saw it, though. He'd drawn a map of Oregon and California and a muscular arm coming out of Oregon. Off to the side of the arm it read: "You Still Fear Me Boy." We'd competed in everything, bringing the best out of each other and often teasing about who feared the other the most.

Chapter 15

Meryl Streep

I was now seventeen, and my senior year wrestling coach, Mr. Wong, felt I was ready to move up from junior varsity to varsity. I weighed in at 169 pounds, and my competition was often bigger than I was. If not for my quick hands, I would have lost every match.

Our team had just arrived at Wilson High School to try to qualify for the state championship. Heavy wrestling mats were laid out evenly, and people had filled the seats from wall to wall. The Lincoln Cardinals were on one side and Wilson High on the other. We rotated against multiple weight classes, wrestling so much that my arms began to feel like Jell-O toward the end of the day.

I faced my next opponent in the center of the mat, standing in a neutral position. My challenger was in such immaculate shape that his wrestling singlet showed popping curves, veins, and muscles straight out of a Superman comic. The referee stood to the side of us. I confronted my challenger in the orange wrestling circle as he stood tall with his wicked eyes gazing down at me, ready to eradicate my very existence.

The referee put his hand between us, blew his whistle, and the match was on. We pawed at each other to find a weakness in a leg, arm, or even a shoulder. During the first two minutes of the match, we wrestled cautiously yet aggressively. Then I maneuvered away from his body, and we began to circle each other. The referee blew his whistle when I left the mat and then signaled us to regroup.

My opponent stepped toward me as I rapidly stepped back. I then moved into range and clutched his right leg with my left arm. We butted heads, and the sweat smeared. He maneuvered free, grabbed my left leg, abruptly took me down hard on my back, and then wrapped his right arm around my neck into a tight headlock. Sweat obstructed my vision, and the pain from the impact was overbearing. The referee hovered over us and quickly dropped to his knees, fixing his eyes for the moment my shoulders would hit the mat evenly.

My opponent's upper body weighed heavily on my head as I pressed my toes deep into the thick mat, and my lower body twisted and turned in circles with him still on top. I poured everything into this round, but I felt both my shoulders make contact with the mat. Instantaneously, the referee slammed his hand on the mat and blew his whistle—a win for my opponent.

After that I was so exhausted, I felt like vomiting. I'd been competing all day, but Mr. Wong said, "Okay, Eddie, you've got one more guy to wrestle."

"One more?" I exclaimed. "Mr. Wong, I don't know if I have any more juice in me."

"You can do this, Eddie. I believe in you. You have to use your quickness on him because he's big, real big. Remember what you've learned. Get low, move fast. He's a pawn, and you're the king. Calculate your next move. Okay?"

"Okay, but who is he?"

Mr. Wong pointed to a gorilla sitting in the center of the challenging team's bench. I could not believe my eyes. He was more like the Jolly Green Giant than a high schooler, with enough hair on his body to use as a blanket. If anyone ever needed a waxing, it was this guy.

He was at least six feet tall and had long, dark, thick hair and acne craters on his face, and his chest extended out. I faced the gorilla in the center of the wrestling circle, and he stared blankly at me, just waiting for the whistle. The referee blew it, and my opponent rushed me as if I were the last chicken on the buffet line, lifted me up, and practically threw me flat on my back. "Ugh!" I gasped as he instantly pinned my shoulders to the mat.

The referee dropped to his stomach to see if my shoulders were flush. He counted, "One, two, three!" and slammed his hand on the mat.

It was over. Magilla Gorilla had won. My quickness had its advantages in the sport, just not with those last two competitors. I think Mr. Wong thought he had a prodigy on his hands and was just testing the waters.

***

Being in the class of 1985 was great, but the best part was that I met a girl. Kristina was undoubtedly the most striking girl I had ever seen in my life. She had a hint of Meryl Streep in her—deep, ocean-blue eyes and a smile that could brighten anyone's day. I never thought she'd be interested in me, but I fell for her so hard that if I didn't try to know her, it would have been a crime.

She drove a Volkswagen Scirocco, which was a big deal since the average senior didn't have a car. It was a warm Monday night, and a group of us walked to the McDonald's on Burnside after a football game against Grant High School. Kristina came along with a friend and ordered strawberry shakes, and they sat across from us sipping on their straws.

I became captivated by her presence, trying to swim in her eyes whenever I had the chance. "So how'd you like the game?"

"It was fun. How about you?"

"I think it's time for us to win at least one."

"Yeah," she replied then smiled. "Seems like we never win."

"But it was a cool game, though," I said. "Maybe we'll win the next one."

"Yeah, real cool," a friend of mine, Jay, added. "We only lost by a zillion points."

I turned to him and said, "Yeah, but we had heart out there, man."

"Oh, yeah, a lot of heart, Eddie," he replied, looking at me like I was crazy. "I'm hungry now."

"It isn't the game, it's the guts!" I exclaimed, with a tight-fisted pat to my chest.

Jay joined in, "Yeah, guts!"

Kristina and her friend smiled. We flirted and chatted until late. After that blissful night, there wasn't a day I didn't want to breathe her into my life. It was like a part of me was missing whenever she wasn't around. I thought of any reason to be near her.

That following Friday, Kristina invited me to her house near a Portland landmark called the Pittock Mansion, near West Burnside Street and up a very steep hill. I'd heard how nice the mansion was, but I'd never been there. Since I didn't have a car and didn't want to take a bus, my other source of reliable transportation was my legs. I threw on my running shoes and sweatpants, grabbed my Walkman and two dollars off the kitchen table, and of course picked up my *Rocky* tape.

I began my journey toward West Burnside to Kristina's house, running past small shops, Fred Meyer, and my favorite place, Baskin-Robbins. With many cars zooming past me, it was a dangerous climb but a small sacrifice considering what was waiting for me. When I got closer, I was in disbelief at some of the houses I saw

114

around me. *If Mom were alive, she would love to have that house, or that house, or even that house.*

I didn't know which driveway was Kristina's— suddenly, I saw her standing by a mailbox at the end of a driveway. She was blooming with happiness.

"Kristina!" I said with excitement. "Hey, what's up? I couldn't find your house."

"That's why I waited down here."

I asked, "You live up here?"

"Uh-huh. Follow me," she said, grabbing my hand as we hiked up the long driveway. Around the corner I noticed a red, glossy 1965 Porsche parked and a basketball pole embedded in the concrete.

As we entered her home, I commented, "Wow, what a cool place."

"You like it?"

"Do I like it? This is sweet!"

"Come on. I'll show you around."

I never thought in my wildest dreams that people actually lived like this. They even had their own bathrooms. The whole house was laced with beautiful, cultured paintings on the walls, coffee tables made of solid wood, a fireplace, and every imaginable gadget to make anyone's life easier. Part of the house was laid out in white, plush carpet, and every souvenir, appliance, and television was of high quality. She had a separate entertainment movie room with a cozy loveseat just for two. It was like *Lifestyles of the Rich and Famous*.

Then Kristina brought me outside to her patio, and it was nothing like the porch that overlooked our brown grass on Albina Street. It was made of red brick that stretched at least a hundred feet long with a panoramic view of downtown Portland.

"Are you okay?" she asked.

"Yeah, uh, I'm okay," I answered, still in awe of everything around me. The truth was I felt out of my league.

"Well, this is my house." She gently held my hand. "You like it?"

"It's a very, very nice place. Are your parents wealthy?"

"Well, they do pretty good. Dad owns a Porsche and Audi dealership."

"How does it feel to have all this?"

"You get used to it."

I asked, "Can you get whatever you want?"

"Not whatever, but I get nice things," she replied, as if it wasn't a big deal.

"It must be really nice to live here," I said, walking around the patio, looking at the scenery, and dreaming of what it would be like if I lived there. We went into the movie room. "What kind of movies do you have?" I said, "I love movies."

"We have a few down here," she answered, sliding open a drawer and showing me neatly stacked rows of VHS tapes. "Pick your choice."

"Cool. It's like my favorite thing to do," I said. "How's this one?"

"*An Officer and a Gentleman*? That's a really good one. You wanna watch it?"

"Yeah, let's check it out."

Kristina asked, "Would you like something to drink?"

"Sure."

She left and came back with a Coke. My gaze roamed around the photos and small tennis souvenirs noticing just how organized everything was. It was as if they had a maid—from the looks of it, housekeeping there would be a full-time job.

She popped the tab and said, "Here you go."

"Thanks."

She sat near me, "Where are you from, Eddie?"

"New York."

"How did you like it?"

"It was all right, I mean, considering," I answered in an evasive manner.

"What part of New York?"

"Manhattan."

I didn't say Lower East Side because I didn't want her to judge me in a way that might ruin my chances with her. I inched closer for a heated moment of silence, and then she brought her soft lips to mine.

"Wow," she said softly, "that was…was nice."

"Is it okay with you?" I asked gentleman-like, hoping she would let me continue.

"Yes. I liked it a lot," she replied with a smile and advanced toward me for another kiss.

I asked, "Um, what time's your mom coming?"

"Why?"

"Well, I really like being here with you."

"I like being here with you."

We kissed again.

"You, uh, kiss really well, Eddie."

My head blew up to about the size of a mountain. I began to carefully slide my left hand around her waist, but I sensed she was now tensed. "If you don't want me to do this, I won't."

"No, it's…it's not that at all. I've just got this feeling inside my stomach."

"Is it a good feeling?"

She nodded.

"I'm glad you like it," I said, leaning toward her once more. "You wanna watch the movie?"

She laid her head on my shoulder, and we began to watch the movie. By about ten p.m., Kristina drove me back down the hill and dropped me off at the Fred Meyer parking lot.

As I stepped out, I said, "I'll see you at school?"

"I'll see you at school," she said gently. "I had a nice time."

"So did I. Yo, Kristina? Um, you know, I really like you—a lot."

"I like you too, Eddie—a lot."

I shut the door and said, "Hold on!" I hurried around the front of the car to the driver's side, reaching my head into the window to kiss her one last time.

**

There was no better place to have a party then the biggest park in Portland: Macleay. If you said, "Beer," the kids at Lincoln came running, ready to pay for a cup. The best spot for a keg was past the first bridge but right before a place called the witch's castle. Urban legend says that witches and paranormal activity surrounded the castle, but the truth is, it was an old stone public toilet built in the 1930s.

One of the funniest partygoers I knew at school was named Butler. He reminded me a little of Carlton back in New York because of his size and strength. He weighed in at about three hundred pounds, had dark thick hair, thick eyebrows, and more hair on his body than the gorilla guy I wrestled. He was a half-Gypsy gargantuan who could keep a party alive and drink anyone under the table if they dared to challenge him. Once he drank forty-eight sixteen-ounce cups of beer at Kristina's birthday party we had at Tom's house. He got so sick that he laid his body out on the driveway and vomited from the side of his mouth as the puddle crept down between the pebbles toward the sidewalk.

Tom's mother, Leonila, walked outside to see what was going on. When she saw him, she ran back into the house and hysterically yelled with her broken English, "Ay! Tommy, Tommy, Tommy! Butler vomit all over floor, outside!"

Tom calmed his mother down and quickly went outside to see if Butler was okay. "Butler, get up, man. People think you're dead out here."

He let out a long belch and replied, "Okay, man. You gotta a dip o' Copenhagen?"

Tom chuckled. "Yeah, man. But first you have to come inside."

Butler struggled awkwardly back into the house with his hand on his stomach. "You have any food?"

Tom grinned, motioning to the kitchen. "Yeah, in the fridge."

"Butler, you hungry?" Leonila asked, lifting a piece of birthday cake off the table and waving it in front of his face.

Butler replied with a nauseous look. "Nah, Leo, nah. I don't want cake."

Leonila kept forcing the cake on him, saying, "Butler, you eat. It's good for you—you feel better."

"Nah, Leo. I can't, Leo. I don't want cake right now."

"Butler you eat, eat," she insisted, putting the cake even closer to his sickened, drunken face.

Finally he grabbed the cake and threw it against the dishwasher, splattering it all over the sink, refrigerator, and the linoleum floor. Leonila ran frantically around the house yelling, "Ay! Tommy, Tommy!"

***

Lincoln had honor courses for those kids who were above average academically. I sometimes walked

119

past those kids with their books in hand, seeing how confident they looked, wishing I could be that smart, that important. But my grades just weren't good enough. Which made me think, *Why am I so different? Don't I have the capacity to learn as much or do as well?* I couldn't come to terms with it, so I stuck with what I did best: sports.

One night I came home and stood by Dad's door. He was sitting on the edge of his bed when I said, "Dad, can I talk to you?"

"Yeah, son," he said, in a sympathetic tone. "Come sit by me."

"Dad? Why am I so different? I mean, I'm sick of being in these dumb classes. I'm sick of being poor and watching all my friends with new cars, clothes, and nice homes. It seems like I go two steps forward and one step back. I try to save, but the money I make is nothing."

Dad placed his hand over mine. "Eddie, there's no such thing as a dumb class, and you can do anything you want if you put your mind to it. You just gotta believe in what you want and do it. Keep going to school, son. I wished I'd stayed, but instead I enlisted and came out struggling for my place in life. You don't have to go down that same path. You have choices."

"What am I supposed to keep trying to do? I don't know what I'm good at."

"What do you like the most?" Dad asked. "What makes you happy?"

"I don't know." I brought my head down. "I can't answer that."

"Eddie, do you know what the secret to success is?"

"What?"

Dad replied, with certainty in his voice, "Hard work. You gotta work harder than anyone you know, and I promise you will be good at whatever it is you want in life.

All it takes is the will and the promises to yourself that you are better than you think. Besides, you're only seventeen. You still have time. There's one thing about you even you don't know about yourself, and that's your heart, Eddie. You have a spirit that many try to acquire all their lives, even people who have it all.

"There's no amount of success, cars, or money in this world that can teach you that. You're born with it, and in a world where there's so much hurt, being in some honor class should not be the goal in your life. You think rich people are happy all the time? I've seen people who've had nothing all their lives and have more than those who have it all. Remember, sometimes those who have it all continue to strive into the wind for happiness. Your destiny will come, but don't give it a time. Instead, let time give you what you need."

"I guess you're right, Dad. I just, I just promised Mom—"

"Eddie, if your mother were here today, she would be so proud of you just the way you are. You've got nothing to prove except that you can continue to be a good man."

"Thanks, Dad." I hugged him and headed for my room.

"And Eddie?"

"Yeah?"

"Never, ever forget that the only time you were poor is when you didn't know how rich you were."

***

Over time Dad's health began to deteriorate, and his increase in weight caused blood clots in his calves, which then spread to his ankles and feet. An in-house nurse would come by twice a week and treat them, but that only helped a little. He'd bathe himself with cornstarch to

121

help with the chaffing on his body because he couldn't take many showers. He was afraid of slipping in the bathtub. I'd offer to bathe him, but he felt ashamed that he couldn't do it himself and never accepted my offer.

Fortunately, he was still able to walk but not without effort, and he soon had to use a wheelchair in the house. His recurring obesity became the center point for harassment too. I remember once when he came back from the Sentry Market by Jefferson High School, where some kids were calling him names and threatening to kill him. They didn't know my dad, but they hated him simply because he was overweight. I thought if these kids had caught him in his prime, they would have had a lot more respect for him. But Dad came to God the same way fate drew me to Portland, and even if he could've hurt those kids, divine intervention would have stopped him.

Dad's philosophy about hate was that it could only breed more hate and that the act of forgiveness was more powerful than the act of violence. I asked how he could be so kind and patient with people like this, and he would always say, "This is the way Jesus would have wanted it done." My father was a man of love and kindness, and never once did he judge anyone.

Chapter 16

I'm Sorry

It had been three years since Ed went into the military. He had successfully made it through the first phases of his training, which included nine weeks of boot camp and several more weeks of Advanced Individual Training. He was assigned to the 75th Ranger Regiment and was ready to begin the US Army Ranger Indoctrination Program and eventually Army Ranger School.

The final test would start once he completed the Ranger Regiment program, which was all about selecting soldiers who had what it took to be Army Rangers. Ed wrote about how happy he was to have made it that far into the program and said that a normal day in Ranger School was typically twenty hours of grueling training, all with sixty-five to ninety pounds of equipment on his back. He was expected to exert himself like this on two meals a day and an average of three and a half hours of sleep a night.

I had no doubt that if anyone could succeed, Ed would. Most people knew him as someone who had an overwhelming amount of discipline and lion-hearted courage that was conditioned to do anything he put his mind to.

As a reward for completing his training, the army gave Ed a two-week leave of absence to visit his mom. I was so excited that prior to his arrival, I went out searching for a new watch for him. I headed downtown to Meier & Frank and found a nice Timex watch with a black face and a black stainless-steel flex band. It cost about twenty-five dollars, and I had thirty in my pocket. I couldn't wait to see his face when I gave it to him.

On June 27, Betty drove me to the airport. We waited in the terminal for Ed to disembark from his plane. It seemed like it took forever to see my best friend come around the corner and down that narrow corridor.

Then there he was, a slender soldier wearing his uniform with Ranger wings on his lapels, spit-shined black shoes, a black beret tilted to the right of his perfect haircut. He didn't have a million bucks, but he damn well looked like he did. I embraced him as if he were my brother.

"Ed! What's up, man?!" I threw a few playful punches at him. "You look great, bro! Look at you, dawg."

Betty hugged Ed. "How's my sweet boy? I've missed you so much. How do you feel?"

"I feel great, Mom. I missed you."

"Ed, I want to give you something," I said, pulling the watch from my inside jacket pocket. "Here, man. This is for you."

"What is it?" He glanced down at a Timex box I had in hand. "You crazy Puerto Rican! What'd you get me, now? Damn! This is *fly*, Eddie. Thanks, brutha."

"No, problem, man. I thought you would like it."

We shook hands in a fashionably funny way and then drove to DeNicola's pizza restaurant and just caught up on good times.

For the two weeks Ed was visiting, I noticed a few things about him that were different. He cussed more, which he had never done prior to joining the military. He

124

also seemed a little sad and secretive. We could be hanging out and Ed would start singing military songs and become more political in his speech. Then he would speak of how he learned to "kill and utilize a weapon against the enemy." I started feeling he had lost the sense of innocence he once had. It was a side of him that was hard to accept.

The next day Ed grabbed an old basketball, and we caught the bus to Wallace Park. We sat under the shelter near the court and made up for lost time. Several guys and a girl we'd never seen before were playing. It was kind of cool to watch her hold her own against a bunch of bigger, sweatier, slightly taller, and even faster guys.

Ed watched her every move. "Who's that girl?"

"I don't know. We should catch the next game with her."

With a gleam in his eyes, he replied, "I want to meet her."

"I've seen her around at Couch Park."

After the other guys' game, Ed shot some balls to warm up and then introduced himself to the girl. I couldn't blame him for being interested because she was stunning. At that moment I thought, *What is she like as a person?* She had blond hair, very red rosy cheeks, blue squinty eyes, and lips that were so shapely that even I wanted to lay one right on them.

Ed started talking to her, and then they both walked over for Ed to introduce me to Paige. She wiped the drops of sweat off her forehead and said, "Hi. You guys come here often?"

Ed replied, "Yeah, we do, usually to play football. She plays pretty good ball, doesn't she?"

I replied, unable to take my eyes off of her, "Yeah, she's pretty good. You come here a lot?"

125

"I just started, but I live just up the road."

"Cool."

She smiled. "Maybe we'll see you again."

Ed replied, "Yeah, we'll be back."

The guys on the court called her out for another game. Paige hurried away and said, "I gotta go, but maybe I'll see you guys later."

"Count on it," Ed said, glancing at me, then back to Paige. "Are you going to be in the park?"

"I'm having a little get-together with some friends at my house—give me a call."

Ed quickly asked, "What's your number, Paige?"

Paige gave it and said, "See ya!"

Ed looked over and pumped his chest into the air, "That's right, homeboy, I *gots* her number."

"Ed, man, she's gorgeous," I said. "I don't know what the heck she sees in you."

"That doesn't matter now, homeboy, as long as I got her digits."

We laughed, and Ed shadowboxed with his hands. That was his way of showing me he was extremely excited.

In the second week of July, Betty and I drove Ed back to the airport. We sat down in the terminal and talk about what seemed like everything, but mostly about Paige. He glanced over to the oversized terminal window at the American Airline dock and said, "There it is, Mom."

Betty began to cry. I held her in my arms and said, "It'll be okay, Betty. We'll see him again."

Ed lifted his green duffel bag over his shoulder, adjusted his beret, and gave his mom a long hug. He then looked over and said, "Hey, Eddie. I love you, man. I'll see you when I visit again, okay? And thanks for the watch, homeboy."

"Okay. I'll be strong, man," I joked. "But don't think you'll be able to beat me in the three-thousand-meter run when you get back."

Ed smiled. "When I get back, I'll wipe your Puerto Rican wetback ass all over Portland."

We laughed, but it was a disguise for the hurt of knowing we were going to be apart.

The door to the plane opened, and people began boarding. Ed hugged us both and said, "I love you guys." Then he headed down the corridor into the plane. He waved a last goodbye and gave me a thumbs-up.

Betty put her arm around me and with her sweet, tender voice said, "My Ed might have left, but my other son is here with me now."

Later that evening, I went to Lincoln and jogged six miles in flat shoes around the track, knowing this is what Ed would have done for me.

***

It had been several weeks since Ed left, and I had become closer friends with Paige, finding myself wanting to be near her. I would ride my ten-speed from my Albina Street home to Northwest Thurman where she lived in a two-story home, just blocks away from the Thurman Bridge, the same bridge overlooking Macleay Park where we had our weekend parties. We'd sit for hours in her kitchen talking about anything—except Ed.

Then one evening my phone rang. "Eddie?"

"Oh, hi, Paige."

She asked, "Whatta you doing right now?"

"Nothin'. Just hangin' out. Why?"

"I'm bored."

I said, "Well, you want me to come over?"

"If you want, but I'm actually babysitting right now."

I asked, "Really—where?"

She replied, "Just up the street from my house."

"So, did you...did you want me to come over?"

"Sure. No one's here, and they won't be home until tomorrow."

I said, "Okay, but it'll take me awhile to get there."

"No problem," she said. "Here's the address."

I grabbed my ten-speed bike and rode down Mississippi Avenue, passing the cross streets, over the Broadway Bridge, and then finally into Northwest. I rode over the Thurman Bridge and, when I got to the house, walked up some very mossy steps.

Paige was as excited to see me as I was to see her. "Hi, Eddie! I'm glad you came. Come in. You want something to drink?"

"Yeah, sure. I'm pretty thirsty." I looked around and asked, "Whose house is this?" curiously touching anything within arm's distance.

"It belongs to a friend of mine."

"It's a cool place."

I stood behind the breakfast bar while she sat on a stool across from me. When we glanced at each other, we had a connection, but I turned my attention to the homeowners—really, anything that might steer me away from what I really had in mind. I asked, "So, the people who own this house, what do they do?"

"I think the dad's a civil engineer or something, and I'm not sure what his wife does."

"Oh, that's cool."

She asked, "Does that really interest you?"

I laughed quietly and replied, "Well, I guess not."

We maneuvered toward the leather sofa, and Paige sat near me. I looked at her pretty, blue eyes and asked, "Do you have feelings for Ed?"

She replied sadly, "Yeah, I do. But I feel alone sometimes."

I knew by her saying those words, something was going to happen. I'd had thoughts of how I wanted her, and now I was torn between doing the right thing by Ed and doing what my heart felt was right.

"Paige, do you think it's good for me to be here?"

"Do you feel uncomfortable?" she asked. "Do you want to leave?"

"Well, something inside me says yes, but it also says no."

"I know how you feel, Eddie. I'm having mixed emotions about everything." Paige worked her hand over mine.

"Wow, I guess I didn't expect this."

She replied softly, "Neither did I."

She slowly reached over and kissed me, and instead of pulling away, I reacted with a kiss. She grabbed my hand tighter and said, "How do you feel?"

"Nervous."

All I wanted was her in my life. She stood up and guided me toward the nearest bedroom door, slowly pushing it open, and said, "Come in," gently holding my hand in hers. "It's okay."

I felt like I was losing myself in her world. "I feel...I feel really—"

Paige said, "I know."

We kissed passionately as I melted in her favor.

As I rode my bike back home, I cried because I cared for Paige but I loved Ed.

Chapter 17

I'm an Airborne Ranger

The teachers at Lincoln genuinely cared about my education. One I'll never forget was Mrs. Pat Walker. She treated us with love and patience while also pushing us academically, teaching us a passion for learning and the drive to finish whatever we started. I sometimes felt like she was family.

After school I would take a ride in Butler's new red Ranchero, which he'd customized with white metal pointed teeth on the front. Everyone knew who owned that car and stayed far away from it because it was Butler's pride and joy. I loved driving it.

Riding in nice cars, going to parties, and having friends, however, didn't fill the gaping void from missing Mom. Instead of focusing on my studies, I experimented with alcohol and skipped classes. Eventually, I would not graduate with the class of 1985 and would go back for another year. Embarrassing as returning to school was, not getting my diploma was not an option.

Ed was about twenty-one years old and on another visit to Portland. He wanted to finish up his time in the military, go to college, and work with his hands—building homes was his dream. I knew he was visiting, but I waited to call him because of the guilt I felt about sleeping with Paige.

I was staying out one night with Tom, Butler, and Joey under the shelter at Wallace Park when suddenly I saw a bright headlight slowly make its way onto the basketball court. At first it was hard to see, and then I could tell it was Ed on a motorcycle honking its horn.

I stood up, surprised. "Ed, that's so cool, man! This is badass! When did you get it?"

"You wanna go for a ride?"

"Hell yeah! What kind of motorcycle is this?"

"A Honda Interceptor 500."

I was awed by the red, white, and blue colors as I climbed on the back. "Let's go! Let's go ride."

Ed carefully rode the bike out of the park and onto the road toward Friendly House. My eyes watered from the warm wind.

I shouted over the roaring motor, "Ed, you know, I saw Paige the other day."

He glanced over, "Oh yeah? How she doin'?"

"She's all right. Are you going to go see her?"

"It's over. She wrote me a letter and said she no longer wanted to see me."

I couldn't help but think that I'd had a part in Paige's decision. I could tell it hurt him simply by how he casually ignored talking about it during our cruise.

Ed exclaimed, "Wanna see what kind of power this thing's got?"

"Go 'head. Tear it up, man. I bet it's gutless."

Ed kicked it into low gear and gave it throttle. I nearly fell off the back seat.

"Whoo!" I yelled, nearly peeing my pants.

"Told you this thing had power!"

We rode until late that evening and met up outside Tom's house to drink beer and reminisce. A pretty, petite

Spanish girl named Jovana walked by and said, "Hi, Tom. You're having a party and didn't invite me?"

"Hey! Jovana, what's up?"

"You tell me, Tom. You didn't even tell me about your party."

"Nah, nah, it's not like that. Come here let me introduce you to my Airborne Ranger buddy. Ed, this is Jovana."

Jovana sized him up like you would an ice cream cone and said, "Hi. Nice to meet you."

Ed replied, "Nice to meet you."

Tom offered, "Wanna beer, Jovana?"

"No, thank you. I have to move on, but we'll see you later."

I didn't know Jovana, but I did see her around the park, often standing on the sidelines and watching us play football. I could see Ed liked her right on the spot, especially as he leaned toward Tom to say, "She looks fine, dude. Is she taken?"

Tom replied, "I don't know."

"She's cute!"

Ed hurried up to Jovana and began talking in his Casanova way, using mannerisms only an American gigolo could get away with. Moments later, he came back and said, "Eddie, she wants to hang out with me, right now."

"Ed, c'mon, man. Are you serious? I thought we were hangin' out with the boys tonight."

"C'mon, man. We're just gonna kick it for a while," he said. "Don't worry. I'll catch up with you later."

Joey piped up, "When a man leaves his buddies for a skirt, you know there's a problem, dude."

We all laughed as Ed sped off with Jovana on his new motorcycle.

Before Ed went back to the army, I was able to finance a 1985 Kawasaki Ninja 600R along with a red, white, and blue leather riding jacket and a helmet. Now we could ride together on two of the coolest, fastest bikes known to mankind. Long rides on crazy buses were a thing of the past.

**

Several blocks from a park called Council Crest up in the hills in Southwest Portland was a suburban, well-kept neighborhood lined with contemporary homes. Every day, a white, skinny kid named Woody from the Council Crest neighborhood would park his '63 white Ford Thunderbird on the east side of Lincoln, where it was a focal point of discussion. It sported white-walled tires, white leather upholstery, black stitching, and a bright-red steering wheel.

It was absolutely immaculate, and we all loved riding in it. Woody quickly became our friend. Meanwhile, Tom purchased a new 1970 Ford Maverick with a custom built 302 V8 and a three-speed transmission. Every time he sped off in it, the hairs on the back of my neck would singe from the fire it blew from its tail pipes. If speed had a name, it would've been called Maverick.

Woody had a bash at his house, and it seemed like the whole senior class showed up. After Ed parked his mom's car, we walked toward the front of the house, past a fountain with a statue of a naked man in it and lush flower beds.

We walked in and heard "Tarzan Boy" by Baltimora playing in the background. Butler was mixing piña coladas in the kitchen, moving back and forth like a bartender serving a bunch of unruly drunks.

"Woody," I asked in a surprised tone, "where'd you get all the beer?"

He paused from showing Tom his new big-screen television. "From Trenton. I gave him two hundred bucks, and he bought it and kept the change."

News spread quickly about the party, and even Kristina showed up with her best friend, Michelle. There was a half gallon each of Bacardi Mai Tai and California Coolers spaced out on the counter. I opened the refrigerator and saw that the food had been removed just to fit all the partygoers' alcohol, including stacks of Budweiser cans above the fridge.

I grabbed a cold one and watched Butler mix the drinks in a blender. "You know what you're doin'?"

"It's real simple, Eddie," Butler said, grabbing a sixteen-ounce red plastic cup from the counter. "You see, you gotta hold to your convictions when you mix up this here shit. This here's a man's job. That's why Woody gave it to me. First you take the Bacardi and a cup, and you fill it with the Bacardi. You follow, Puerto Rican?"

"Yeah, I follow you. Damn! That's too much," I blurted. "It's gonna taste like crap!"

"No, no, it's the right amount, homeboy," he said with confidence. "You put it in the blender, grab some ice, put it in the blender, grab the mix, put some in the blender, and top it off with a little bit of this magic gold beer—grab me the Tabasco sauce."

"What! Tabasco? You already messed it up with the beer," I said strongly as I handed him the Tabasco. "This is whack! I tell you—now I ain't drinking that poison."

He continued, "See here? I put a few drops of this Tabasco in—boom, boom—mix it, and voilà! I'm done."

"There's no way I'm gonna drink that," I said. "No way."

"No, here, try it. Try it!" Butler insisted, practically shoving the combustible drink into my face.

A crowd gathered, including Ed, so I said, "Look, man, I'll try a little, but that's it."

He held the cup directly in front of my face. "We're all waiting."

I seized the cup, reluctantly sipped, and almost spat it out on Woody's cream-colored tile floor. "Oh my God! You should be sent to jail for this awful piss."

Butler poured sixteen ounces of it into another cup, exclaimed, "Watch this piss go into my gut," and guzzled it as if it were a can of frosty Coke. "Damn! That's strong. I think I'm feeling a little buzz now." His face looked disgusted as he rubbed his stomach.

"I told you. Ain't nobody gonna drink that crap. I'll just stick with my beer."

Ed came up from the living room, opened the refrigerator, and snatched a beer. He saw Butler sweating profusely and asked, "What's wrong, big boy?"

I interjected, "Oh, well, Butler thought he could be a big man by drinking a cup of that nasty mix, and now he's paying for it."

Ed smelled what was in the blender and blurted, "Damn! That's nothing but Bacardi. What's that brown stuff in there?"

Butler acted like he felt lightheaded, rubbing his stomach and saying, "I gotta sit down, bro." He struggled awkwardly into the living room, crashing his massive body onto the sofa.

Ed and I grabbed several more beers and sat on some steps outside Woody's house, staring at the naked statue. It was quiet outside, but inside sounded like *Animal House* with laughter and slurred dialogue.

I sipped my beer and said, "Hey, Ed?"

"Yeah."

"Have you ever killed anyone out there in the bushes?"

He looked at me strangely, drank a big gulp of his beer, and replied, "Nope. But I've seen things I wish I hadn't."

"Like what?"

He shook his head, stared at the ground, and sadly replied, "Hungry kids, oppression, you name it. You know, I really didn't know how lucky I was till I enlisted and saw how much hurt was out there."

"Do you regret enlisting?"

"Nah. I regret not making something out of my life," he said sadly. "Here I am drinking beer, and I don't feel like I'm going anywhere. You know, one day I'm gonna get married, spit out a few kids, watch 'em grow up, and build houses."

"Married?" I asked. "Man, I can't imagine either of us getting married. It seems like that only happens to parents."

"We have to. It can't just all be drinking beer and going nowhere. There has to be more to life."

"You know, my dad always says if you follow God, you'll never need to look for anything else. Whatta you think?"

"I don't know, man. Maybe. I do know I'm fittin' on downing this beer right now," Ed said theatrically, lifting the can to his lips and gulping it to the last drop.

I nudged him and said, "That's messed up! I could down a beer faster than that, homeboy."

"Well, c'mon, Missing Link," he said, making a funny face. "That sounds like a challenge to me."

We rushed inside and got six more beers out of the refrigerator and laid them across the kitchen counter like a row of dominos. I looked into the living room and called, "Butler! Woody! You guys, come 'ere! Ed and me are gonna have a slamming contest."

Butler brought his body up from the sofa, paced up the stairs, and said, "I gotta see this."

136

Everyone else followed. Ed grabbed two beers off the counter, pulled both tabs and handed me one.

Andrew, a close friend who lived in a house just past the Thurman Bridge, was there watching the challenge. He wasn't the average stuck-up rich kid who looked down on anyone. We felt he'd been shunned by his parents because he didn't follow in the same path as his sister. He didn't mind being the black sheep of his family, however, since he had now found a new family with us. It often seemed as if nothing ever bothered Andrew. He could be insulted, thrown down, and beat up, and he would simply laugh it off and move on. The one thing about Andrew that only his closest friends knew was his sensitivity about his huge head and long neck. This is why we gave him two nicknames: Charlie Brown and Bottleneck.

Andrew barged between us and said, "Okay, wait. I'll give you guys the go-ahead. No sipping. No cheating—that means you, Eddie."

"Man, shut up, Bottleneck! I ain't gonna cheat."

Ed and I each held a can of beer close to our lips and waited for Andrew's signal.

Butler said, "Y'all just a bunch of bitches. I could slam two of those faster than both of you put together."

I sipped the foam off the top, and Tom accused, "You're cheating, Eddie! No cheating."

"I'm not. Chill out, Castro."

Kristina said, "Eddie, don't do it. You're gonna get sick."

"Don't worry, baby. This is for you," I said, acting as if I had control over the challenge. "This here is for my girl."

Andrew proceeded, "Okay, drinkers get ready, get set. Go!"

I tilted the can up and felt the beer drizzle past my lips while I swallowed as much as possible.

Butler was cheering, "Go! Go! Go!"

I got down to my last guzzle and beat Ed by a couple of seconds. Butler handed us two more beers, and this time, I could see in Ed's eyes that he was determined to win the next round.

Butler said, "Okay, drunks. Ready? Cans to your lips, get set, go!"

I gulped as fast as I could, but Ed was taking bigger swallows as beer trickled down the sides of his mouth.

"Go! Go! Go!" the crowd cheered for Ed since I'd won the previous round.

I glanced at Kristina from my peripheral as she rooted me on. "C'mon, Eddie! You can do it!"

We tilted our cans farther back, and seconds later Ed crushed the can with his hand and yelled out an Airborne Ranger shout, "Hooah!" Then he sang, "Airborne Rangers lead the way, Airborne Rangers lead the way. Deep in the battlefield covered in blood, lies an Airborne Ranger dying in the mud. Airborne Rangers lead the way. Those silver wings upon his chest tell America that he's one of their best. Airborne Rangers lead the way! Hooah!" Then he threw his can on the floor.

I felt a heavy buzz come on and almost had to take a seat on the floor. That didn't stop Ed from proclaiming his victory over me, proudly poising his finger directly over my head. "You see, boy, you're just a squirrel tryin' to get a nut in a big man's world. You will never be me! Hooah!"

I retorted, "Okay, punk ass, another one. I challenge you to another one."

Butler said, "Wait! I got an idea. Woody, do you have two empty two-liter bottles?"

"Yeah, there under the kitchen sink."

Butler grabbed them, snatched a knife from the kitchen drawer, and cut them in half.

138

"Okay, you guys think you know how to slam? Well y'all gonna have to drink outta this!" He declared, victoriously holding the two plastic bottles up over our heads, handing them to us. Ed and I each took one, brought the spout snug to our lips, and tipped the bottoms up. I said, "Go ahead and pour it in, Butler."

Butler continued, "Okay, I'm gonna get two beers and pour them into the containers. First one to drink it empty wins. And no cheating, Negros." He pulled the tabs and held them over the two-liter funnels.

Ed and I tilted our heads farther back and anxiously waited for the beer to rush in.

Butler announced, "Alcoholics ready, get set, drink!"

He poured both cans, and I could see the strain in Ed's neck trying to take in every ounce he could.

Woody shouted, "Go! Go! Go! Man, I can't believe they're doing this."

Butler ordered, "Woody! Open two more and bring 'em here!"

He tossed the first two cans onto the floor and pulled the tabs off the ones Woody gave him, pouring those into the funnels. My throat felt like a dam had broken and a flood of rushing alcohol came running through it, but I wasn't about to cry uncle.

Butler demanded, "Woody, get me two more goddamn cold ones—quick!"

Woody popped two more, brought them to Butler, and urged, "Here! Take it!"

He tossed the empty cans to the floor, and before Ed and I could finish drinking the previous round, had Woody grab a fourth round of beers from the fridge. As he started pouring, people cheered, "Do it! Do it! Do it!"

Suddenly, I couldn't drink another drop and jerked my head down, ran to the sink, and spewed everything from my mouth into the basin.

Ed continued drinking the beer as everyone cheered, "Ranger! Ranger! Ranger!"

He brought the bottle down, let out a long belching sound, and exclaimed, "Hooah! You don't know how to drink it—that's what it is. Rangers lead the way!"

"Ed, man, I'm feelin' messed up, dude," I said, arched over the kitchen sink, dry heaving. "I need air."

He patted me on the shoulder and said, "Maybe next time, young'n." He walked away as I heard indistinct laughing.

It was about eleven thirty p.m. when Kristina approached me, reaching her hands around my waist. "Eddie, I have to go home now."

"Why? The…the party…the party's just startin'," I slurred. "Come on, stick around."

"You're drunk."

"Nah, I'm—I'm not drunk. I'm just feelin' a little uncoordinated," I said, swaying, trying to stay in one place. "See, look?"

"I gotta go. Call me tomorrow."

"Don't go, Kristina. Are you upset with me?"

"I just don't like seeing you this way."

I followed her outside to her car. She slid into it, rolled the driver's window down, and said, "Bye, Eddie. And please don't drive home, okay?"

"C'mon, Kristina…you really think I'm that du-dumb?"

"Eddie, this is no joke. If you drive home, something could happen. Promise me you won't drive."

I reached my head into her window. "I promise. I promise," I said and kissed her.

Kristina said softly, "I love you. Be safe."

"I will, I'll be fine. See you tomorrow."

She drove off as I watched. I went back inside and into the living room.

Ed asked, "Where've you been?"

"Outside taking care of business."

"Oh, yeah, I know what kind of business you've been takin' care of," Butler gestured a masturbating motion.

"Man, y'all wish you had some business you could take care of."

Ed pitched me a beer. "Here, have another one. It'll take the edge off. Besides, I gotta go, man. I gotta go home and get sobered up."

"Why, man? You're too messed up to go anywhere."

"'Cause, I gotta...gotta get my u-uniform."

"You gotta get your uniform? What the hell for?"

"I have to. I'm going back in the next couple days."

"I don't know, dude. I promised Kristina I wouldn't drive."

"No, dumbass. I'll drive."

"Ed, we're too jacked up, but if you know what you're doin'—"

He wrapped his arm over my shoulders and confidently said, "I know what I'm doin'! Now, c'mon, Missing Link. Hey, Woody, I'm going back to my house."

Woody nodded.

"What?" Tom exclaimed. "You're not going anywhere, Ranger!"

Tom search Ed's pockets, looking for the keys to the car. "Where are they? Where'd you put your keys?"

"There in uh...safe place," Ed said, casually pulling a can of Copenhagen from his back pocket, dipping a pinch full, and shoving it in his bottom lip.

"C'mon, quit messin' around," Tom said. "You're in no condition to drive."

Ed pushed Tom away and said, "All right, all right. I won't go. Just chill out."

"You promise?" Tom asked, pointing his finger at him as if he were a child.

"Yeah, I promise!"

"I'll watch 'im, Tom," I said. "If he tries to go anywhere, it'll be with me."

Ed dashed toward the front door like a shoplifter running from the scene, beating us to the car and then locking himself in.

"Ed! C'mon, man, and open the door!" I pleaded, firmly tapping on the window.

Andrew marched to the back of the car and leaned on it, crazily jumping up and down on the bumper.

Butler stood in front of the car and declared, "Negro's gonna hafta go right through me first."

"C'mon, Ed. Get out!" Tom demanded, beating on the driver's door.

Ed was teasing us with the keys in his hand as if he was going to start the car and drive off.

Tom pressed his hands against the driver's window, "Okay, Ed, I'll let you follow me down the hill, and if I think you're driving okay, I'll let you drive the rest of the way."

"What? Dude, are you nuts?" I said. "He's too whacked! Even I know that."

"I'm using psychology on him," Tom whispered. "Just go along."

Ed cracked the window. "You promise you'll let me drive down the hill?"

"I promise," Tom answered impatiently. "I promise I'll let you drive down the hill."

"Don't fuck me, Tom. Don't you ever fuck me," Ed said, sounding like Al Pacino in *Scarface*. We laughed hard.

Then I hurried to the passenger's side and urged, "Ed, Tom will let you drive, but you gotta let me ride with you."

He opened the door. "C'mon in, Missing Link."

Tom said, "Eddie, you help him steer down the hill if you see he has a problem."

"Got it covered, Castro. Don't worry about it."

"I'm serious, Eddie. Watch him! As soon as I see you guys not driving right, I'm pulling you over."

I laughed and said, "Okay, I got it, man. Quit holding us up, Mr. Wannabe Officer Dumbass."

Tom hurried to his Maverick and started it.

Ed commanded, "Put it on KGON. Find KGON on this piece of shit."

"I can't. This radio's just AM," I replied, pushing all the buttons on the stereo panel.

He rolled down the window and pinched a glob of chew out from his lower lip, tossing it onto the pavement. Butler jumped into Tom's car, and they slowly drove off, taking the lead.

Tom waved his arm outside his window and yelled, "C'mon! Follow me."

Ed's heavy foot jerked on the gas pedal, and my head whipped back. The car sped down the hill away from Woody's house. I was so drunk that my head dropped underneath the dashboard as we drove down Southwest Chehalem Avenue then past Council Crest Park and along the curvy hillsides. As my head swayed with the car's movement, I knew that if I didn't sit up to help steer, we were going to wreck.

We followed Tom onto Southwest Greenway Avenue into an unforgiving downward abyss that led us into a hell of a ride down Vista Hill. I felt the car weave and heard the tires screech just before I smelled smoking rubber. Then we spun 360 degrees and a couple hundred feet down Vista Avenue.

Ed shouted, "Oh shit! Oh shit!" trying to recover control of the car. It spun again and again and suddenly came to a halt just inches from the edge of a hill. I vomited

143

in the car, and when I looked over the dashboard, I saw a stone wall.

"Wha'...what happened?"

Ed replied excitedly, "I was handling it! Handling it! Did you see that? Did you see that?"

"What the hell happened? Where are we?"

Ed said, in an animated tone, "We're on Vista Avenue, dude! Did you see that? You missed it. We almost went over the cliff!"

He tried to restart the car, but it wouldn't turn. Cars maneuvered around us while Tom made a quick U-turn and sped back up toward us. His car came to a halt with the headlights shining directly at us. Then Butler pushed open his passenger door and quickly rushed to our aid.

"Ed! What happened?" Tom asked. "You guys okay?"

Butler pulled my door open. "I can't freakin' believe what happened."

Ed replied, "Yeah, man. Did you see that, Tom? The car spun several times down the hill, homeboy."

"Yeah, we saw it. At first we thought it was a cop car with its lights on.

Butler said, "Tom, we gotta get this car outta here before the cops come."

"Okay, I'm gonna drive Ed's car, and you drive my Maverick back up to Woody's."

When we got back to Woody's, we partied longer to the scratchy LP sound of "Louie Louie" by the Kingsmen. We locked our arms as we formed a line and slurred every one of its lyrics, dancing from side to side, taking turns falling to the ground. When the party died down, Butler crashed on the sofa while the rest of us slept on the living room floor with no blankets or pillows.

At nine a.m., a ringing doorbell woke me up. I had a severe hangover but managed to move unsteadily toward the front door. Betty was standing there with a baffled look and said, "Oh, my Lord."

"Hi, Betty." I let out a loud belch that smelled like alcohol. "I'll get Ed."

"Are you okay?"

"Yeah, Mom. Hold on."

I sauntered into the living room, but Ed wasn't there. "Ed?" I called. "Where are you?"

"What?" he replied from the bathroom. "I'm over here."

"Dude, your mom's here. She's at the front door, man."

"I know. I called her to come pick me up."

"You called her? Why? She's gonna know we've been drinking."

"I need to go home. I'm tired of being here."

Betty walked in and saw crushed beer cans and mangled cups scattered over the floors and counters, and a line of cups strung from the ceiling like a chandelier. She was at a loss for words and patiently waited for Ed to finish.

Once they left, I struggled into the bathroom, splashing water over my face. As I hovered over the sink and looked up into the mirror, I saw the reason for Betty's reaction: when I'd fallen asleep, the guys used my body as a human billboard, running mascara under my eyes, scattering smiley faces over my half-naked body, sloppily painting lipstick over my lips, and scrawling the word *loser* on my forehead.

Chapter 18

Home for Good

  Two great things happened for me that year. Michael had another baby girl, Naomi, and Ed was coming home for good. I put together a surprise party for him at my house. Tom, Butler, Joey, Jimmy, Kristina, and Jovana hung out at the house while waiting for us to show up from the airport. I remember thinking, *Now my best friend is here to stay.*

  Ed walked down the corridor wearing his black beret, the silver wings pinned to his lapels once again symbolizing the rank of an established soldier. His rosy-red cheeks, clear hazel eyes, and slender body were signs of a true athlete who had just completed the hardest regime in the world. We greeted him with open arms.

  He kissed his mom on her cheek.

  Betty was crying. "Hi, baby. My beautiful son is home for good."

  The kissing and hugging lasted for several minutes before I chimed in, "So you think you're a tough Ranger now, huh?" I grabbed his duffel bag, and we walked toward the car parked outside the terminal. "How's does it feel to be home?"

  Betty got in the car as I loaded the trunk.

  "It feels good, Eddie" Ed said. "I'm glad I'm out of there, knowing I'm gonna be a civilian again."

146

"Why, was it too tough for you?" I said jokingly.

"Boy, I'm an accomplished Ranger, and you betta show me respect!" he declared, with a closed-fisted right hand to his chest. "Don't forget it."

We got into the car and headed to my house.

"Where we going?" Ed asked.

"We're going to the base where the rest of the soldiers are!" I grunted, pretending I was an authoritative figure from the military.

"You'd be a good sergeant, Eddie. You should join. It's not just a job, it's an adventure!"

"No way, man. I don't think I'd like it if a sargent yelled spit in my face all day."

Ed said, "You wanna see something?" He unbuttoned his left shirt sleeve past his elbow and showed me a tattoo of a black panther stealthily pawing down a bed of rocks.

"Whoa. When did you get that?"

"In Germany. You like it?"

"Yeah, it's cool, but I'm surprised you did that."

He jiggled his arm to give off the impression of it moving and said, "Well, it's there forever now."

When we arrived at my house, I said, "C'mon, Ranger, time to see my ol' man."

Ed led the way to the front door, and I noticed how excited he was to see Dad, whom he loved and admired. Many times Ed had called him collect from the barracks to ask questions about the Bible, and Dad had recited scripture to him.

We had walked several feet into the dark hallway, turned left, and headed toward the living room when Ed asked, "Why is everything so dark?"

That's when the lights came on and everyone shouted, "Surprise!"

Dad sat in his old, beat-up chair, wearing a blue cotton hat and oversized pants and suspenders with streaks of cornstarch on them.

There was a crayon-colored banner pinned to the wall above the entrance to the kitchen that read: *Welcome Home, Ed!*

I showed him into the kitchen and said, "See what we made? There's lasagna, garlic bread, white rice, chips, and plenty of soda pop and beer, man. It's an all-you-can-eat buffet in the 'hood, brutha."

"Looks good," Ed replied. He walked over to Dad, hugged him and said, "How you doing, Al? It's good to see you!"

"Hey, Ed, thank God you got home safely," Dad said, holding the Bible. "I prayed for you every day."

We mingled and took turns talking to Ed while the music played.

Betty said to Ed, "I have to go now, honey. What time will you be home?"

"Later, Mom. I just wanna spend time with my brother Eddie cause he ain't heavy." Betty smiled because she knew Ed was referring to the song by the Hollies, "He Ain't Heavy, He's My Brother."

"Okay, you stay with your brother and call me if you need a ride."

Kristina stood quietly in the small, crowded living room while I spent time with Ed. Meanwhile, Butler, Jimmy, and Tom were in the kitchen, digging their forks into a plate of lasagna when I said, "Hey, Jimmy, you should try coming up for air, man."

He laughed and replied, "Man, this is grubbin'!"

A couple of hours passed, and everyone had left except for Kristina and Jovana. When Ed slipped into my room with Jovana, Kristina and I tried to keep my dad talking so he wouldn't get the urge to go to his room and catch them kissing. Dad was at a high weight and usually

148

bedridden. Every day he maneuvered his wheelchair from his bedroom to the living room in front of the television.

Dad had lacked enthusiasm since Mom passed away, but I couldn't blame him. At some point in our lives, we became weary of the way the world is layered with imperfect people and the struggle of just trying to live. I think he was tired of how people treated him and fighting to be better. When you're already downtrodden by life and then someone you love dies, you die with them.

Kristina talked with Dad about his life as I went into the kitchen to clean up, spooning the leftover lasagna into plastic bowls and covering them with aluminum foil. After a while, Ed and Jovana came out of my room, Jovana's hair slightly messed up.

"Hey, Al." Ed walked over to Dad and wrapped his left arm around his obese shoulders. "I missed home. I missed a lot."

My dad asked, "How'd you like your party?"

"It was awesome! All the great food, my beautiful mother, my buddy Eddie—it was awesome. Awesome!"

"Good, good. You know, we all worried for you and prayed for your safety." Dad patted Ed's lower back. "Especially when they sent your battalion to Libya. That worried all of us."

"I worried for you guys too." As Ed said this, he eyed the pretty, graceful Spanish Jovana standing in the hallway. "Yo, baby, why don't you bring your fine self over here?"

Jovana fluttered her eyelids, giggled, and said, "Whatever."

Ed caught my attention. "Where's your Ninja?"

I motioned at the back door. "In the garage."

"Oh, you mean the shack. Let's go check it out," he said, stepping into the kitchen and unlocking the back door.

Kristina grumbled, "Oh, okay, the girls will just sit right here like little dogs."

In a Don Juan manner, I responded, "Nah, baby, that's not how it is. We'll be back."

We walked outside past the naked branches pointing at the gray sky and across the brown patchy grass, into the run-down garage behind the house. Spring was close, but the trees seemed hesitant to bring up new life.

Ed glanced at my motorcycle and asked, "Did you just clean it?" running his hand over the bike.

"Yeah, the other day."

"Looks real good!" Ed said, lightly touching the front fender.

"We should go riding tomorrow, if it's nice," I said, jokingly gesturing my right index finger over his head, "unless you're afraid of the Ninja, homeboy."

He smiled, "The Interceptor rules, baby. You know that." Ed had a serious look.

"Something up?"

Ed straddled the motorcycle, aimlessly staring at the gauges on the bike. "Nothing's wrong. Just that, well, I just missed home real bad."

"I know man. We missed you as much as you missed home."

"Kristina seems like a nice girl. Is that her car out front?"

"Yeah man. Nice Audi, huh? Can you believe it? She'll probably never have to work day in her life."

"Why's that?"

"Her mom and dad are pretty well off. They let her drive any car she wants. You know it would take us a million years to have one of those cars."

"A rich girl going out with a poor boy," Ed said, grinning widely. "Yeah, that's what I'll call you—poor boy just like those po' boy sandwiches."

150

We laughed and I replied, "Ah, man, that's cold blooded. Not cool."

The serious look on Ed's face came back. "Hey, Eddie, I gotta tell you something. I think Paige is pregnant."

My heart skipped a beat then pumped at a thousand miles per second. All the guilt I felt about being with Paige that night came back to haunt me. "Wh-whatta you mean?"

"I think she's pregnant," Ed repeated in a low tone.

"How? Did she call and say this?"

"She wrote me a letter and said she might be pregnant."

"You're kidding, right?" I hesitantly asked, "Do...do you know for certain the baby's yours?"

Ed slumped over the gas tank and wrapped his hands over his bowed head. "I don't know. I don't know what to do."

I asked, "Well, are you sure about this?"

He sat up and sighed, "That's what she said. It's probably some other guy's, and now she wants to blame it on me."

"I don't think so, Ed. I don't think she would lie," I continued. "You gotta talk to her, man; you gotta find out what's going on. What about Jovana?"

"She doesn't need to know. I haven't told her anything. I'll deal with it. I'll talk with her."

"You will? Even if you guys are no longer on speaking terms?"

"If I have to, I'll take care of the baby. I'll do what I gotta do."

"Ed, let's not get ahead of ourselves."

I sat on the edge of the concrete foundation that held up the garage, sunk my head down, and sighed. "Damn, this is messed up. I'm not sure what to think."

"Don't worry about it. Like I said, I'll deal with it." Ed stood off the motorcycle and said, "It seems like I'm becoming a man faster than I thought."

I stood up, slipped my hands into my jeans pockets and walked around the motorcycle beside him. "Whatever I can do, man, I'll be here for you. You know that. We're brothers."

Ed shook my hand. "Thanks, Eddie. You're a good man."

I knew the ice was broken and suggested, "How 'bout we go riding later instead of tomorrow?"

"Yeah, let's do it."

As we walked back I asked, "You gotta name for him?"

Ed smiled at the idea of being a father and replied, "Twinkle Toes. I'll name him Twinkle Toes."

"Well, that's a good name."

The next day, Ed wanted to pay a surprise visit to see his dad, who he called Buzz, so I borrowed my dad's white 1965 Ford station wagon, and we drove to the Columbia Villa complex searching for him. The Columbia Villa was in a low-income neighborhood, much like the projects I used to live in, but row houses. It was located in North Portland, close to the industrial area, a place most people didn't care to visit.

The same neighborhood was patrolled by an anti-gang Portland police unit because of the Crips, which were spreading through the area. Because Buzz and Betty were separated, Ed hadn't seen his dad since he'd been stationed in the military, so at first he was little nervous.

We drove to a home with partially hanging, rusted gutters and spray-painted gang signs laced along the sides of it. It was the closest reminder to where I had come from in the ghetto, but in my opinion, this tough neighborhood was not quite as dangerous. We walked over areas of

152

patchy brown grass and stepped in front of the house with different shades of paint chipped over the door.

When Ed knocked on the door, a corpulent black lady wearing a tight, netted outfit—bulges of fat squeezing through the netting like a hefty mountain of pancakes—answered the door. "Yeah, what?"

The place smelled of marijuana, and four partially naked, barefoot kids stood beside her.

"Do you know someone they call Buzz?" Ed asked politely.

"Who?"

"His name is Buzz. He...he's my dad. I think he lives in one of these homes, but I'm not sure which one."

"I haven't seen nobody name Buzz 'round here. Try that apartment over there." She pointed to another door across the brown fallen leaves and unseeded soil. "He might be over there."

"Thanks," we said and walked across the grass to knock on that door. A fat, tall man with messy hair, a chipped front tooth, and a bottle of Night Train in hand answered. "Yeah?"

"Does Buzz live here?" Ed asked.

"Buzz?" the man replied in his abrasive voice. "Oh, yeah, yeah. Hold on."

"Who is it?" someone in the background cried out. "Who's at the goddamn door?"

The tall man opened the door wider, looked behind him, and said, "Someone's looking for you."

A short, stocky man wearing striped boxer shorts with holes in them stood up from a cut-up, urine-stained sofa and walked a few steps closer. That's when I saw the welts on his fatigued, drunken face. He was surprised to see the only family who ever came to visit and exclaimed, "Craps!"

For some strange reason, Buzz's nickname for Ed was Craps.

Ed replied, "Hey, Dad!" as he walked in to hug him. "How you doin', ol' man?"

Chairs, newspapers, and old cardboard boxes were strewn across the place, and wine bottles lay everywhere. To the left of us, a small black-and-white television sat on an old kitchen table. Buzz proceeded to slur, "This is m-my drinking buddy, Judd."

Ed nodded.

Buzz insisted, "Sit down. Sit down," as he cleared some clothes from the sofa. "So, what've you been doing, Marine punk?"

Ed chuckled. "I'm an Airborne Ranger, Dad. Just like you were, remember?"

"Fuck the Rangers! Goddamn pussies!" Buzz raised both his hands into a karate pose and said, "C'mon, Craps. Let's see how tough you are."

Ed laughed, copied his dad's moves, and jokingly said, "Dad, I don't wanna show you my Ranger skills. I might hurt you."

"Oh, yeah? C'mon, Craps. I'll tear you a new asshole."

I began to laugh.

Ed helped his dad back to the sofa, saying, "Dad, I could kick your ass all over this apartment. Sit down over here before you have a heart attack and let's just talk."

"Eh, screw it!" Buzz said, "I'm too tired to kick your ass anyway."

We laughed.

Ed asked, "So what've you been doing with your life?"

"Drinkin' booze and more of it," Buzz replied, with a drunken smirk on his face. "How 'bout y-you?"

"Drinking booze?" Ed said, "You know that stuff's not good for you."

"Whatta you talkin' about? It's better than sex!"

"Is it?" I chimed in.

154

"Goddamn right it is!" Buzz said, standing from the sofa grabbing a can of Hamm's beer from the rickety kitchen metal table, giving Ed a lesson in beerology. "See this can here? It doesn't talk back to you, bitch and whine at you, call you a liar, judge you for who you aren't—heck, it's everything a man could want in a woman."

Ed smiled, but I knew better. I knew his smile was only covering the hurt he felt seeing his dad this way. "Come back and sit down, Dad. So whatta you gonna do today?"

Buzz sat down and demanded, "Get me a woman."

That amused Ed. "And who's going to be the lucky woman? I thought you said booze is better than sex."

"It is," Buzz confirmed, licking his wet lips ready for another drink.

"Then why do you want a woman?"

"'Cause I do it better when I'm drunk."

Ed said amusingly, "How do you know you can still even get it up?"

"Whatta you mean? I could be unconscious, and I would still be as hard as a rock!"

Ed laughed, stood up, and reached for the television dial. "Dad, you're crazy. What's on the tube?"

"Nothing, as usual, or you could put it on that fat bitch, Oprah. There's nothing ever on," Buzz said. "Hey, why don't you get me a woman?"

"Dad, I'm not gonna get you a woman. Besides, the woman I would get would be a slut. You don't want that."

"How do you know what I want? You don't know shit, Craps!"

Ed said, "Dad, you'll just get a disease or something, then you won't be able to have sex at all."

Buzz said roughly, "I'll put a rubber on."

"Let's talk about something else," Ed suggested. "I'm tired of talking about women."

155

"Ah," Buzz said to his roommate. "Hey, Judd, get me another drink."

Ed sat close to his dad with his arm over his shoulders and a solemn look on his face, not saying much to anyone. I pulled a chair from the kitchen table and watched reruns of *The Muppet Show* for the next hour.

By now I was bored. "Hey, Ed, we should probably go."

Ed asked, "Is there anything you need, Dad? Anything besides rubbers?"

"Yeah, yeah, why don't you get me some wine down the street?"

"Some wine? You don't need wine. Look at that gallon you have sitting on the table."

"That's my backup bottle."

Ed and I laughed. Ed said, "Backup? That bottle should last you a few weeks."

Buzz smiled then slurred, "I c-could drink that bottle in twenty minutes. So why don't you go to the grocery up the street and get me a bottle of, uh, Night Train?"

Ed stood up. "We gotta go, Dad. I love you."

We walked toward the door, and I opened it. Just then, Buzz clinched the back of Ed's jacket. "You need some money—food stamps or something?"

"No, Dad, I don't need any money. Why don't you use that to buy some underwear?"

"What's wrong with my underwear?"

"They've got built-in air conditioning all over them!"

"I just wear these around the house, you know. Don't you have a pair like these?"

"No, I don't. We gotta go. I love you," Ed said, leading the way out of the apartment.

"Come see me again, Craps!" Buzz yelled out as we walked toward the car.

When we got inside the car, Ed didn't say a word, but it didn't take a rocket scientist to know what he was thinking. He was sad, upset, and possibly even ashamed. I really didn't know what to say, so in order to break the silence and make some light of a sad situation, I asked, "Why do they call your dad Buzz? Is it because he's always buzzing?"

Ed grinned. "No, man, his formal name is Edmond, like me. Though I never thought about it that way."

Chapter 19

For Mom

The day finally came for me to receive my diploma. Dressed in my finest slacks, pink long-sleeved dress shirt, and polished black loafers, I confidently stepped on the bus to the Keller Auditorium downtown. It was around the corner from the Cookie Cabana where Gerard worked as a baker. West from the auditorium was Keller Fountain, which consisted of several manmade concrete waterfalls and steps.

When I arrived, Kristina was waiting outside. Then she ran toward me, embracing me with a kiss. "You made it. I'm so proud of you."

"Thanks, babe. Have you seen Ed and Betty?"

"No, are they supposed to be here?"

"Yeah, I thought they'd be here by now."

We walked across to the fountains and admired the tumbling waters gracefully splash into drops of music, "This is beautiful," I said, drawing closer to her glistening eyes. "I'm glad you're here with me."

"I wouldn't miss this for anything," she replied, kissing me. "You worked hard for this."

"Hard to believe that, well, I'll be outta high school. Not sure what I'm gonna do."

"Now you're going to move on to bigger things. Just follow your heart. You'll find your way, Eddie. You'll find it."

"You know, my dad says that to me."

Kristina pulled me closer. "I'm sure whatever does happen, it's going to be good."

As we headed back to the building, I saw Ed standing out front with his mom.

As Betty and Kristina turned toward the auditorium, Ed and I walked across to the fountains. He swung his arm around my shoulders and said, "I'm proud of you. Your mom would be too."

"Yeah, I wish she was here right now."

"She is, Eddie. She is. She's watching down from heaven saying, 'There's my little Puerto Rican, wetback son. I'm so proud of him.'"

"You think so?"

He answered, in an understanding tone, "You've come a long way from being a New York kid who had nothin'. Who knows where you'd be if you were still back there? We probably wouldn't have become homeboys if you didn't come to Oregon. Everything happens for a reason—everything." He placed his hand on my shoulder. "By the way, I found out Paige is not pregnant."

"That's a relief," I said, but I noticed he seemed sad. "What's wrong?"

"I just wonder what it might've been like to have a little one."

"You think you were ready for that?"

"I don't know. Maybe."

"Well, like you said, everything happens for a reason, right?"

"I suppose. You know, Tom's enlisting into the Marines."

"He told me. I wish he wouldn't," I said, shaking my head. "Hey, Ed?"

"Yeah."

"You think you and me will grow old together?" Ed joked. "What? Are you homo or something?"

I chuckled. "No, man, I mean, you think you and me will always be best friends no matter what?"

Ed pointed to my chest. "I will always be right here 'cause you and me is homeboys. We're one and the same, so you never have to worry."

"Hey, I can still whip your Ranger ass. You know that right?"

"Shut up, po' boy," Ed said, as we threw a few playful punches at each other. "C'mon, let's go inside and get this over with."

We swung our arms around our shoulders and were headed back when I said, "Hey, Ed?"

"Yeah."

"Maybe we should both build houses."

Ed smiled. "Sounds good."

When we got inside, I saw Butler, who was also graduating. We couldn't find our seats along with the other students, so we held up the ceremony for several minutes. The announcer came out and gave a speech about the class of 1986. One student a few seats down threw his graduation cap up in the air and yelled, "Whoo!" before the speech was over. The announcer commented, "I'm not embarrassed—they're *your* kids." Everyone laughed.

After the speech, the seniors went backstage and waited to receive our diplomas. A staff member came up to me and asked, "Eddie, how would you like your name to be announced?"

"Um, how 'bout Eddie Stallion Regory?"

"Is that what you want?" he asked in a hurried manner.

"Yeah, that's how I want it."

When it was time for my name to be called, the announcer said, "Eddie Stallion Regory!"

I rushed out in front of all those people, received my diploma, did a two-step dance, and headed off the stage.

When the ceremony ended, the school had a senior pizza party with card games, bingo, and other activities that lasted all night at the YMCA. The next morning, we had breakfast on the *USS Kansas City* on the waterfront. On the bus ride back home, I rested my head against the window, peering into the downtown streets of Portland, watching people waiting at bus stops and moving about. Then images of Mom flashed through my mind, especially the times we had living in New York. I quietly muttered, "This was for you, Mom. This was for you."

***

Ed and I rode our motorcycles everywhere. It became a ritual for us to get up on those hot summer days and ride through the streets of Portland, taking in the green trees, passing over the Fremont Bridge, and stopping at Wallace Park for one-on-one basketball. We rode side-by-side like Poncherello and Officer Jon Baker did in that 1970s show *CHiPs*. When we felt the need for speed, we zoomed down windy roads or up the Burnside hill. It was like moving at the speed of light as people watched us weave in and out of traffic. The road belonged to us, and we knew it.

Early one summer morning, we were riding and decided to stop near the Thurman Market across from Friendly House to play Asteroids and Pac-Man. Afterward, we stopped at Friendly House and saw Hazel and Tatiana and challenged them to several games of foosball.

By about eight thirty p.m., Ed said, "Let's go riding."

"Where to?"

"Anywhere. Doesn't matter. The wind is calling us, man."

I looked over to Hazel. "Good seeing you. You gonna be here tomorrow?"

She smiled. "Maybe."

We grabbed our helmets and riding jackets and stepped out of the center. We rode past Wallace Park down Raleigh Street, passing the Gypsy Restaurant and Lounge, and Cinema 21 on Northwest 21st Avenue.

"Hey, Eddie?" Ed called out, trying to get my attention through my helmet. "Let's go play tag at Couch Park."

"Serious?"

"Yeah," he answered. "It'll give us something to do."

We parked our bikes near the basketball court where I'd first met Ed, and we played tag on the structure until the streetlights came on. Shortly after dusk, a police car drove slowly through the park and stopped in front of the structure. A black, heavy-set police officer stepped out.

"Hey!" he hollered. "You need to get down and leave the park, now!"

I stared down. "Why? It's not even ten p.m. yet. Doesn't the park close at eleven?"

Ed stood by, watching the commotion before stepping off the structure.

I continued, "That's not right! We shouldn't have to leave the park if we're not making noise or bothering anyone."

The officer became agitated and quickly pulled his billy club from its holster. He clenched his hand tightly around the handle. "Get down or get hurt!"

Ed started to walk away when the officer demanded, "You stay right there! You don't go anywhere. I want to talk to you."

I nervously proceeded down the structure toward the officer as he'd requested. He held his club close to his body while I stood there wondering what was going to happen next.

The officer asked, "Why didn't you come down when I asked?"

I stammered, "I-I-I don't think it's right for you to push us around, man."

He shouted, "Get on your stomach, now!"

I didn't think that was wise because where I came from, getting on your belly for a cop could mean losing your life.

"Why?" I asked.

That's when the cop grabbed me by my shirt and threw me down to the cement, shouting, "Get down!" With his heavy foot on my back, the heel of his boot pressed firmly against my spine. I felt the point of his club solidly pressed against the small of my neck. He did a pat-down search and declared, "Stupid kid."

At this point, I didn't know where Ed was. Then I heard him yell, "Leave my friend alone! Leave him alone! We didn't do anything to you."

The officer released his foot. I quickly stood up and saw Ed holding a huge, heavy steel garbage can lid. The officer put his hand on the grip of his gun.

I shouted, "Ed, run!"

I ran the opposite direction, glanced over, and saw Ed running faster than I'd ever seen.

"Hey! Stop! Stop!" the cop yelled, calling for backup.

I ran behind the back yard of the William Temple Church, but it was dark and I couldn't see a thing. I suddenly came to a complete stop when my neck ran into a clothesline.

"Ugh!" I gasped before landing flat on my back.

I grabbed my neck, rubbing it to soothe the pain, and stayed there for a minute. The officer didn't know we'd ridden to the park, so I knew Ed would have the sense to meet me later by our motorcycles. I wandered around the neighborhood and then walked to the Quik Stop next to Cinema 21.

I waited until the clock in the mart said it was one a.m. and then went back to the park to see if Ed was there. Sneakily glancing across the basketball court, I saw him sitting on the same railings where we'd first met.

I whispered loudly, "Ed!"

"Eddie!" he answered.

"What happened? Where's the cop?" I asked. "Where'd he go?"

"Man, Eddie, I was scared. He called for backup, and they looked for me in a building. I hid by Fred Meyer."

"You mean that building on Everett?"

"Yeah, that one," he said. "That cop was an asshole!"

"You telling me, man," I said. "Why do you suppose he was pushin' us around like that?"

"I don't know. I really don't know."

"Then what'd you do?"

"I hid," Ed said. "But before I got to the building, I stopped and looked at the cop straight in the eyes and pointed my finger at him and said, 'The laws of justice will put you in your place.'"

"What'd he say?"

"Man, I just ran after that, fool. That fat cop couldn't catch me."

We laughed.

"Damn, dude. I can't believe what you did," I said. "You were moving out."

Ed replied, "I never ran so fast in my life."

"I know. One second you were there, the next about three blocks down the road."

"Let's get outta here 'fore he comes back," Ed said.

We rode to the 7-Eleven on Southeast Powell and bought two Big Gulps and nacho cheese chips, loading it with jalapeños, onions, tons of cheese, and chili. When we got back to Ed's place, I could see he was a bit distressed. He slipped off his running shoes and sat on his bed.

"Ed, you okay?"

"Yeah, I'm just ticked off," he replied, bringing his head down. "Why'd he have to come at us like that? It's just not right."

"Because he was a prick!" I said. "It was a slow night, and the bully didn't have anything else to do. Besides, the doughnut shop was closed."

Ed switched off the lights, turned over into his bed, and fell into a troubled sleep.

At about five thirty, he was screaming.

I woke from the noise, but my eyes weren't adjusted to the dark. "Ed, Ed, what's wrong?"

I was startled, but not surprised, only because I'd seen him do this before. He mumbled some words and went back to sleep. Ed thought his violent dreams were because of the spicy foods he ate.

The next day Ed went into the kitchen to make breakfast. I stepped out from a well-deserved rest, rubbing my eyes. "What's up, bro?"

"Nothin'. Have a seat. I'm making some energy food."

"What is it?"

"It's my power breakfast. Frying up some white bread with eggs, cinnamon, vanilla extract, and butter."

"Sounds healthy," I said sarcastically. "Whatta you call it?"

"Peanut butter French toast. We put the peanut butter on last." He set two plates of French toast on the table and grabbed a jar of Adams peanut butter. "This is the best peanut butter in the world," he said. "Try it on your toast."

"You want me to put this on my food?" I asked, leery of what it might taste like.

"Yeah, go ahead. It's good. Try it," he insisted. When I hesitated, he picked up a butter knife and spread some on my French toast. He then opened a new bottle of aunt jemima syrup and poured some over my toast.

"That's enough, man," I said. "That's way too much."

Ed looked over to his mom sitting near the TV and watching the *Today* show. "Mom, did you know Eddie's dad met his wife at sixteen? Right, Eddie?"

"Yeah," I replied, still eating my breakfast.

Betty said, "Well, he must've loved her very much to see her at sixteen. You tell him I love him."

"I will." I said, looking over to Ed, "Say, man, this is awesome! Where'd you come up with this peanut butter French toast idea?"

"A guy from the barracks showed me how to do it." Then Ed suggested enthusiastically, "Hey, why don't we take the bus downtown today?"

"The bus? Are you crazy! We've been taking buses for years, and now that we have wheels you wanna take a bus? No way, man. Not me. I ain't doin' it."

"C'mon, man. It'll be good for us," he said. "We'll go see that new *Heartbreak Ridge* movie with Clint Eastwood."

"All right, but we'll have to come back and get our bikes because I'm not stayin' out all night without my wheels."

After breakfast, Ed slipped his boots on, and we caught the bus downtown to the Fox Theatre on

166

Broadway. It was about three p.m., and the movie wasn't starting until five fifteen. We walked into the nearby Newberry's, where they had a pet shop on the basement level, and played with the animals. Then we headed to Old Town just north of Burnside.

There is where we saw homeless people lying against dirty alleyways and roaming the streets with cheap bottles of wine snuggled into their unwashed clothing.

"I bet my dad's down here," Ed said. "How can a country so rich not help these people?"

"I don't know, man. It's just the way it is."

Ed moseyed to a homeless man sitting against a storefront and asked, "Hey, buddy, you hungry?"

The man, with his dirty, long beard, wrinkled face, holey shoes, and tired eyes, looked up and nodded.

"C'mon," Ed said, helping the man to his feet. "We'll take you to get some grub."

We took him to the Burger King on West Burnside. Between the both of us, we had enough money to see the movie and buy snacks, but Ed didn't think about any movie. His purpose now was to give this man a warm meal and whatever else he needed.

The man was a bit incoherent, so Ed ordered for him. "Hi, uh, how 'bout two Whoppers and fries."

We sat down and watched him eat. He didn't say much, although you could see in his eyes that he was thankful.

Ed wrapped his arm around the man and said, "Hold on there, buddy. You're gonna choke if you don't slow down."

The man smiled while he finished his food, and by the look in his eyes, I could see he was thanking Ed for saving his life for that one day.

Ed asked, "Hey, buddy, you want us to take you back?"

The man nodded.

Before we left, he looked at Ed with his wrinkled eyes and quietly said, "George."

"George? Good to meet you, George," Ed said. "Eddie, give me some money."

"Why?"

"Because I'm gonna give it to him."

"But he'll buy alcohol with it."

"Does it matter?"

I handed him my last five-dollar bill. Then Ed reached down to untie his army boots and forced them off. He handed them to the man and said, "Here. You need them more than I do."

I said, "Ed? You gave him your boots? Whatta you doin?"

He replied, "The right thing."

We skipped the movie and walked to Keller Fountain.

Ed bent over to rub his feet, "Now my feet are getting cold."

"You did an amazing thing, Ed. You really did."

Ed said, "You know, I gotta quit drinking. After seeing that guy, I don't wanna be like that. My father is like that."

"Well then, let's both get in better shape like we used to be," I said. "You know the one thing I'm afraid of?"

"What?"

"When my mom died, I promised her I'd do something with myself, and here I am, doin' nothin'."

"You ain't a bum, Eddie. Just give it time."

I said, "Don't you ever wonder where you're going or what you're gonna do with your life?"

"Yeah, I do all the time," Ed replied quietly. "I just turned twenty-three, and I don't even have a job yet."

"You're twenty-three, and I'm twenty. Maybe I'll write our story," I said. "My dad always said I had the gift of gab."

Ed laughed. "What would you write?"

"I don't know. Maybe I'll write about you—how you wish you were like me and that I have enormous power over your weak, Airborne Ranger ass." I kept teasing, jostling him as if I was going to push him into the fountain of water.

Suddenly, Ed jumped into the cold, running water with his clothes on and his hand stretched toward the sky. "I have been baptized!"

In disbelief, I yelled, "Dude! You're fuckin' crazy!"

"C'mon in," Ed invited. "The water's cold."

At first I hesitated, then jumped in.

We were like kids splashing in the water. When it was time to leave, our clothes were dripping wet on the bus back home. People looked at us like we were crazy, but we didn't care. We later stayed up to watch *The Tonight Show with Johnny Carson*. I glanced over and realized I loved Ed so much that even giving my life for him would be a small price.

***

The next evening we rode our motorcycles to Wallace Park and sat under the shelter, the whole time watching Tom play basketball against Butler and Joey. Whenever we played, Tom's bony elbows would flail like helicopter blades at our faces, so we'd end up forfeiting the game to save our teeth.

I saw headlights slowly making their way into the park. As it got closer, we knew it was a cop car. Butler quickly said, "Hide the beers!"

I tossed them in a nearby garbage can. The car made its way onto to the court, and two cops stepped out. At first I couldn't see their faces, but when they stepped closer I saw them clearly. Ed and I looked at each other and thought the same thing. One of them was the same black officer who had harassed us at Couch Park.

"Whatta you guys doin' out here?" the officer asked.

"Nothin'," I replied nervously. "Just playing hoops."

I wouldn't look him in the eyes so he shined his light into my face. "Have you guys been drinking?"

"No, we haven't. We've just been playing hoops," Joey answered in a cool manner. "Just chillin' and playing hoops."

The cop was paying more attention to Ed. "I think I know you. Yeah, you're, you're—"

I politely interrupted, "Officer, we can leave now if you'd like."

"I know you," the cop continued. "You're the same guys who were at the Couch Park location."

"Other park?" I questioned, acting like I had no idea what he was talking about. "I don't know what you mean."

"You just cut your hair, didn't you?" the cop said to Ed. "Stand up. Do you have ID on you?"

Ed pulled out a thin black leather wallet from his jeans pocket. The cop shined his light onto the ID and looked up at Ed. "Turn around and give me your hands!"

He handcuffed Ed and read him his rights, put him in the police car and questioned him awhile longer. Then he came back to me and said, "I'm taking your friend to the Portland Precinct. He'll be going in front of the judge in the morning." The cop's partner kept a careful eye on the rest of us.

They drove down Raleigh Street. When I got home, I thought about Ed's actions the night he saved me from that cop at Couch Park. He'd demanded the cop stop threatening me even though all he had for protection was a garbage can lid. Ed was protecting what he loved the most—just as that cop would have done if he were saving his own family.

Chapter 20

My First Puff

Tom had already left for basic training, and I managed to get a new job at the Lloyd Center Theater in Northeast Portland working the graveyard shift as a janitor. The bright neon signs, huge theater screens, and THX sound gave me the feeling of being in Hollywood and helped me escape from my problems. I'd always had a passion for the movies. The black and whites, the color movies, the stupid movies, and even the animated ones were great.

I'd often invite Dad to go see one with me, but he felt he was too fat to fit in the seats and thought people would think he was a freak. I assured him I wasn't embarrassed and didn't care what people thought, but I often wished he was healthier so we could do more together.

He did enjoy working with wood and would cut out animal photos from magazines to use as patterns for his next project. Then he'd give the wooden animals to neighbors or anyone who liked them. It was a way for him to keep his sanity, especially after Mom died.

Sometimes we'd have long talks about her, and he would suddenly cry, wishing she was still alive. I felt helpless in trying to comfort him, sitting on his bed and powdered with cornstarch. I'd wrap my arm around his

172

obese back, showing him the love a son should give to his father. When Dad was in the mood, he loved singing opera while in the kitchen washing the dishes. I'd be listening in my bedroom and encourage him to continue, but he would always say it took too much air out of him.

We didn't always get along, though. Once I arrived at home upset and angry and Dad noticed.

"What's wrong, son?"

"Everything, Dad. I'm tired of just getting by, seeing everyone else get ahead. I'm sick of all these minimum-wage jobs, never having enough money to get what I want, barely making my motorcycle payments."

"You'll get yours someday. Just give it time. Life's not like the movies." He patted his bed for me to sit near him, "Come here, son. Sit down. Some people work a lifetime to achieve things, but you still don't realize that your biggest achievement is your desire to be more than those who just give up. Eddie, you have many talents, but the best gift of all is you've got your mother's heart."

I said, "I'm tired of working hard. I work and what do I get? Nothing," I rested my elbows on my knees and brought my head down. "Why do we have to be poor? Why couldn't you make things better for us?"

"Son, I tried! Don't you think if I had the money, I would give you whatever you need? Don't you think if I could've given your mother a better life, I would have? I would've helped your sister and brothers. I hate living this way! I can't even afford a pair of decent underwear because I'm in hock up to my ears. Who knows, maybe I could've had your mother live a little longer. My poor wife, she didn't deserve to die! I should've been the first one to go. Me, Eddie, me! I failed her, and I failed you guys. I'm sorry."

Dad struggled back into his wheelchair, rolled himself into his room, and cried on his used-up handkerchief.

173

Afterward I felt terrible, so I entered his room and said, "Dad, I'm sorry. I didn't mean those things. They were wrong of me to say."

"It's not your fault. You're right. All my life I've worked nothing but labor jobs, barely getting by, praying—hoping—for something better to come along. But nothing's gonna knock on your door, son, and hand you a dream," he said, blowing his nose with his handkerchief. "You gotta go out there and earn it. You gotta want it so bad you can taste it. But if you live your life the way I did mine, you'll never want anything but death."

"Dad, don't say that. It's not your fault. Life's not so bad. I just see people like Kristina who have all these nice things and new cars, and I wish I had a piece of that lifestyle."

He said, "It's funny, people with money wish they had more time with family, and poor people wish they had more money. Don't you see the irony in it, Eddie? Money doesn't make you happy; giving is what makes us happy. Money won't pay for honor, your self-respect, or even honesty." Dad grabbed my hand. "All money can ever do to people who want it is either destroy them or make them forget who they are. Is that what you want, Eddie? To forget where you came from and what we sacrificed for you and Joey?

"A man isn't measured by the money he has but how he got it. What does it all matter if you don't have God in your heart? You could die tomorrow, and then where would you take your money and cars, Eddie? Do the important things in life, and the rest will follow. You've got your mother's will and ambition; you've just gotta believe—believe you can do anything." Dad paused, sighing deeply. "Now I'm tired and want to go to bed."

I moved closer. "You're right, Dad. I shouldn't have gotten so upset."

174

"It's okay, son. Come here," he gently laid his hand on mine. "Eddie, you have the most precious, wonderful gift in the world. You have your health. When you've got that, nothing can stop you. If I were a rich man today, I'd give it all away to be with your mother. I would not think twice about it." Dad blew his nose.

I brought my head down and quietly said, "Dad, you really think we'll see Mom again?"

"Yes, I do, son. I do with all my heart."

***

A week before Kristina's graduation, Larry, Kristina's dad, loaned me a red 1987 Porsche 944 Turbo with spoilers. It was a dream come true to drive this streamlined piece of machinery. I felt like the king of the road. That same week, Kristina went looking for a prom dress. My tuxedo wouldn't be ready until the day before the prom.

I drove the Porsche to Ed's place, hurried to the front door, and knocked.

"Hey, wetback, what's up?"

"Ed, come check this out!"

"What?"

"Come out here," I said, motioning him to follow me. "This is gonna trip you out."

He begged, "Come on! Just tell me what it is. Can't you just tell me what it is?" Suddenly, his eyes opened wide, focusing on the bright red Porsche parked along the street.

"Whatta you think?" I asked.

"Whatta you mean?"

"What do I mean? This is my ride for Kristina's prom. I have it for the week."

"No way! Are you serious?"

"Dead serious," I said. "Come on, I'll take you for a ride, po' boy."

He grabbed a cassette tape from his house, rushed back, and nearly dove into the car. We cruised south on 82nd avenue past the Clackamas Town Center mall and then merged onto the interstate, hitting a high speed of 137 miles per hour. Ed put the tape in the Blaupunkt stereo, and we blasted the sounds of "Take On Me" by A-Ha as we raced back to my house. When we arrived, we parked the car in the garage so no one would see it on the street and break into it.

We entered the side door and saw Dad sitting in his chair watching television.

"I dig your shades, Al," Ed said sarcastically, referring to the black garbage bags stapled over the living room windows.

I stood there laughing at his comment.

"Hey, man, they work," Dad replied.

"You too poor to buy real blinds?" Ed said, with a funny expression. "I gotta couple of bucks. Let me help you out."

"Yeah, I'm poor. You got money? You gonna buy me some?" Dad said, slightly leaning forward with his hand out and eyes wide. "Tch, man, you're not gonna buy me spit."

"Yeah, Al, I'll buy you some."

Ed was making me laugh so hard, I couldn't breathe. "Oh, man, I gotta sit down. This is too funny. Ed, you gotta quit."

He wrapped his arm around my dad's shoulders. "Youza poor Negro needs me to buy you some blinds."

"Nah, man. I don't need you to buy me nothin'," Dad said proudly. "I like my poor man's blinds."

Ed chuckled then walked into the kitchen to get something to eat. Seeing a boiling silver pot simmering on the stove he asked, "Whatcha cooking, Al?"

"Old recipe my mom used to make: ham hocks, chicken bones, chicken feet, beans—all that good stuff."

"Mmmm, sounds good, yeah. I like body-part soup."

"You know, you don't have to eat it, Ed," Dad said. "I'm not proud. I'll eat it—all of it too. You know, you come into my house and start talkin' trash about my blinds and food. You can leave! The door swings both ways."

I interjected, "Dad, you'd eat anything that had a food label on it."

He pointed his finger. "Ah, you see, you forget where you came from."

"No, Dad, I didn't forget. I just know I have never eaten that crap before."

"As far as I care, both you guys can starve!" he said. "I don't care."

"Say, Ed, let's go out for tacos," I suggested. "There's a Taco Time up the road."

"Yeah, maybe we can throw the tacos in with the soup," Ed added.

I laughed. "That's cold. That's cold blooded."

"Go 'head. Make fun if you want," Dad said. "But when you're hungry and your stomach is tight and bloated, you'll eat my body-part soup then."

"Al, I ain't ever gonna eat that soup!" Ed said, laughing. "You couldn't pay me to eat that soup. In fact, my Army rations look better."

"You wanna burrito or something, Dad?" I asked.

"Nah, man. I'm gonna eat my soup and be content."

"Okay. But once we head out that door, it'll be too late." I looked to Ed. "Let's go, man, and leave him with his soup du jour."

We drove to the Taco Time on Interstate Avenue and had two crispy burritos. Then we cruised around until

177

two o'clock in the morning before heading back to my house.

"Let's flip a coin to see who gets the floor," I suggested.

"That's okay. I'll sleep on the floor. It's good for the back," Ed offered, pulling some blankets from my closet and laying them neatly on the floor.

I said, "Thanks. You da man. Hey, turn off the light."

"You afraid of the dark, sissy boy?"

I said, "Nah, man. I just can't sleep with the light on. Hey, Ed?"

"Yeah."

I said, "You know what I feel like right now?'

"What?"

"I feel like I'm on top of the world."

He replied, "Great. You can be on top of the world while I go to sleep."

I smiled and closed my eyes.

By about five a.m., I heard a loud scream coming from Ed, who was still asleep with his eyes closed. He sprung up and sprinted through the house like a madman. I then heard a shattering noise.

Dad was sleeping in his chair when this happened. I turned on the bedroom light and ran out into the living room. Ed had just awakened, standing in an incoherent state of mind over the broken television on the floor.

"Ed, you okay?"

He panted quietly and shook his head. "Yeah, yeah." He wiped the sweat from his forehead, retreated to the bedroom, and went back to sleep. I pieced the television back together and put it back on its stand. Dad looked shocked by what had just occurred.

"Dad, you okay?"

"He's not sleeping here anymore. There's something wrong with him."

I knew he didn't mean it. He loved Ed like a son. As I headed back to my room, I saw a hole the size of a fist in the wall on my left. I turned the light off and crawled into bed.

The next day we drove to Ed's place, and I asked, "Ed, remember what happened this morning?"

"What?"

"Dude, you went crazy in my house."

"I did?"

"Yeah. Don't you remember?"

"Sort of." He turned up the radio.

"I can't believe you don't remember," I said, dropping the subject.

When we got there, we straddled our motorcycles and rode to a friend's house in Northwest Portland. Ed and I walked downstairs into the basement area. It was the usual scene with beer, marijuana, and cocaine laced over the bar and the sounds of Jimi Hendrix playing in the background.

We maneuvered our way to the sofa to watch Madonna on their big-screen television. I later saw Ed at the bar talking to Phil, the owner of the home.

"Ed, let's go," I urged him.

"Hold on," he replied, cutting up lines of cocaine with a razor blade. "I'm busy."

"Whatta you doing?" I asked. "Whatta you doin' that for?"

"Hold on," he said. "I'm trying to finish this."

He pulled a half-cut straw and quickly snorted two lines. At first I couldn't believe my eyes, but then I was curious. "What's it feel like?"

"It numbs your nose," he answered. "It's no big deal."

"Why you doin' it, then?"

"Nothing else to do."

"Let me try it?"

"Nope. It's not good for ya."

Phil said, "Just let him try it, Ed."

"If I give this to him, he'll start trippin'."

"Man, I'm not gonna trip. You're the one who's trippin'," I said, motioning like I didn't care about trying it anymore. I sat back down to watch MTV, thinking about how Ed was now trying cocaine.

***

It was a hot July afternoon, and the skin on my shoulders was peeling from lack of sunblock. Kristina invited me to go swimming at her grandfather's house. I was having a good time doing belly flops and backward dives in the Olympic-size pool in the backyard. Her mother was sipping her margarita near the pool house. Strangely, her grandfather never introduced himself. At first I didn't think much of it, but as the day progressed, I realized that even though I had been invited, I felt my presence wasn't welcome.

After a couple of hours of playing in the pool, I was so hungry I would've eaten liver. I heard Kristina call from the patio, "Eddie, let's go!" I leveraged myself out of the pool and wrapped a white plush towel around my waist. She said, "Put your clothes on too."

I followed her into the house, and they were preparing hamburgers. My mouth was salivating, and I could feel the hunger coming on stronger. If I were at my house, I'd be picking the meat straight out of the hot frying pan.

Kristina said, "Follow me."

"Where are we going?"

"I'm going to take you home."

"Why?"

"Well, my grandfather wants me back up here."

"What? Why? I don't get it."

She hesitated and then answered, "He wants me to eat with them."

"I thought you were gonna eat with me? Wait a minute, wasn't I invited up here? I'm confused."

"I'm sorry, Eddie," Kristina said. "H-he told me to take you home."

I vehemently said, "What the hell! Why? Are you guys short on burgers or something?"

"No, Eddie. He just wants to make it a family thing."

"Kristina, I don't know where your family's from, but where I'm from, when you invite someone to your home, you treat them as a guest, not like shit! And that's the way I feel I've just been treated. Didn't you say something to him? Didn't you think it was sort of wrong? Or did you cower away again because you didn't want to hurt his feelings or whatever?"

"What's that supposed to mean?"

"You know exactly what I'm talking about. Why should you stand up for me? You get everything anybody could ever want, freely! Why should you care about me? You've never been able to be your own person, always trying to please them instead of yourself."

"I don't need to hear this! It's not what it looks like. He doesn't hate you."

"How could he? He doesn't even know me."

"Eddie, stop," she said. "What am I supposed to do? What do you want from me?"

"Kristina, don't you have any control of your life? You could have told him he was wrong. When my dad does something wrong, I tell him. But I think it's deeper than what I'm saying. I think you're afraid because he's got your future in the palm of his hand. Why should you blow your future on a nobody? I've got no rich future for you. I've only given you my love and my heart, but I guess that wasn't enough."

She began to cry and sat there quietly for the rest of the ride home. When we arrived, I hurried out and slammed the passenger door. Kristina rushed after me.

"Kristina, just leave! Leave!" I shouted. "I'll go to McDonald's or something."

"Eddie, wait!" she urged, trying to stop me from opening the front door to my house.

"Don't you get it? There's no more waiting. You've made your decision." I pushed open the door then shut it behind me.

She knocked heavily. "Eddie, open the door!"

"Kristina, go home. Go home to your rich daddy and mommy," I yelled from behind the door. "You think I like knowing I've got nothing to offer you? You think it's easy for me to not be accepted into your world?"

Moments later I heard her car driving away. I leaned against the door and thought about everything in my life, realizing I was lying to myself that I could belong in a world outside of my own.

A couple hours later, I picked Ed up in my dad's car and headed for Phil's.

"Hey, guys, party's downstairs."

We saw Butler relaxing on the sofa, watching television, and drinking a Hamm's. "I see you've upgraded your beer, man," I said sarcastically.

He retorted, "Yeah, just like I upgraded your girlfriend."

We laughed.

"Why you gotta go there?" I said. "Not cool."

"You asked for it."

I looked over and saw Ed and Phil taking bong hits together. "Say, man, let me try that?"

"You don't smoke," Ed said. "Besides, it's not good for you."

"You guys don't know how to smoke that shit. That's the problem," I said. "Ed, let me try it, c'mon."

"It's not a good idea," he said, exhaling smoke into my face. "Just watch me."

Phil passed me the bong. "Let him try it. Don't be such a hard ass on the guy."

"Whatta you want me to do with this?" I asked.

Phil said, "Just suck it!"

Ed laughed and said, "Yeah, suck it."

"Seriously. Show me."

Phil brought the bong close to his lips and said, "Make sure you seal your lips around it, and then suck the shit out of it like this."

He inhaled the smoke from the long tube, held it for a few seconds, and then exhaled.

"That's it?" I asked.

"That's it," he said. "Child's play."

I brought the bong to my lips and inhaled more smoke than I wanted. For about twenty minutes I didn't feel a thing, and then everything started to spin and my legs began to feel heavy.

"Ed, man, something's happening. I can't breathe!" I said, walking unsteadily toward the sofa. "This is weird."

"Just relax," Ed said. "Go lay down."

I was unable to control my actions and kept laughing at anything and anyone. Then I got to a point where I felt like I was going to die.

"Let's go home, stoner," Ed said, grinning widely.

I moved slowly off the sofa. "Damn, this isn't gonna go away, is it?"

"Just give it time. You smoked a lot at once."

He grabbed the keys from me and led me to the station wagon. We merged onto I-5, and I saw the freeway sign to Seattle. "Ed, I keep seeing the Seattle sign, man. There it is again! Ed, what's goin' on?!"

"Just relax," he said. "It's the pot trippin' you out."

Everything seemed like it was in slow motion. It took forever to get to his house, and all I remembered was flopping down on his sofa.

Chapter 21

The Encounter

When Kristina left on vacations, I would write her letters, and she kept every one I sent in a red shoebox hidden on her top closet shelf. This time was more than vacation, though. She would be leaving for college, and we both knew that once she left, she would finally become independent from me and perhaps her parents.

Her mother felt this was an opportunity for Kristina to finally get rid of me. In fact, she had once referred to me as the downtown guy and Kristina as the uptown girl. I didn't see much of her father either. He was always playing tennis or working at the dealership.

In my opinion, the only time Larry wanted to play dad was when he was nosy about Kristina's private life. Then one night Kristina called me crying.

"Kristina? What's wrong?"

"Eddie, this is embarrassing for me to say, but, my dad…my dad found my box."

"And?"

"Eddie, he found out I was on the pill and confronted me."

"What? Well, what'd you say?"

"I didn't know what to say. I was too embarrassed. I-I'm sick to my stomach. He said he was ashamed of me."

"Kristina, he has no right to be prying into your business like that. Put him on the phone!"

"No, Eddie. I don't think that's a good idea."

"Kristina, I'm going up there!"

"Eddie, please! Don't come up here. It'll only make things worse."

I sighed, debating what to do. "Okay, I won't. But are you gonna be okay? Do you want me to meet you somewhere?"

"No. It's okay. I'm going into my room to stay in there forever," she said. "I've got to go."

I couldn't stand feeling helpless, so I called a cab and proceeded to Kristina's with the intention of talking to Larry on a mature level. In the cab, I rehearsed what I would say. The driver glanced into his rearview mirror but didn't care. When we approached the long driveway to Kristina's, I asserted emphatically, "Stop right here, right here."

I reached in my back pocket for my wallet, realizing I'd left it home. "Damn," I said angrily. "Look…um…can you wait here for me?"

"Yeah," the driver said. "But the meter's gonna be running."

"Fine." I rushed out, jogged up the driveway, and knocked firmly on the door.

"Eddie?" Kristina was shocked. "Wh-what are you doing here?"

"I just wanna talk to your dad, please. I'll be calm."

"I don't know. I don't think it's a good—"

Larry called from the living room, "Kristina, who's at the door?"

I tried to step in, but Kristina blocked my path.

"Kristina, I just wanna talk to him."

Larry heard the tone in my voice and said, "Kristina, is that Eddie? Let him in already, and close the door."

"Larry, I wanna talk to you, now," I demanded in an authoritative voice.

"What?" Larry replied. "You need to tone it down, Eddie."

"I wanna talk to you. I don't appreciate you going into Kristina's personal box. You should mind your own business."

"Don't you talk to me like that in my house," Larry said angrily. "How dare you!"

"I'll use any goddamn language I please!"

Larry hurried from his chair, and I could see his face burning with anger.

Kristina's mother stood there, baffled, as Kristina pleaded, "Stop it, Dad! Stop!"

I barged my way closer to Larry and yelled, "Why did you have to pry into Kristina's box? Tell me."

"What?" he shouted. "Who the hell do you think you are? Get out of my house!"

"I'm not going anywhere till you tell me."

"You little punk!" Larry said, then grabbed me by my throat and pushed me up against an imported Japanese painting.

The glass shattered. I grabbed Larry's hands, pushing them off of me, and demanded, "Get off!"

We wrestled each other into the living room onto the plush white carpet.

I continued, "You wanna mess with me, ol' man? C'mon!"

I knew I could hurt Larry and, from the looks of it, he sensed it too. I rushed forward and punched him in his jaw. Blood spurted from his lip as Kristina's mother stepped between us. "That's enough!" she screamed. "Larry, that's enough!"

Kristina grabbed my hand. "Eddie, come on! Let's go."

Before we left, Larry glared icily and shouted, "I'm gonna sue your ass off, Eddie!"

I threw my hands up. "Sue me for what? I got nothin' anyway!"

Kristina pointed firmly at him saying, "No, you're not! I don't think so."

I thought, *For the first time, she stuck up for me.* We hurried outside and down the driveway.

She said, "I can't believe what you just did."

I saw the distressed look on her face. "Kristina, I-I'm sorry. I wanted to tell him how I felt and how wrong he was, but you were right; it got worse. I didn't mean for it to turn out this way."

"Eddie, I can't believe what you did, but...well, he's had it coming for a long time. Please go and I'll call you tomorrow."

She walked me back to the cab.

"Kristina," I asked slightly embarrassed, "I forgot my wallet."

She reached into her jeans pocket and handed me money. "Here," she said and quickly headed up the driveway.

I got in the cab and rolled down the window. "Kristina."

She turned.

"Thanks for standing up for me."

She smiled and walked away.

***

All the next day, Ed and I rode our bikes. Around one a.m., we headed onto Southeast McLoughlin Boulevard toward the Ross Island Bridge. We noticed an old blue half-ton truck pull in front of us. It had three guys in it, one of them wearing a cowboy hat. We sped past them, but before we knew it, the truck passed us. We were always up for a good race, so Ed passed it again. The race quickly got out of control as we sped past the other cars.

The truck tailgated Ed's motorcycle—inches away from his back tire—then got behind me and zigzagged. It didn't have as much low-end torque and therefore wasn't as quick as our bikes, but it must've had a powerful engine because it was definitely faster. I saw Ed motion his hand at a nearby closed gas station. Understanding the signal, I kicked my clutch into low gear and sped sharply into the station as the truck abruptly stopped behind us.

Three guys stepped out, tensed and their fists clenched, but that didn't scare us. We approached them, and I thought, *Oh, God, this isn't gonna be a fair fight.*

Ed rushed toward the man he thought was the leader and shouted, "You could've killed us, asshole! What were you thinking?"

"Well, why were you trying to race us?" the leader slurred, as if he'd been drinking.

The guy in the cowboy hat had a speech impediment and went along with whatever his leader friend said. "Yeah, yeah. Uh, why were you racing us?"

It appeared we were dealing with some rednecks, and I was afraid one might head back to the truck and pull a weapon. I also thought this was a bad time to get Ed angry, since he had been feeling upset about Paige.

I moved between them. "C'mon, Ed, forget it. These guys are out of it."

"No, Eddie! No. They could've killed us! Did you know that, asshole?" Ed turned and yelled at the leader. "You could've killed my best friend because you decided to ride on our asses with a two-ton truck! You're lucky I don't snap your fucking neck."

"Well, we didn't know," the leader replied.

Ed cringed, pointed at the leader, and asserted, "Don't you ever—ever!—get close to anybody ridin' a motorcycle! You have a truck, and I'm on two wheels. We could've gotten killed. And you could've run over us. Don't you ever do that again!"

They backed up, and the leader said to his friends. "Let's go. Come on. This guy's crazy."

After it was over, I felt proud of Ed's courage. He had more of it now than before he'd enlisted in the military.

He grinned. "Did you hear the way that guy with the cowboy hat talked? 'Duh, uh, duh.'"

"He was a joke, but they were scared," I added.

We continued our ride over the Ross Island Bridge past Powell Boulevard. We stopped at the 7-Eleven and had our traditional nachos.

Chapter 22

True Friendship

When I got home the next day, Yoko was wagging her tail, excited to finally see me home. Dad was in his chair watching a rerun of *ALF*. He loved watching his sitcoms, especially *The Bill Cosby Show*.

"Where have you been?" Dad asked.

"I've been out with Ed. Why?"

"Why do you think? I was worried."

"I'm sorry. I should've called."

"Jeez, man, yeah, you should've. You could've been dead for all I knew."

"I know. I'm sorry."

"Hey! Why don't you take me to Fred Meyer to look at the tools?"

When Dad felt strong enough, he loved going to Fred Meyer.

"Really? You wanna go to Fred Meyer?"

"Yeah, man. I wanna go! Go get my slippers and beige pants and checkered shirt, the one with the Velcro."

"Dad, you always say the shirt with the Velcro, and it's the only shirt you have."

"I know," Dad joked. "It makes me feel like I have more clothes."

I rolled my eyes, went into his room, and grabbed a pair of bear-claw slippers Anna bought for him.

"You want me to iron your shirt?" I asked.

"No. As long as it's clean."

"It's all wrinkled."

"So what, man? Just give it to me."

"Dad, you're not really gonna wear those slippers, are you?"

"Yeah, man, why? What's wrong with them?"

"Well, Dad, people are gonna look at us crazy."

"These are all I got."

"Well, what about a pair of my shoes?"

"My feet are too wide. Besides, they help my feet breathe."

"But they have claws on the front of them."

"Man, are you gonna take me, or are you gonna worry about my foot attire?"

"Look, Dad, let's be reasonable. I'm not gonna take you through Fred Meyer with feet that look like bear claws. We're gonna have to get you another pair of shoes."

I heard a heavy, quick knock on the front door. Yoko barked as I went to answer it.

"Ed!" I said, surprised. "Whatta you doin' here?"

He walked in, and Yoko was excited, wagging her tail and waving her paws in the air for attention.

"Quiet, Yoko," I demanded, following Ed into the living room.

"I'm gonna go to my room to get my Anacin," Dad said, maneuvering his weight into the wheelchair and then pushing himself to his room. "Move outta the way, Ed. I'm a fat, old man. Move!"

I was still surprised by Ed's sudden appearance. "What's up? Whatta you doin' here?"

"I made a surprise visit to Paige's and found her diary," Ed replied, as he sat on the sofa and showed me a small, black book.

My heart skipped and blood raced through my veins. My first thought was, *Is he gonna find out about Paige and me?* I had to think of something to say or do to stop him from reading it.

"Ed, that's not right. Maybe you shouldn't read it. It's personal."

"You don't think so?" he asked suspicious like. "Why?"

"Well, I mean, diaries are private, right?"

"Yeah, but I've been trying to find this since she told me about it," Ed said. "She even asked once if I wanted to read it."

"Sh-she did?"

"And she had this out where I could see it." He skimmed through the pages reading whatever caught his interest. I stood there quietly, hoping I wasn't in there. He became silent, stood up with a somber look, and then gradually turned away.

"Ed, are you okay? Wh-what's up, man?"

"Yeah," he replied sadly with his head down. "I'm okay."

He went out the door without saying another word, leaving me there empty. I heard the roaring sound of his motorcycle take off. My reaction was to call Paige. I ran to the phone and dialed, but no one answered.

"Eddie, are you ready to go?" Dad called from his bedroom.

I stepped into his room and said, "No, Dad. I'm sorry. I can't take you to Fred Meyer right now. I-I'm not feeling up to it."

"What's wrong, son?"

"Nothing."

I went outside and felt sick to my stomach knowing I had hurt the most important person in my life. I just wanted to die. My whole world had caved in, and there was nothing I could do.

It had been days since I'd heard from Ed. Meanwhile, Tom was in town for a couple of weeks. I drove Dad's car to see another friend named Jeff, who lived near Clackamas Town Center. When we were younger, Tom and I used to take road trips in his '67 Pontiac Firebird and spend the night at his house in Eugene. As much as we liked seeing Jeff, we loved his dad's cooking even more. He would create a breakfast that even a chef would have been inspired by.

Jeff was intelligent about politics, cars, and about stereo equipment. In fact, I think he was the only person in our clan of friends who read books, reminding me a little of Salvador in New York. When I got there, I knocked on the door.

"Eddie! What's up, man?" Jeff said loudly. "Come in."

I walked into his spacious apartment and saw a big-screen television to my right showing *NFL Primetime.*

"What's up, Jeff? I heard Tom was here," Tom stepped out from the bathroom. "Hey Cuban!" I embraced him. "When did you get in?"

"Yesterday. Where's your better half?"

"Oh, Ed, he's probably riding somewhere."

"Where's your weak Ninja?" Jeff smirked. "How come you're not ridin' with your sidekick?"

"Aw, it's just me tonight, man."

"Hey, I'm thinking about getting a Honda Hurricane," Jeff said. "What do you think?"

I said confidently, "It'll never be faster than the Ninja! You know that, Jeffrey boy."

Jeff pulled open the refrigerator door and asked, "What's your flavor? We have Henry's and Labatt's."

"Thanks, but I'm not drinking tonight." I slouched on the sofa.

"Why not? You wimpin' out on us?" Jeff said jokingly.

"Yeah, wetback," Tom added.

"Man, shut up, Tom. At least I didn't come to America on a boat made out of toothpicks."

Jeff laughed and joined in. "Yeah, Castro. Go back to Cuba, toothpick boy. I'm tired of you being in my country."

We talked and played cards until about two a.m., when the subject of Ed came up again.

"You haven't seen Ed at all?" Jeff asked.

I replied, "No. Not really. He hasn't called you guys at all?"

"Probably out gettin' laid." Tom patted me on the shoulder. "Why don't you join the Marines, Eddie?"

"I'll never join the military!" I said, resentful. "They fuck with your brain, make you think you're gonna be somebody, but then you get out. Then no one respects or cares about you."

Tom said, "It's for your country, man. It's discipline and loyalty."

"It's bullshit!"

"You're a communist," he said smugly. "You just don't have the stamina."

I threw my hand in front of his face, "See, they already got you brainwashed."

"Can we get back to playing cards?" Jeff chimed in. "I'm tired of hearing you girls whine."

I stood up. "Well, sissies, I gotta get home anyway. It's late."

"You're just tired of losing your money," Jeff exclaimed, shuffling cards and pretending to be some big-shot card dealer. "Why don't you go steal some hubcaps, sell them, and then come back and gamble some more?"

"Sure, I'll start with yours and sell them back to you."

We laughed.

"I gotta go too," Tom said. "I'll walk you out, Eddie."

"Thanks for coming by," Jeff said, "and if you visit again, don't bother bringing that gutless motorcycle of yours, 'cause I'll have the Hurricane by then."

"Okay, you get your motorcycle and we'll race on Highway 26. Then we'll see who has a gutless bike."

Tom and I shut the door behind us. "What are you doing tomorrow?" Tom asked.

"Nothing. Let's hook up."

"Give me a call," he said. "I won't be going back until next week."

We went our separate ways, and I merged onto I-205, then I-5 north toward my house. It was about three a.m., and I was dozing off behind the wheel. To avoid falling asleep, I held the visor with my right hand and the radio turned up. I merged on the Killingworth exit, took another left at the flashing red light, and quietly uttered, "Almost home. I can make it."

Then I blacked out. I woke up three blocks down, smashed into a parked car, which had crashed into a steel mesh fence behind a house. I tried to get myself together as I looked over the bent iron steering wheel. I could see the front end of my car underneath the back end of the other.

I forced open the driver's door. Smelling gasoline, I rolled out of the car and crawled into the street. My chest was in pain as I lay on the yellow-painted street lines, groaning.

Then a hand gently touched the back of my shoulder. "Are you okay? Hey, buddy, are you okay?" someone asked.

I heard sirens and indistinct chattering around me as paramedics arrived at the scene.

The paramedic carefully touched my shoulder, "I don't want you to move, okay? Tell me, can you feel this?" He touched my fingers and toes.

"What?" I replied incoherently. "What'd you say?"

"Can you feel this?" he repeated. "Can you hear me?"

"Yeah, I can f-feel that," I replied, noticing the reflections of the ambulance lights glimmering off a police officer's badge. "I can feel that."

"Do you have insurance?" the paramedic asked.

"No, no, I don't."

He continued, "We're gonna have to take you to the hospital."

"No, no. I don't need any hospital," I said. "See, I'm fine, I don't need it." I hastily stood up and walked around, trying to rub away the pain on the left side of my chest. Then I sat on the curb, close to the totaled car, and swayed forward and backward.

The officer bent to one knee, "Do you have a driver's license?"

"Yeah, uh, it's in the car."

The paramedic came to me again and proceeded to say in a calm voice, "Look, there may not be any bleeding outside, but there could very well be some inside of you."

It seemed as if everything around me was surreal and all the speech was fragmented as people in their pajamas gawked at me. Still swaying and rubbing my chest, I asked, "Are you trying to s-say that…that I could be fucked up inside?"

"There is a possibility," he answered, setting his hand on my shoulder.

No matter how much pain I was in, I kept thinking about what it would cost to fix me up.

The paramedic urged, "So, what's it going to be?"

"Okay."

They put me in a neck brace and lifted me onto a stretcher into the ambulance. When we arrived at Legacy Emanuel Medical Center in North Portland, the paramedics rushed me into emergency and put me through a CAT scan.

"Nurse?" I said, inside the CAT scan.

"Yes."

"I really need to pee."

"Just a minute," she said, handing me a urinal. "Use this."

After what seemed like hours of testing, the nurse brought me to my room. She turned on the TV and said, "Here you go, Mr. Regory. If you need anything else, just hit the button on the bed panel."

"Thanks."

At that moment I thought, *I was sitting in a living room with Jeff and Tom playing poker, and now I'm laid up in a hospital bed watching a rerun of* The Facts of Life.

Later that morning, Michael rushed to the hospital, easing his way into the door.

"Hey, Mike, what's up, bro?"

"How you feel, bro?" Michael asked in a soft-spoken voice.

"I'm okay. How'd you know I was here so soon?"

"Dad told me."

"How'd he find out?"

"Cop came to the house."

"Man, I can't believe I wrecked the car," I said disappointedly. "I was only a few blocks away from home, next thing you know, I was out in the middle of the street in pain. How's the car, man?"

"We sent that thing to its grave," Michael replied in a funny way. "I wouldn't worry too much about it."

"I bet Dad's pissed."

"He ain't pissed over some dumb car. Don't worry about it," he said. "What's important is you, not a car."

198

"Look at all this crap they hooked up to me." I motioned to the wires and white patches attached to my chest. "This is crazy and probably expensive."

"Well, you're lucky you're not dead. I saw the car on the way to the hospital, and you shouldn't even be breathing."

"You saw the car?"

"Yep. And it didn't look good."

I sighed. "Damn."

"It's not the end of the world, Eddie."

"Where's Joey and Gerard?" I asked.

"They're at home, still sleeping. They'll be here later when I tell them."

I warmly looked up to the same angel who'd once protected me from the struggles I faced living in the ghetto—the brother who I could never be ashamed of being like. "Hey, bro, I appreciate you being here. Thanks."

Michael inched beside me, gently laid his hand on my head, and said, "I love you, Eddie. You're my little brother, and I'll always be here for you. You understand?"

"Yeah."

"I gotta go now, but I'll be by later with the family, okay?"

"Okay."

When Michael left, I pushed a button on the bed panel to turn off the lights. I lay back on my bed with my hands under my head, staring blankly at the ceiling dimly illuminated by the streetlights shining into the window. I thought of my life back in New York, wondering how Nanny, Louie, and Carlton were doing now. I thought about Joey, Anna, and Gerard.

Then I felt an empty feeling whisk through my weary body, and I remembered that once I left the hospital, Mom still would not be there for me. Dad used to say that being in a hospital can be a time to reflect about the important things in life. He was right.

Later that evening, my eyes slowly opened to see Gerard and Joey poised over the bed rail.

"How do you feel?" Gerard asked.

I was still weak, but I managed to talk. "I feel better. W-what's up, bro?"

"Why don't you get out of that bed and quit faking it?" Joey joked.

I chuckled a painful laugh. "Hey, Joe. What's up?"

Joey said, "You okay?"

"I think so." Then I asked, "Hey, has Ed come by the house?"

"Haven't seen 'im. But I think he called Dad. Why?"

"Just wondering."

Gerard walked around to the foot of the bed and glanced at the clipboard attached to the railing. He was smart at double-checking and questioning everything. Whenever he was around, I could be assured that he had my back. It was one of several reasons why the family considered him as the peacemaker.

"Am I okay?" I asked.

"Yeah, it doesn't look too bad," he replied, setting the clipboard back in its place.

I said, "Michael told me about Dad's car. Guess it's pretty jacked up."

"Yeah, you did a number on it," Gerard said. "But the car doesn't matter."

"That's what Michael said, but I know Dad."

"Hey, Eddie," Joey spoke up. "What did it feel like being in an ambulance?"

"It's no fun, man. Besides, you should know. Don't you remember that day in New York behind the building?"

Joey said, "Yeah, I remember that day. I saved your life, man." He pulled a chair close to the bed and sat in it. "Did the doctor say when you can leave?"

"About three days."

"Ah, you just want the attention." Joey smiled. "I know you."

Gerard shook his head. "Shut up, Joey."

***

The next morning, after my hearty breakfast of cherry Jell-O and scrambled eggs, I turned on the television and, because there was nothing else better on, forced myself to watch *Days of Our Lives*. I noticed the door crack open. A hand with a toy motorcycle inched its way into the room. The person pretended he was riding that toy motorcycle, making all the necessary sounds to bring out the realism of it. I became excited because I knew who it was.

"Ed!" I exclaimed happily. "What's up, man!"

"Where'd you get your new ride?" I gestured to the toy.

"Fred Meyer," he said. "You're lucky you weren't riding your Ninja."

"Yeah, I know. Where've you been?"

"Here and there. What happened? How'd you wreck?"

"Oh, I fell asleep," I replied, chuckling to myself. "I mean, dude, I was just blocks away from the house and then bam! There I was sucked under the ass of another car. It was a trip."

"Fell asleep? Dumb, dumb," Ed said, making a funny face at me. "Well, this should show you not to fall asleep again at the wheel."

I chuckled and shook my head, "Got that right. Hey, did you know Tom was in town?"

"Yeah, I thought about dropping by his house later." Ed rested his hands on my bed rail with care. "You know I love you, right?"

"I love you too, Ed."

Then Ed changed his tone to something more forgiving. "Don't think I'm mad, 'cause I'm not. The past is the past."

I said, "Homeboys?"

He replied, "Homeboys."

I solemnly gazed at Ed and then expressed with the deepest regret, "Thanks, Ed...thanks."

He stood around for a couple of hours flipping through channels on the TV and then stood up. "Well, I gotta go. I promised my dad I'd go see him. You get well, okay? We'll go ridin' when you get out."

"Okay. Hey, you're gonna go see the Buzz man?"

"Yeah, he's lonely. Called me begging for me to come over, said he'd treat me out to Loaves & Fishes."

I laughed. "Are you kidding me? You mean that free Meals on Wheels place?"

Ed laughed. "Here, take this." He handed me the toy motorcycle. "It'll keep your spirits up and ready to ride again."

I thought, *My heart is now at peace.*

Chapter 23

Risky Business

It was the year 1988, when Mike Tyson became heavyweight champion of the world and knocked out Michael Spinks in the first ninety-one seconds of the fight. Ed wanted to hit my TV with a baseball bat because of it. Instead, we left the house on our bikes.

It was sunny and after racing our motorcycles over the Freemont Bridge, we met up with Andrew at Wallace Park near the courts. Butler, Tom, Joey, and Adora—Andrew's new Spanish girlfriend—were playing cards in the back of the Battlewagon, drinking California coolers. Andrew drove the Battlewagon down Highway 26 reaching speeds of up to eighty-five miles per hour to Seaside beach. Ed and I accelerated our bikes past Andrew's car to see whose could go the fastest. I could see Ed speeding near the Battlewagon, coming within suicidal distance, then reaching his hand out to daringly touch the side-view mirror.

When we arrived at Seaside, we rode up Broadway Street past Pig 'N Pancake, Portland Fudge Company, the carousel and strip mall, Phillips Candies, and Funland Arcade. Families were walking on both sides of the street, cooling down with vanilla ice cream cones, and the kids bobbing their balloons in the air. We cruised slowly around the oceanfront promenade, passing the Shilo Inn on our right.

We stopped near an open gravel parking lot across from the hotel. Excited about feeling the warm Oregon sand between our toes, we rushed toward the volleyball nets and on to the open beach, where we played like kids in a sandbox.

By about ten p.m., Seaside had become a ghost town, and we found a secluded area north of the beach, started a campfire, and drank beers till midnight.

"Let's get outta here," Ed whispered to me. "I wanna go riding."

"And go where?"

"Back to Portland. I just feel like flying through the wind right now."

"Party's just starting; let's stick around here for a while and slam a few more cold ones."

"I don't wanna stick around here. C'mon, po' boy! Let's go."

"Couldn't we ride around here instead?" I said. "We'll have to ride sixty miles back, man."

"If you don't go with me, then I'll go by myself."

"All right, all right, come on," I said, dragging my feet through the cooling sand and finally onto the road where the bikes were parked.

We slipped our helmets and leather jackets on and rode back. Once in Portland, we headed northbound on Union Avenue, taking in the night lights and midnight walkers enjoying the warm breeze.

Ed sped closer, flipped his helmet visor open, and shouted, "Let's get a hooker!"

"What?! Are you serious?" I replied, trying to keep my motorcycle straight.

"Yeah. Let's get a hooker."

"Ed, aren't you afraid of getting some disease or something?"

"We won't get any disease," he said. "Let's just try it! I got condoms."

Never in my wildest thoughts had I considered paying for the services of a prostitute. At first I wondered how we were going to do this. We patrolled our bikes up and down the strip, carefully eyeing one tall mulatto woman in a Superwoman-type outfit.

We slowed down and almost stopped when she signaled for us to meet her around the corner. "Hey! Hey! Lookin' for action? Over here."

We stopped our bikes.

"How much do you charge?" Ed asked.

"For both of y'all? I charge fifty dollars," she replied with a sassy attitude. "That's my price."

"What? Fifty dollars? You have to be kiddin' us," I said, sizing her up. "C'mon, Ed. We don't need her for no fifty dollars."

"Okay, okay, hold on. Twenty-five!" she exclaimed desperately. "Twenty-five."

"Well, whatta you think?" Ed asked.

I leaned over and whispered, "She's not my type."

"Yeah, me neither," Ed said. "Well, thanks anyway."

We quickly rode off as the hooker called, "Okay, okay, ten dollars...ten dollars!"

Several blocks down, we noticed a girl patiently waiting at a bus stop wearing a fur coat. She had this innocent look as if she didn't belong in this neighborhood.

Ed signaled for me to pull over near a curb and said, "Whatta you think?"

"You mean about that girl at the bus stop?"

"Yeah."

"I don't know. She looks like she could be one, but she's waiting at the bus stop."

"Dude, she's out at three in the morning. You really think she's waiting to catch a bus?"

"I don't know, man. Maybe."

Ed motioned for me to follow, "Let's go ask her."

"Okay, I got your back."

We circled around the block several times before Ed stopped. "Nice night," he said, looking up at the dark sky. "So, what's your name?"

The girl asked properly, "What are you guys looking for?"

Ed stammered, "I, we're looking for, um—"

The girl interjected, "You guys looking for action?"

Since we were on the main street, we had to act fast.

"Yeah, we are," Ed answered in a matter-of-fact tone.

"I'll meet you around the corner," she said, signaling us to move our bikes away from the bus stop.

About half way down a quieter street, we stopped our bikes and turned off the engine. "Whatta you charge?" I asked.

"Depends on what you want," she declared, with her eyebrows up high and her arms interlocked.

"Don't worry. I'll pay for it." Ed asked, "Where we gonna take her?"

"I don't know."

"Let's take her to your house," Ed suggested casually.

"What? Are you on drugs? No way, man! If Dad found out, he'd kill us both!"

"Well, we could maybe take her to my house."

"What about your mom?"

"She won't know. I'll tell her she's my girlfriend or something."

"You're serious?"

The hooker snickered and patiently waited for our solution to this crazed idea of ours.

206

"Yeah, let's just take her to my house."

I asked, "Where we gonna put her?"

"Get on my bike," Ed said to her. "C'mon, get on the back seat."

"You want me to ride on that?"

Ed replied, "Yeah, is there a problem?"

"Nope, no problem," she said. "This is crazy."

"By the way, my name's Ed, and this is my best friend, Eddie."

"Both of you are named Ed?"

"Yeah," Ed said. "Two Eds are better than one."

The hooker smiled and proceeded to get on Ed's bike.

Her fur gray coat and purple, high-heeled shoes were more eye catching than the colors on Ed's motorcycle. We rode south on Union Avenue and took Powell up to 37th, paranoid the whole time that a cop might see us. When we got to Ed's, I was relieved, but not for long.

He reached into his pants pocket. "Eddie, I forgot my house key."

"Whatta we gonna do?"

"I'm gonna have to knock on the door," he said. "Damn! I didn't wanna wake my mom."

"Wait! What if your mom asks who she is?"

"You're right. What's your name?" Ed asked the hooker.

"Patty."

Ed said, "Patty, when my mom answers and if she asks, tell her your name, and I'll say the rest."

"Okay, but I can't believe this." Patty grinned. "You guys are crazy."

Ed knocked softly. Moments later, Betty looked through the peephole and opened the door. She was happy to see him and said, "Hi, sweetie. Who's this?"

Ed replied, motioning to Patty, "Mom, this is Patty, Eddie's girlfriend."

I couldn't deny it, so I went along.

Patty said, "Hi, nice to meet you."

"Well, hi, Patty. It's very nice to meet you too," Betty said, looking over to me. "Hello, my second son."

"Hi, Mom."

We walked inside and sat in the living room for a while.

Before heading back to bed, Betty asked, "Would you like something, Patty?"

Our attention was now on Patty as she replied, "Uh, no. No, thank you."

"Are you sure?"

Patty confirmed with a nod. "Yes, I-I'm sure."

Betty hugged Ed and me. "Goodnight, and goodnight to you too, Patty."

"Yes, uh, good night," she said. "Nice to meet you."

Betty went back into her room, and we waited until she fell asleep.

"Eddie, you go first," Ed insisted. "Go ahead."

"Me? Why me?" I said. "You go first. I've never done anything like this before."

"No, go ahead. If my mom comes out, I can say you're in the room with Patty."

"Man, what am I supposed to do with her?"

"Whatever you want. I'm paying."

I ushered Patty into Ed's room and, before I closed the door, said back to Ed, "I don't appreciate you saying she's my girl, either."

I quietly shut the door and stood there. Patty sat on the bed, waiting for me to take charge. I walked around the bed and cracked the window open.

"Well, what do you wanna do?" she asked.

"It's kind of warm in here. How much did you say it cost for…for—"

"Look, just relax. I'll take care of everything for you." Patty stood up and grabbed my hand. She brought me to her and unzipped my pants. "You like that?"

"Do I have to answer?"

"So, what do you want?" she whispered in my ear, kissing my neck.

I answered her.

She replied, "I can do that."

"This isn't gonna work," I said. "Let's just forget it."

"You want me to stop?"

"I guess," I replied, uncertain.

She tried other ways, and I said, "Look, I know this isn't gonna work."

She stopped and said, "You know, your friend is paying for this, so you gotta do something." She pulled her shirt off and seductively lay back on the bed. Her motions began to excite me.

After it was over, I stood up, threw my pants back on, hurried toward the bedroom door, and said, "Thanks."

Ed had all the lights off except for a few lit candles on the kitchen table.

"Well, how'd you like it?" he quietly asked.

"It was okay."

"What'd she say?"

"Nothing," I said. "It's your turn now."

He carefully lifted the candle from the table and proceeded into the bedroom.

I asked, "Whatta you doin'?"

"I wanna make this special," Ed whispered, opening the door then shielding the candle from the warm breeze whisking through the bedroom window. "See you in a bit."

At first I thought he was nuts, but if Ed felt any moment was special, he made the most of it.

I anxiously sat on the sofa and waited, worried about Betty waking up. Ed finally came out. As Patty was getting dressed, he pulled some money out from his wallet and said, "Here."

"Thanks," she said, stuffing the money into her bra.

"Where would you like us to leave you off?"

"The same place is fine," she replied, combing her hair with a bristle brush she pulled from her coat and layering more makeup over her face.

We took her back to the same bus stop, then rode to the nearest 7-Eleven and ordered nachos.

Ed said, "Man that was the best orgasm I've had in a long time!"

"You mean?"

Ed nodded.

"What did you pay her?"

"I gave her a hundred bucks."

"What? Are you kidding me? I didn't go that far with her."

Ed replied in disbelief, "You didn't?"

"No, no, I didn't. Didn't she tell you?"

"Well, she was worth it," he said, shrugging his shoulders as if the money didn't matter.

I laughed and said, "She was one expensive ho, but at least she was better looking than Superwoman."

The next day, we rode our bikes back to my house, and Butler was there talking to Dad. "Hey, Butler! Whatta you doing here?" I asked, happy to see him. "How was the party at the beach after we left?"

"What's up, Negros! It was fine. By the way, why'd you guys leave?"

Ed glanced at me, and I knew he wasn't going to say a word about the hooker with my dad sitting there, so I said, "We were just tired. By the time we got back to Portland, we crashed."

Butler joked, "Together, homos?"

"Yeah, right."

Butler motioned to the kitchen. "You're retarded! I bought a case of Bu-Bu-Busch for you guys."

I shifted my attention. "Hey, Dad, did I get any calls or mail today?"

"Who do you know that knows how to dial a phone?"

I signaled my head at Ed. "He does."

Dad said, "Ed couldn't find his way out of a garbage bag."

Butler requested, "Eddie, get me a beer."

"What do I look like to you?"

"Like a reject," Butler said, laughing. "Now get me a beer."

I stepped into the kitchen, grabbed a beer, and snapped the tab. "Ahhh, you hear that? That's the sound of Buschhh."

"Here. Give it here," Butler demanded, drinking the whole can in seconds.

"Damn!" I remarked. "You didn't even come up for air."

"Hey, why don't you give me one of those?" Dad asked.

"Nah, Dad. It's not good for you," I said. "You might croak or something."

"Give him one," Ed said. "It won't hurt him."

"Ed, you know if he drinks that, he'll fall down and have a heart attack."

"I'm not gonna have no heart attack!" Dad insisted. "Just give me one, silly."

"Hey, Al, watch this," Butler said, grabbing a beer and guzzling it to the last drop.

"That's cold blooded!" Dad shook his head. "And I treat you like family here."

Meanwhile, Ed made his way into the kitchen and grabbed three beers.

"Here, Al." He tossed a can.

"No, Ed, you shouldn't give him that. Okay, Dad, I'll tell you what, I'll hold the beer and you can take a sip."

"Tch, man, you gotta be kidding me," Dad replied disappointedly. "I'm not some kid. You treat me like a baby, man."

"C'mon, it's for your own good," I said, opening the can of beer and holding it with both hands. "Okay, you ready?"

"This is ridiculous," he said. "I'm a grown man, and I'm being treated like a kid."

"C'mon, are you ready or not?"

"Yeah, yeah, I'm ready."

I inched the can closer to his lips, and Dad wrapped his hands around mine. He quickly started to drink it, and I lost control of the can.

"Dad, Dad! You promised!" I yelled in laughter. "C'mon!"

"Go, Al, go! Do it!" Butler cheered.

Beer was trickling down the sides of Dad's mouth, but he wasn't about to let go of that can.

I shouted, "Dang! You see, next time you ask, I'm not gonna trust you."

"Man, youza sucka! You shoulda known better than to trust your ol' man," Dad said, wiping the foam off the sides of his mouth.

The whole time, Butler and Ed couldn't stop laughing.

"You see, Dad, because you drank that whole can of beer, you're gonna have a heart attack and die a slow death," I said, pointing my finger at him.

Easily distracted, Ed pointed at a water gun in Dad's window. "What's the water pistol for, Al?"

"It's for the dogs in the neighbor's yard. I keep it by the window so when they bark a lot, I squirt them. Besides, they like it on the hot days."

"Let me see," Ed said, trying to grab the water pistol.

"Don't touch it," Dad said. "Whatta you wanna see it for?"

"I just wanna check it out."

"No, dummy. Don't do that," Dad said, pushing Ed's hands away.

Butler said, "I wanna see the dogs too."

"Why do you wanna see them for?"

"'Cause."

"No, no," Dad said in a funny way. "What part of *no* do you not understand—the *n* or the *o*?"

"C'mon, Al," Butler begged. "Let me see the dogs?"

"No!" Dad said. "Now leave me alone."

Ed held my dad's arms and yelled, "Eddie, Eddie! Pull the shade!"

"Man, you guys. Don't mess up my shade!" Dad implored. "Please! Okay, okay, I'll let you see the pit bulls, but don't tear my plastic shade, man."

Ed released his grip. Dad carefully pulled each staple holding the shade to the wall so it wouldn't damage the plastic.

Butler said, "Why the hell do you have a garbage bag for a shade, anyway? This ain't no shade."

"It works," Dad said. "See, they're just minding their own business."

Ed tugged at the window, but it was stuck.

"C'mon, Ed, you said you just wanted to see the dogs," Dad said, trying to grab his hands away from the window.

Ed finally lifted the window partially open. One pit bull was chained to an iron pole about ten feet away. He lifted the window further then pointed the water pistol at the dog. The pit bull sat there guarding its turf, its ears erect, its muscular body uneasy, tensed.

Suddenly the dog sprang forward with a deep, loud bark. It came to an immediate halt inches away because of the thick choke chain tied around its burly neck.

Ed squirted the pistol at it. The pit bull went silent for a second, looked confused, and backed up. It came at the window a second time, and Ed squirted it again. Butler and I laughed the whole time this was happening. The dog backed up and sat beside his post, wagging its tail when it realized there was nothing it could do.

Dad tried to stop us. "C'mon, that's enough, you guys! Leave them alone."

"Let me try!" Butler said anxiously.

"No, man. No, Butler," Dad said, trying to grab the water pistol from Ed.

"Okay, guys, time to grow up," I said, closing the window. "Let's shut this thing."

"Spoiler," Ed exclaimed with a funny expression.

"One day that dog's gonna be off its chain and bite your hands off," Dad warned.

"I'll just slap him around," Ed replied.

"Yeah, sure." Dad looked longingly down the hall. "I'm going to bed," Dad said, with an exasperated tone. "All this excitement made me tired."

I got a small buzz from the beer, and Ed sat on the sofa watching Pink Floyd on MTV. Butler was in the refrigerator trying to stir up some edible concoction.

I asked, "What kind of nasty poison you making now?"

"Man, you ain't got nothin' in this fridge," Butler whined. "All you got is eggs."

"We haven't been shopping yet. We should go to the store and get some grub," I said. "Whatta you think, Ed?"

Ed was too absorbed by the TV.

Butler wasn't going to give up on finding food, so he looked in the cupboards, grabbed several bags of Ramen noodles, and declared, "Now this is the one staple no poor Puerto Rican should be without!"

I pulled out the steel pot. "You're not gonna make all this weird shit like you usually do 'cause I'm hungry."

"This'll be good. Grab me the cheese?"

"Cheese? Man, Butler, you said—"

"Eddie, trust me. You'll like this," he said, shaking the noodles and chicken spice from the packages into the pot and then filling it with tap water. Right when the noodles were done, he shredded about a quarter block of medium cheddar cheese, cracked four eggs, and mixed them in with a touch of Tabasco sauce.

I said, disgusted, "Man that looks gross! Who's gonna eat that now?"

"Taste it!" Butler held a fork dripping steaming melted cheese and Ramen noodles up to my face.

"No way!" I said, backing away from it.

"Ed," Butler called. "Come 'ere and try this."

Ed stood from the sofa to see Butler's creation and sarcastically said, "Mmmm, looks good, Butler."

"Just try it!" Butler demanded as he proceeded to guide the fork of food into Ed's mouth.

Ed reluctantly tried it. "That's not bad."

"All right. I'll try it," I said. "But it better be good."

Butler dipped the fork into the steaming pot of noodles and said, "Here!"

"You're right. That's not bad. You lucked out, man," I said, grabbing an extra fork for Ed.

We began eating out of the pot.

Butler brought a finger to his mouth, "Hey, this is missin' something."

"Like what?" I hesitantly asked.

"More...more Tabasco!" he exclaimed, with a gut-bursting laugh.

"Wait! Wait! Before you do that, I'm grabbin' me some more," I said, and washed a dirty bowl from the sink. "Here. Put it in this."

"Me too," Ed said, doing the same.

Butler was happy he had the rest of the pot to himself. I grabbed the TV remote and sat on the sofa.

"C'mon, put it back on MTV," Ed pleaded. "I was here first."

"Nope. It's my turn to put it on my channel," I said, turning it to HBO. "I wanna watch boxing!"

We hung out all day drinking beer and watching TV, making enough noise to wake up the neighborhood.

"You guys keep it down! I'm trying to sleep," Dad cried from his bedroom.

I whispered, "Let's keep it down, guys."

But we kept laughing and roughhousing, even wrestling in the living room and almost knocking the TV over several times.

Ed slipped into my room and turned on the radio. "Take On Me" by A-Ha drifted down the hall as Ed pretended he was riding on his motorcycle, moving his body to the beat of the music.

Butler went to check on him, "Whatta you doin', moron?"

"Riding."

"Shut up, retard," Butler said, clearing a spot on the floor. "Move over. I'm going to bed." Ed and Butler lay on the floor like newlyweds while I prepared my own bed.

Butler said to me, "How is it that you get the bed, and Ed and I have to sleep on the floor?"

"That's how the rules work here. You guys sleep on the floor, and I sleep on the bed. Been like that for centuries."

Butler said, "That's some bullshit."

"Goodnight," Ed said. "Pleasant, pleasant, pleasant dreams."

We were about to fall asleep when this loud noise on my bedroom door occurred. *Bang! Bang! Bang!*

"What the fu—!" Butler exclaimed. "Who the hell is that?!"

"Hey!" Ed said, nearly jumping to his feet.

Dad waited for us to fall asleep and then banged his wooden cane against the closed door.

"C'mon, Dad," I pleaded, from the bed, covering my head with a pillow.

"Nah, man. You, you guys wouldn't keep quiet when I asked." He laughed. "I begged and pleaded, but you wouldn't stop. Now it's my turn."

Ed smothered his head with a pillow.

"C'mon, Al, we're tryin' to get some sleep," Butler whined but was laughing too.

Dad kept laughing and banging on the door with his wooden cane.

"All right, Dad, we're sorry!" I yelled. "We won't do it again."

Dad was having such a good time torturing us, he decided to make music with the thumps of the cane hitting the door. "La-la-la," he sang over and over.

I finally slipped out of my comfortable bed, turned on the lights, and opened the door. "Okay, Dad. That's enough!"

"Are you bums gonna do it again?"

"No. We're not gonna do it again!" Butler said, in an impatient tone.

"You promise?"

I said, "We promise, Dad. We promise."

"I didn't hear Ed say he promised."

I said, "Say you promise, Ed."

"I promise," he muttered from under his pillow.

"Okay," Dad said, turning his wheelchair around and rolling himself back into his room, laughing. Dad then cried out from his bedroom, "Next time you'll know better than to mess with me. I'm like a Mafioso. I may not get you now, but I'll get you later."

Butler said in a theatric tone, "Ooh, a Mafioso, I'm scared. Next time I'll kill the Mafia."

Ed and I laughed and eventually fell asleep.

Chapter 24

On My Own

Kristina had left for college. I was twenty-two and headed out for a good time with Tom, Andrew, and Donnie, another friend. We drove to several clubs downtown to drink straight shots of tequila and vodka, and by eleven p.m., we were ready for a strip club. We hurried into Andrew's Battlewagon and drove to Harpo's.

The Battlewagon's speakers blared "We Don't Have to Take Our Clothes Off" by Jermaine Stewart. The car shook because of our jumping, dancing, and singing along. We sloshed and spilled beer over the floor and seats, even on our clothes. When we got to Harpo's, Donnie forced open the side door and vomited onto the parking lot.

"Ed! Ed! Wait up, man," I shouted, as he headed toward the front door.

"C'mon you pansy-ass pussies!" Andrew said, laughing at us.

"Andrew, give me a chew," Ed demanded, feeling up Andrew's pockets, trying to find his can of Copenhagen.

I said, "Ed, "What if some fine girl wants you and you got that in your mouth?"

Ed pinched a glob between his fingers, pressed it into his lower lip, and casually said, "Well, then, she'll have to kiss me with it in my mouth."

Andrew opened the door, and Donnie walked in first as the rest of us followed. Wooden pillars stood on both sides. We sat a few tables away from the stripper stage.

Ed pulled out his wallet and said, "Tom, get some *cervezas* for us," handing him some money.

"What kind?"

"Doesn't matter, you stupid Cuban," Ed joked, sitting down. "Get whatever."

A stripper signaled for Ed to come closer.

"Ed, don't go up there," I said. "She just wants your flow, dude. She's ugly anyway!"

He stood up and slithered his way around some chairs and tables toward the stripper. He glanced back, saying, "I'm just gonna see what she wants."

I smiled and said, "C'mon, let's go play some pool."

"In a minute, in a minute," he replied, sitting on a rotating stool at the stage and watching her every move.

I reluctantly stood up and sat next to him, watching the stripper slowly take off another piece of clothing to a different song. My stomach churned at the sight of her wrinkled face, cellulite legs, tattooed body, and sagging breasts.

I turned to see Ed's reaction, but he seemed content. He reached in his pants pocket, pulled out a one-dollar bill, and folded it in an erect position on the stage. The stripper showed Ed more attention and proceeded to squat over the bill, making sexual gestures at him. She squatted further onto the bill and swallowed it up. We couldn't believe our eyes. We looked at each other and laughed.

"Whoa! Damn!" Ed bellowed.

I vehemently declared, "This is nasty!"

The stripper scowled at me. We both watched this freak show, and she came back and danced some more. This time, Ed reached into his pocket and pulled out a five.

"Ed, don't give her that."

"It's all right," he said, laying the bill on the counter. "She deserves it."

I grabbed the five back off the counter. "She deserves it? Whatta you, nuts? You're wasting your money!"

The stripper eyed me and shouted, "Why don't you leave him alone and let him put his money where he wants?"

Ed laughed. "You just got served."

I dramatically shouted back to the stripper, "Well, if you weren't so fat and didn't smell, maybe I would." I looked around to see the other patrons' wide-eyed reactions to my comment and turned my head back just in time to see her pick up an ashtray to throw at me.

"You asshole!" she yelled. "You betta get the hell outta here!"

I dashed from my seat and ran for cover behind the nearest pillar. Suddenly, some biker guys stood from their chairs, their rugged faces and cold eyes sizing me up. There was a moment of silence, and then Andrew blurted, "We betta get the fuck outta here!"

Donnie was laughing as the rest of us hurried out the exit.

The waitress said firmly, "You're all eighty-sixed! Don't come back!"

The biker guys watched to make certain we left. Ed was laughing so hard he could barely breathe. It began to sprinkle as we hurried inside the Battlewagon. Andrew sped out of the parking lot and recklessly drove west on Powell.

The music got louder and the partying in the back of the Battlewagon intensified.

I looked out the window to see a girl with blond hair and yelled, "Yo, baby! Yo! What's up? Wait! Where you goin'? Can we come with you?"

Ed tried to slide the door open while Tom held him back.

"What the hell are you doin'?" I asked, pulling Ed away from the door.

"That girl…that girl was awesome! Did you see her?"

"Ed," Donnie said, "we can find some fine bitches somewhere else." He passed a half bottle of tequila around.

"Give me that! Give me that bottle!" Ed demanded, grabbing it away from Donnie's hands.

"Here, fuckhead!" Donnie laughed. "Take the whole fuckin' thing!"

Ed tilted the bottle and guzzled it.

"Man, what the hell?" I said in disbelief.

"I'm an Airborne Ranger with a black beret!" he exclaimed proudly.

"Airborne nothing. You're a damn idiot!" I said. "Give me that!" I gulped a quick shot. "Bottleneck!" I called over the music bouncing off the small, paneled walls of the Battlewagon. "Bottleneck! Bottleneck!"

"What?"

"Where we goin'?"

"How the hell do I know?" Andrew said. "Tell Ed to give me some chew."

I looked over and yelled, "Ed! Andrew wants your chew."

"Tell him to kiss my Ranger ass!"

Andrew laughed. "Ed, give me a chew!"

Ed tossed me the can, looked over to Tom, and asked, "Whatta you lookin' at, you Fidel Castro piece of pie hole?"

Tom went quiet for a second and replied, "Nothin', you Marine wannabe."

"Bottleneck, where we goin', man?" I asked impatiently.

"We're going to the opera," Andrew said.

"Seriously?"

"Back to Harpo's."

"Quit messin' around," I said, irritated. "Where are we goin'?"

Andrew glanced over and yelled, "Ed, where we goin'? Tom, you know where we're goin'?"

Ed shouted, "To the moon, Alice, to drink some tee-quila!"

I heard this banging sound in the back, and when I looked over, I saw Ed wrestling with Tom, trying to pull his pants off.

"Donnie, Donnie, help me take his pants off," Ed urged, laughing uncontrollably.

Donnie tried to help, but the once-scrawny, frail Cuban kid was now the tough Marine who would not let it happen easily. He fought back with strength and purpose like I've never seen a 135-pound Marine fight.

"Ed, stop!" Tom begged, using all his strength against them.

Neither of them gave up as they laughed so hard tears slinked down their drunken faces.

"Eddie, Eddie, help us!" Ed yelled. "We almost got 'em off."

I rushed over, but Tom didn't have another ounce of strength in his average-size arms and gave in. Andrew almost hit several parked cars.

"Okay, guys," Tom said, dropping his voice to a lower pitch. "Give me my pants back."

223

"Hey, Tom, you Marine guys sure are tough," I said, holding my stomach in laughter.

"Bottleneck, stop the car!" Ed demanded. "Now!"

Andrew pulled over by Couch Park and Ed quickly pulled the side door open. He rushed over to Tom and grabbed him by his jersey, forcing him out the Battlewagon in his underwear.

"Ed, no!" Tom yelled, frantically trying to fight his way back in, "C'mon, Ed! No, no, no!"

"Holy shit!" Donnie said. "That's cold."

Ed slammed the door shut.

"C'mon, Ed. Let me back in!" Tom pleaded. "C'mon! I'm out here in my underwear."

Andrew peered out the passenger side and yelled, "Hey, Tom, what are you doing out there in your underwear, you sicko?"

"C'mon, you guys, open the door!"

Minutes later, Ed unlatched the door and opened it. Tom rushed back into the Battlewagon and exclaimed, "Man, that was messed up. You're all assholes!"

Andrew pressed on the gas, peeled rubber, and drove up Northwest 21st past the Silver Dollar Pizza Company. I whispered a few words in Donnie's ear and, when ready, he was going to do what I had secretly suggested.

The rain came down harder as it was almost time for my cue to Donnie. I grabbed Ed from behind. "Donnie! Help me!" I yelled.

Tom didn't know what was going on, but that didn't matter because if it was against Ed, he was in. Donnie tackled Ed's legs, knocking him down, while I pulled his arms over his head, locking them with my legs.

Tom clinched Ed's pants from the sides and pulled with all the muscle he could muster. Ed squirmed, kicked, and fought with three of us on top of him. We had them halfway off when Tom and Donnie gave up.

We were just blocks away from Wallace Park when what had started out to be wrestling for fun became a fight between Ed and me. We fought until we felt the Battlewagon come to a screeching halt. Our bodies abruptly rolled forward to the front.

Tom shouted, "Damn, Bottleneck! You made me spill my beer!"

Donnie tried to break it up. "Stop, you guys! Stop! This is dumb!"

"Stop, you guys! Stop!" Tom echoed.

Andrew forced open the side door. Donnie pushed us out, and Ed and I fought through the streets. I glanced around and noticed we had stopped on the corner of 25th and Pettygrove. Our clothes were soaking wet as heavy drops of rain bounced off our faces. We rolled near the curb where the water was deeper.

"Ed! Eddie! Ed, you guys stop!" Tom begged, trying to break us up.

Cars with shining headlights beeped their horns at us. I grabbed the back of Ed's hair, drenched it in a dirty, deep puddle, and shouted, "C'mon! You wanna fuck with me! C'mon!"

I saw the hurt in his face and pulled back, letting his head slip away from my hands and watching it drop into the dirty water. Donnie and Tom pulled me off.

Donnie shouted, "I can't believe you guys! You're fuckin' friends."

Ed spit the chew out from his mouth and didn't say a word. He stepped toward me, and Andrew said, "No, no, no. I'm not gonna let you go over there if you're gonna be a bad boy."

"I'm cool, I'm cool," Ed said, moving Andrew aside. "Let's walk."

"Cool," I replied.

He swung his arm around my shoulders.

Tom was going to follow us, when Andrew said, "No, Tom. Let 'em alone."

We walked over the soggy grass toward the basketball court. Ed pulled his wet, slightly cracked can of Copenhagen from his back pocket, flipped the lid, slipped a pinch in his lower lip, and said, "You know, you fight like a girl."

I went quiet, then laughed. "I kicked your ass all over the street. Whatta you talkin' about?"

"You didn't kick my ass," Ed scoffed. "If I wanted, I could've snapped your neck!"

"Ah, man, I had your head in a puddle of dirty water. Your ass was drownin'. Even the paramedics had to help you."

We hugged and walked back to the Battlewagon when Ed said, "That was fun. We should do that again sometime."

"Cool with me."

I knew there was nothing on earth that would separate our friendship, not even a fight. Afterward, we drove to 7-Eleven to eat some nachos, and from there, Andrew drove me home.

Anna with Yoko

Eddie's mother, Santa Regory

Top left: a friend, lower left: Eddie
Middle: Albert (father) lower right:
Joey in New York

Michael Regory

Ed Jerome hugging a homeless man

Jimmy Duncan and Eddie Regory

Gerard Regory

Mike Butler and Eddie Regory

Risa and Joey Regory on their wedding day

Eddie's best friend, Tom Utrera age 15

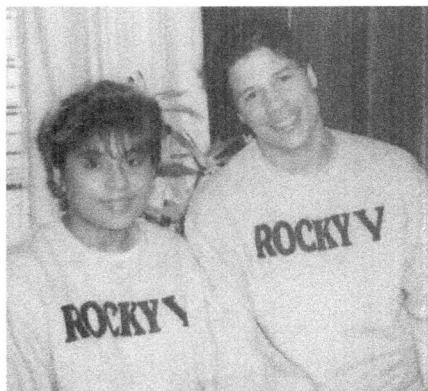

Hazel and Eddie at the Rocky V premiere

Eliana Regory

Hazel, Eliana and Eddie Regory

Doyle and Gladys McCranie (Hazel's Parents)

Ed Jerome

Eddie and Hazel at Washington Park

Chapter 25

Big Chance

It was 1989, and the smell and feel of autumn, especially the scattered leaves through the streets, reminded me of those moments when I arrived in Portland. It was time for me to get a job where I could use some of my artistic abilities—something that would make me feel good about being at a job, about myself.

One morning I walked into an office building somewhere downtown and saw a large directory that showed the office locations of people who had professional practices. Knowing this wasn't for me, I got back on the same bus to head to Sandy Boulevard. On the way I noticed a white building with *Jones Sports Company* on its sign, located on Northeast Sacramento Street. I walked in and saw the receptionist wearing a light gray scarf and a blue blouse.

"Hi, um, my name's Eddie, and I was wondering if your company was hiring."

The receptionist was startled by my forwardness. "Just a minute. I'll get someone for you," she motioned to a wooden bench. "Have a seat over there, please."

"Thanks."

I was dressed in a Norwegian white handmade sweater that Kristina had given me, brown corduroys, and penny loafers. I heard heavy boots clomping toward me, but I could not see who it was, so I tried to stay calm and confident. An older man with a gray beard and an authoritative, loud voice said, "Hi, I'm George. I hear you're looking for a job."

I stood up. "Yes, sir."

He asked, "Well, what do you know? Do you know anything about screen printing?"

I felt if I didn't fabricate just a little, I would lose my opportunity, so I fibbed, "Yes, I do. I'm familiar with the process."

"You are? Okay, come with me."

I followed him into the warehouse, passing Asian women sewing golf bags and using cutting machines of all kinds. He brought me to the back and pushed open some swinging doors, which led us into an art department.

"This is where we do all of our printing. Do you think you'd like to do this?"

"Yes, yes I would."

"Jim!" George called loudly at the supervisor. "This is Eddie, and he's looking for a job."

He walked away, his shoes still clomping.

Jim was a small man who had dark hair and an unshaven face. He sized me up and asked, "So, how much do you know about screen printing?"

Instead of saying how much I really didn't know, I told him of all my accomplishments in the field of art, which was really only copy drawing on white sheets of paper from comic books.

"Well, I've developed a board game and tried to screen print it myself, and I started reading up on stuff about the process. I also graduated from Lincoln High School. I'm ambitious and a fast learner too."

"Oh, wow, so you're into making games, huh?"

"Yes, sir."

"Just call me Jim."

He showed me around the semi-clean shop and introduced me to the ladies, including a deaf woman who

235

did the embroidering. She signed to me with her hands, "Hi."

"So, when do you think you can start?"

When I heard this, my heart was pumping with excitement. I wanted to tap my feet together in the air like in that Toyota commercial. "Right away! I can start right away!"

"Well, how 'bout Monday since it's the start of a new week?"

"That's fine. Perfect!"

"Okay, so, we'll see you Monday."

"Great. Thank you very much. Monday it is."

Jim escorted me out the front doors and shook my hand. "Welcome aboard."

"Thanks." I couldn't wait to get home and tell Dad. I thought, *Yes! I got me a real job.*

My first day on the job, I dressed in jeans, a blue, loose-fitting shirt and the same bandanna I always wore when I went jogging.

Jim greeted me with, "Hey, Eddie. You look ready to work."

"Yeah, I'm ready."

Jim showed me to a Hopkins printing press, "So, have you ever worked on one of these before?"

I wanted to impress him but didn't want to sound dumb, "Yeah, um, this is a printing press. I really like the mechanics on this thing."

"Yes, that's right. It's a printing press. So you have worked with one of these?"

"Well, I've seen one of them at work, but never worked on one myself."

I sensed Jim felt I didn't know as much as I had portrayed, but he liked me and was willing to show me the ropes. He pulled a white, cotton towel from a nearby table and placed it over the wooden palette on the press, taking a can of red soluble ink and layering some below the image on the inside of the screen. I watched with interest, eager to learn this new trade.

He said, leaning over the screen, "Get some distance between the palette and the shirt and lightly flood the screen with ink. Bring the squeegee below the image, angle the squeegee, and place the screen against the shirt. With both hands, pull the ink through the image onto the towel."

Jim lifted the screen, and I was amazed by blended shades of color on the shirt. "Whoa," I uttered. "That's cool."

"You try it," Jim said, handing me another towel.

I placed the towel over the palette, stood behind the press, and grabbed the squeegee. "Like this?"

"There you go. You got it," he said. "With a little practice, you'll be busting out these jobs in no time."

I flooded the image on the screen and pulled the ink through. "Wow."

Jim said, "Pretty cool, huh?"

"Yeah, it is."

"Eddie? Let me ask you something."

I stopped and listened attentively.

"You really didn't know how to screen print, did you?"

I brought my head down like a sad puppy. "No. Not really."

"Hey." He handed me another towel. "Doesn't matter. I didn't know either. Everybody needs a start. Here, practice on these towels." He walked away, and I felt nothing but respect for the guy. Suddenly all my feelings of failure and worry about not finding a job I'd like were in the past, all because one special person believed in me.

That week, I was anxious to celebrate with Ed about my new job. I called and said, "Ed! Guess what, man?"

"Whazzup, cuz?"

"I got a job!"

"Hey, that's great. When do you start?"

"I already did."

He asked, "Hey, you know where I'm going?"

"Where?"

"California."

"California? What for? When?"

"In a couple of months."

"Why?"

Ed said, "I just wanna get myself together and quit drinking and do something with my life."

"So how's California gonna help you with that?"

"Well, I signed myself into this rehab center over there."

I forgot about my new job and thought only about how I was going to lose Ed. I asked sadly, "So, how long are you gonna be gone?"

"Long enough to clean myself out, and I'm gonna start running every day again. When I get back, I'll be in really good shape, and we can both start running like we used to."

"I'm gonna miss you, man."

"I'm gonna miss you too, bro," Ed said. "But I'll come up and visit."

"So, what do you want to do tonight?"

"Par-ty!" Ed squealed loudly. "I'll come by later and pick you up."

This time he picked me up in his new Volkswagen bus. We called it Battlewagon 2, or B2 for short. It was about nine p.m., and we partied at an area under I-5 south of the Hawthorne Bridge. It was a place where people would hang out and talk to girls, drink beers, and even arm

238

wrestle over the hood of a car. We'd listen to "Rock the Casbah" by the Clash, "Never Gonna Give You Up" by Rick Astley, or my favorite, "Rock Me Amadeus" by Falco.

It gave me a good feeling to be there by the moving Willamette River, staring at the bright lights reflecting off the multicolored city signs as they blinked and gleamed from the cold Portland darkness.

Jeff, Joey, Butler, and Tom showed up. It was late when I noticed Ed wasn't around. "Tom," I asked, "where's Ed?"

"I don't know. He was here with Jeff a minute ago," Tom said, looking over to Andrew, "Charlie Brown, give me a chew."

"I don't have any more, Cuban."

"Butler, have you seen Ed? Has anybody seen Ed?" I asked.

Butler said, "No, I haven't. I saw him awhile ago."

"Where the hell can he be?" I said. "I haven't seen him in a while."

"Ask Joey. Maybe he saw him," Butler suggested. "He's over there by the wagon."

"Man, where the hell is he?" I paced around the B2, looking out into the dark river. After searching everywhere I gave up and waited, chatting it up with Butler and Joey. Then I saw a shocking look on Butler's face, "What the fu—"

I exclaimed, "Ed? Where the hell have you been? You're soaking wet, man!"

"I know. I jumped off the bridge."

"What? You jumped off what?"

"I jumped off the bridge."

"He did. I saw him do it," Jeff said. "I couldn't believe it either."

"You saw him do it?"

Jeff replied, "Yeah, man, I saw him. I couldn't believe it. Fucking crazy!"

"Ed, did you really?" I asked.

"Yeah," he confirmed, taking the chew out from his mouth. "Charlie Brown! Give me another chew. This one's wet."

"I'm not the chew supplier here," he said, grabbing the can from his jeans pocket and thrusting it to Ed anyway. "Here!"

I didn't know how to respond. I wanted to deny that he could have done such a stupid thing. "Ed, tell me you really didn't do that."

"I did," he replied, in a cavalier way. "Can I use your shoes?"

"My shoes? What am I gonna wear?"

"Wear those shoes in the van. The ones I gave you."

"Those are boxing shoes."

I looked down at his running shoes and saw they were soaking wet. I pushed each loafer off with the ball of my foot and gave them to him. "Here, man. These are my only dress shoes, though, so don't mess 'em up."

He replied, "Thanks, brutha."

I tried forgetting what had happened while I talked with Butler, but it was all I could think about. Shortly after, I was hungry and about to ask Ed if he could drive me to 7-Eleven, but again, he was nowhere to be found. I looked up at the bridge then and saw him walking toward me again.

I yelled across the way, "Ed! Come 'ere, man!"

He appeared a little drained.

I continued, "Where'd you go?"

He replied, almost out of breath, "I jumped off the Hawthorne Bridge again."

By now I was angry. I glanced down at the shoes I'd loaned him and reached over to touch them.

240

"Ed, you kidding me! I just lent you these, man. What the hell are you thinking? Suicide?"

Ed fidgeted his hands and clattered his teeth as he trembled in his dripping clothes. "I did it 'cause I was bored."

"'Cause you're bored?" I brought it down a level. "Ed, what's going on with you inside, man? That jump could have killed you."

He ignored the question, but I could see he was crying for something other than my friendship. Ed blared, "I'm an Airborne Ranger, boy!" He walked away to the rest of the guys near the B2 to brag.

They sort of laughed in disbelief of what Ed had just done, only because none of us had the courage to help him. Instead, I felt we unconsciously became enablers.

By one a.m., Ed and I decided to go to a tavern called the Belmont Inn on Southeast Belmont. We sat several feet from the empty dance floor with the striking sound of pool balls echoing off the billiard tables. A full-figured body, pretty brunette waitress wearing a snug apron with the restaurant's insignia asked, "You guys know what you want?"

I replied, "How 'bout a pitcher of Henry's, um, a side order of onion rings—Ed, did you want something to eat?"

"Nah."

Before she left, I said, "Oh, and, uh, I wanted your phone number, but it's not on this menu."

She smiled. "Sorry, that was yesterday's special."

"Oh, I see. That's a stop sign?"

"I'll be back with your drinks."

"Dude, she was fine," I said, staring at her as she headed back to the bar.

Ed reached into his pants pocket and pulled out his wet can of Copenhagen. We sat there and gazed at the empty dance floor, listening to the oldies music. His eyes were slightly red and glazed over. I could tell he was in deep thought about something—I just didn't know what.

"Here's your pitcher," the waitress said, setting it down with two coasters and two frosty glasses. "Your food will be here soon."

"Thank you," Ed said, pouring beer into my glass.

I took a sip and said, "Give me a dip."

He smiled and gestured like I was crazy. "You don't dip. Last time you dipped, you got sick."

He kept staring at the dance floor. Then "Jailhouse Rock" by Elvis Presley played over the loud speakers. Ed stood up and eased himself to the dance floor with his back facing everyone. He shook his right leg to the beat of the music, lifted his collar over the small of his neck, and started dancing as if he were Elvis himself. The crowd cheered, and some joined in.

The next morning we ate cereal with Adams peanut butter in Ed's kitchen.

"How do you like your breakfast?" he asked.

"It's good." I paused. "Do you remember much about last night?"

He replied, "Kind of, why?"

"'Cause, man, you did some crazy shit."

"Like what?"

"Ed, even *I* wouldn't have forgotten what you did if I did it myself. 'Like what?' Man, you were jacked up." I shook my head. "Ed, you jumped off the bridge. Don't you remember that?"

"Yeah," he said quietly, looking ashamed for what he'd done. "I remember."

"We can't go out drinking anymore if that's gonna happen again."

"I know. You're right. That's why I decided to go to rehab," he said and changed the subject. "Hey, whatta you feel like doing? You feel like rappelling?"

"You know I can't do that."

"That's okay. I'll teach you."

"Nah, man. I'd be too scared. Besides, where would we go?"

"We could go to the Thurman Bridge near Paige's house."

"I don't know. Dude, wasn't last night enough risk for you?"

"That was last night. I'm talking about doing something today."

"I don't think so. Let's go play some pool at Friendly House. Then we'll see what to do afterwards."

"Well, I'll bring the ropes anyway, just in case." He hurried into his room, snatching ropes and clips.

We were driving near Friendly House when Ed insisted, "Let's just head straight to the Thurman Bridge."

"Are you serious?"

"Yeah, we won't be there long. Let's just try it."

"All right," I agreed hesitantly.

The Thurman Bridge overlooked Macleay Park— the same place we'd had our keg parties up the trail. We parked the B2 near the bridge. Ed pulled out his ropes and clips and proceeded to walk toward the center of the bridge. I became excited about rappelling, but also scared.

Ed asked, "You wanna try it first?"

"No way, man."

"I'll go first and then you can try."

I looked over the bridge's railing—seventy-five feet down to the cement. "I-I don't know. This looks pretty scary."

"It's really easy," he explained. "I'll strap the harness around your waist and use these clips and rope. The gloves will protect your hands from getting rope burn."

"It's easy because you know how to do it."

"Let me show you," Ed said, tying a simple overhead knot, fastening some clips and a harness around his legs, making sure everything was tight and secure. He tied the rope to the top rail and stepped over.

"Ed, I don't know, man," I said, nervously watching him hold tightly to the rope and position his body into an *L* shape off the edge of the bridge.

"You see, you hold tightly, and then you push off with your legs." He proceeded to count as I watched with anticipation. "One, two, three!" he cried out, gliding down the rope like an eagle heading straight for its prey.

When I saw how easy he made it look, I was eager to try it.

He landed softly on the ground and shouted up, "See? Told you it's easy."

Ed unclipped himself from the ropes and walked up some stairs, which led him back up to the bridge. He asked, "You wanna try it? You saw how easy it was for me."

"Okay!"

He wrapped the harness around my legs, making sure everything was safe and secure. He held tightly to my shirt as I stepped over the rail. I became tentative to do the same *L* shape off the bridge when Ed said, "Eddie, listen, just leverage the rope against your back and let your hand loose when you're ready to glide down. Don't be afraid. Face your fears. Like I said, the gloves will stop the rope from burning your hands."

"Okay, okay. I-I think I got this."

"Don't be afraid. Just push off."

"I don't know, man."

Ed exclaimed, "Just do it!"

I gradually eased the tension off the rope from my back and began to glide toward the ground. I kinked the rope flush against the small of my back and then stopped about a quarter of the way down.

I released some rope from behind me, but then my shirt tangled into my front clip. I was now halfway between the bridge and the ground. Ed had made certain everything was secure—except my shirt, which was not tucked tightly enough into my pants.

I shouted up, "Ed! My shirt...my shirt is caught."

"What?"

"My shirt is stuck! It got caught in the clip."

"Can you swing yourself to the left, close to the hill?"

"I don't know. I'll try," I answered, swinging as hard as I could with little success. The harness around my legs began to cut off my circulation. "I can't do it. I can't swing hard enough to reach the hill."

"Okay, hold on," he voiced loudly. "I'm gonna have to climb the bridge and get you down." Ed ran back to the car and grabbed a large Army-issued bowie knife and started to climb the bridge like Spider-Man. "Eddie, can you swing toward me so I can grab you?"

"I think so." I recklessly swung forward and backward like you would on a swing, trying to reach Ed's extended hand.

"C'mon, c'mon. Gotcha!" he exclaimed, grabbing the rope. "Hold on. I gotcha. I'm gonna climb back down and swing you over toward the hill near the stairs. I think we have enough rope."

"Hurry up, man. My legs are killing me!" I said, almost crying from the harness pinching around my legs.

Ed followed the rope down with his right hand as he used the left side of his body to maneuver toward the bottom. Once he reached the ground, he yanked the rope several times as I swung in the same direction; Ed reached out and snatched me with both hands.

I was finally able to touch ground. "Damn, get this rope off me, hurry!"

He cut a section of my shirt and loosened the harness. After he gathered all the gear, he asked, "You okay?"

"Yeah, I think so."

When we got to the car, I was extremely sore, and the inside of my legs had red indentations from the harness and ropes.

"You were a little sissy," Ed teased, making this funny crying face at me. "I can't believe you."

I kept trying to rub the pain away from the insides of my legs. "Man, you try having a harness wrapped around your ass for a long time, cutting off your circulation."

"Youza little girl," he said. "At least now you can say you've tried it."

"Man, shut up! I hated it. I'll never do that again. I knew some shit was gonna happen, and guess what—it happened to me."

"Ah, you'll be okay. Now you know what's it's like to be a Ranger."

***

Ed left for California, and after a while on my new job at Jones Sports Company, I received a small raise. I decided to buy my first new car. I was going to buy one of those Yugos, but then I decided to have Andrew help me buy a Volkswagen instead. We visited Volkswagen of America in downtown Portland.

I spoke with a saleslady who seemed fairly nice and worked within my budget. I knew what I wanted because a coworker once allowed me to drive her car to see what it was like.

That warm summer night, I was thrilled about my new ride and its stereo playing "My Prerogative" by

Bobby Brown. I made a phone call, "Butler! I got some new wheels, man. An '89 Volkswagen Fox."

"How much did it cost?"

"About seven thou. I bought a stereo and bra too."

"Come get me!" he said eagerly.

I dashed out the door and drove to Northwest 29th and Vaughn Street where Butler lived, just two blocks away from Macleay Park, and honked my horn.

"Buddy!" Butler exclaimed. "Look here. Nice!" He drew out the word for several seconds.

"Get in, man. Where do you wanna go?"

"Can I drive?" he asked.

"Yeah, c'mon."

He anxiously got in the driver's side and drove around.

"Hey, let's go to Wallace Park," I suggested.

"Why?"

"Because I wanna see who's there."

We parked on the north side of the park and walked up the grassy hill near the court. Players were there picking up games.

I said, "Hey this park reminds me of sixth grade. Do you remember Hazel?"

"Think so."

"Wonder if she's here." I noticed a girl sitting under the shelter watching the guys play. At first it was hard to see who it was, so I wandered closer. "Yo, Hazel! Whatta you doing here?"

She smiled, her face glowing as if she was also happy to see me. "Nothing. Just sitting here."

"Well, how's your sister? How's your mom?"

"They're fine."

When her elegance stood up, she was no longer the pudgy little girl I once passed in the halls of Chapman School but instead a mature, striking, unblemished flower that had flawlessly blossomed.

"Hi, Hazel," Butler said. "Eddie told me to come to the park 'cause he was lookin' for you."

She smiled in a coy sort of way.

I had completely forgotten Butler was there. "Hey, um, I got a new car. You...you wanna drive it?"

"Sure." She seemed surprised I would ask.

"Butler, give me my keys."

He tossed them and said, "Oh, I see how it is.

Hazel and I headed to the car while Butler continued dramatically, "Yeah, sure you will. You found Hazel. You're not coming back, flat leaver."

I hurried to the driver's side and opened the door for her. She gracefully slipped into the seat and then unlocked my door.

"Thanks." I buckled my seat belt. "You know how to drive a clutch?"

She replied nervously, "I-I think so."

"Okay, check this out. This is first gear, second gear; this is third gear, fourth, and fifth. And if you want to put it into reverse, you just push down and over. Got it?"

She seemed confident and inserted the key into the ignition, stepped down on the clutch, and then threw the stick into neutral. "Like this?"

I replied in an animated way, "You got it! Right on. See, you know how to drive a stick!"

She slowly drove down Raleigh Street.

"How do you like it?" I asked.

"It's nice. Where did you get it?"

"Downtown."

Hazel said, "I'm impressed."

We drove past most of our stomping grounds— Lovejoy, Couch Park, Washington Park, and finally back down to Wallace Park, parking the car in the same spot.

Butler saw us and bellowed, "It's about time!" gesturing as if we had taken forever. "Thought you were never gonna come back!"

248

"Hey, I was showing Hazel my new ride, man. Hazel, you gonna be here tomorrow?"

"Um, no, not tomorrow."

"Well, can I get your phone number so I can call you?"

"You have a pen?"

"Butler, you have a pen?"

"Butler, give me the key, give me a pen. What do you think I am? Of course I don't have a pen, dumb shit!"

Hazel smiled. "Can you remember the number if I give it to you?"

"Yeah, yeah. I'll remember."

Later that evening, I realized my time with Hazel that day was different than it used to be. It wasn't one of those random moments when I used to jog from my house and make a pit stop at hers for a slice of cheese or a short conversation. She was no longer the introverted girl with the long, black, lustrous hair and chubby smile I had only glanced at near the Chapman School lunch tables. She was now someone I could not keep my eyes off of. Tonight was a special night because it was my first date in my first car with a woman I felt would be my wife.

***

The following weekend, Hazel and I met at the Lloyd Center Mall. I saw her by the railing overlooking the ice skating rink near the Meier & Frank department store. She was wearing a red leather skirt, black nylon stockings, and a silky blouse. I was dressed in my loafers, a fitted long-sleeved navy shirt, and my favorite Levi's 501s. I snuck up behind her and softly touched her hips. "Yo, what's up?"

She turned, delighted to see me. "Hi."

We moved closer, and I asked, "Where do you wanna go eat?" I suggested, reaching for her hand. "We could stay here in the mall or leave."

"Doesn't matter. Wherever you want."

I wanted to take her someplace nice, but I didn't have much money. Yet she didn't seem like a girl who cared about that. "Well, why don't we drive around and see if we can find a place?"

We headed for Sandy Boulevard and saw Sylvia's, an Italian restaurant. I guessed I could afford it, so we pulled in. Once we were inside, the hostess instructed, "Follow me," and took us to a table for two wrapped in a checkered tablecloth with a candle.

The ambiance and delicate background music brought the romantic side of me out. "So, um, you look great, different."

"So do you."

I said, "Can you believe it's been, like, how many years since we last saw each other?"

She smiled. "Awhile."

After taking our drink orders, the waitress asked, "Are we celebrating anything special today?"

I squinted at Hazel and confidently said, "Yeah, we're celebrating our reunion."

The waitress smiled. "Well, that's a good reason. I'll be back with your drinks."

I opened the menu, saw the prices, and thought, *I should've checked this place out before we came*. I didn't want Hazel to think I was cheap, though, so I said, "Order whatever you want. It's on me." I figured if she ordered first, I would know how much I had left for myself.

The waitress came back and asked, "So, have we decided?"

I motioned to Hazel. "You first."

She said, "Um, I'll…I'll have the Lasagna."

As soon as she said that, I casually glanced over the menu to see the price, but I couldn't find it quickly enough. "I'll just have the soup of the day."

Hazel asked, "Is that all you want?"

"Yeah. I'm not very hungry," I said, patting my stomach. "Ate before I met you." Then the waitress left. "It's been a long time, Hazel, a long time. I miss jogging to your house and grabbing a piece of that famous cheese."

She smiled with her popping brown eyes.

I continued, "You know, uh, I know it was a few years back, but I wanna say I'm sorry for not coming to your graduation. I really wanted to, but...well, I got caught up in a lot of things. I hope you're not pissed at me about that."

"It's okay. It's in the past."

When our food came, the server asked, "Is there anything else I can get you?"

"Nothing for me. How 'bout you, Hazel?" I asked, relieved when she said no.

After that first blissful date, Hazel and I became inseparable. Sometimes she'd visit me at my job in the screen print department and bring my favorite ham and cheese with sprouts sandwich on kosher rye from the Greek deli on Northwest Lovejoy. In the evenings, we'd meet up at one of our favorite places, the Blue Moon on 21st and Glisan, just west of Couch Park. It was also across from my favorite pizza place, Silver Dollar Pizza Company. We'd sometimes stay and talk until closing, even if we had to go to work the next morning.

Chapter 26

Turning Point

After a year of Jim taking me under his wing and teaching me how to screen print umbrellas, golf bags, T-shirts, and caps, it was time for me to leave Jones Sports Company and seek a higher wage in the same line of work. Every day Hazel would encourage me to continue my endeavors to better myself.

During this time, Ed came up from rehab to stay with his mom, but being away from the help he needed gradually threw him back into his drinking ways. Andrew now lived on his own in the Belvoir Apartments a few blocks north of the Vista Bridge, and since I now had Hazel in my life, Ed spent more time with Andrew.

Joey left for San Jose, California, so Anna and Gerard found another place to live on Northeast Freemont. Dad and I moved out of our place on North Albina Street into a one-bedroom house with a big basement just off of Northeast Ainsworth on 32nd. This time we built a wheelchair ramp to the front door and set up Dad's bedroom in the living room. I set the TV near his bed on a wobbly wooden stand that Dad had made out of scrap wood. Our home wasn't big, but Dad was grateful.

It was March 30, and I went to go pay Ed a surprise visit at Andrew's new place. When I tapped on first-floor apartment window, Andrew pulled the shade and forced the old, unbalanced window open. "Hey, Puerto Rican! What the hell are you doing here?"

"Hey, Bottleneck. Where's Ed?"

Andrew turned and called, "Ed! It's Eddie!"

I heard Ed call in a humorous voice, "What does he want?"

Andrew moved away so I could see Ed sitting on the sofa drinking a forty-ounce bottle of St. Ides watching Run-DMC on MTV.

I climbed through the small apartment window because it was faster than walking down a flight of stairs to his apartment. "What's up, man?"

He said, sticking his hand out for our brotherly handshake. "What's up, homey."

I said, "Hey, um, I thought you just came back from rehab?"

Ed snapped, "I did."

"So, what's up?"

"*Nada*," he replied .

"So, why you drinking?"

He shook his head and gestured the palm of his hand at me, ignoring the question.

I stepped away and grabbed a glass from the kitchen.

"Let me have some?" I poured some of his beer into the glass, only to have him drink less. "I thought you were gonna dry up?"

"I did. How's Hazel?" he asked, casually avoiding the subject.

"She's good."

"Eddie's gonna marry Hazel someday," he blurted out to Andrew.

"I heard you got a new motorcycle," I said. "Where is it?"

"Yep. It's the Hondamatic. You wanna see it?" He held his can of beer as we crawled back out the apartment window. "Whatta you think?"

"Check it out, man," I said, with a disdainful look. "This thing's a piece of shit!"

"It's the Hondamatic!" he exclaimed. "This is a fine ride."

"Ed, this is definitely a step down from the Honda Interceptor."

"I think I'm going back to school."

I no longer knew what Ed wanted out of life, but I still supported him. He was like the wind passing from one place to another, trying to find his way back to where it all started so he could make better choices.

Ed continued, "I wanna get into architecture."

I had to stop him from going on. "Ed, why are you drinking again?"

He looked at his can sadly. "I don't know. I know I shouldn't. I know I'm fucking up."

"I thought that was why you split to rehab, so you could clean yourself out. Start a new life—you know." I noticed he was getting irritated. "You know you can tell me anything. We're like brothers."

He straddled his motorcycle, started it, and slowly rode off toward Lovejoy.

"Ed, Ed! Wait, man," I called desperately out as he waved.

The next day I had to make it right with Ed, so I decided to take a risk and see if he was at Andrew's place again. When I arrived, Andrew opened the window.

"Eddie," Andrew greeted loudly. "What's going on?"

"What's up, Andrew. Has Ed been here?"
"He's in the bathroom."

Ed stepped out of the bathroom, tucking his shirt into his pants, and saw me at the window. His eyes were a little red, like he hadn't had much sleep. "Hey, brutha, whazzup?"

"Hey, can we talk?"

"Yep," he said, crawling out the window.

We stood on the hillside with our hands in our pockets. "Hey, I'm sorry, man. I don't know what came over me. I shouldn't have been talking about your drinking and all that. I just care about you."

Ed nodded, assuring me everything was okay. "Forget about it," he stepped forward shook my hand. "So, how's Hazel?"

"She's good. Remember how we used to jog to her house?"

"Yeah, man. I remember those days. It seems like it was yesterday."

I smiled. "You know, sometimes I get scared knowing I don't have control of the future."

"You mean Hazel?"

"Yeah. But I also mean you."

Ed said, "You're lucky. You're lucky you've got someone who loves you, something I've never had in a woman. She's right for you, Eddie. So don't leave this one, because if you do, then I'm the next one in line."

I chuckled. "This is a different kind of commitment, though. I mean, it's like I feel something inside, but I'm not sure what it is, bro."

Ed took in a breath, grabbed my shoulders, looked me straight in the eyes, and jokingly declared, "You can be a man!" acting out a scene from *The Godfather*.

I laughed. "Seriously, man."

"If that's how you feel, then she's the one for you. You'll marry her and someday spit out a few kids. Out of all the girls you've had, I know she's the one. She's liked you ever since Chapman."

I leaned against a parked car. "Isn't it a trip knowing I didn't even think of her then? Who would've known how a girl I once saw as a friend I now see as my wife."

"Eddie, when you came up to me that first day at Couch Park, I knew we'd be best friends. You know why? Because you spoke to me when no one else did—and because we have the same name."

We chuckled.

"Shit, man, that's true. What are the chances of us meeting with the same names and all? Can't believe it."

Ed glanced at the watch I gave him. "This is a nice watch. Every time I look at it, I think of you."

I said, "Hey, maybe you can come over and eat with us at my dad's. We'd love to have you and just hang out with family."

"Sounds good. I gotta go now, but I'll see you tomorrow."

"Yeah. Call me, man. I know I've been around Hazel a lot, but since you're back, we'll hang out at the Avalon and play some video games or something." When Ed straddled his motorcycle and started it, I asked, "Where you going now?"

"To see a friend in West Linn."

"Okay, man," I said, "Hey—I love you, man."

"Luv ya too!" Ed said, speeding off.

Later that night my eyes became watery, dreaming of the days when Ed and I first met at Couch Park, shaping long vines of plastic Gimp at the lunch table and eating peanut-butter-and-jelly sandwiches. I thought about how we'd go to his house and play with his ferret. We even watched those *Rocky* movies we were so inspired by. I still felt a piece of me was slipping away. Now that my life was with Hazel, it was harder to be the kid I once was.

April 1, I woke up early and dressed in my workout clothes to go for a run. I'd just torn a white strip of shirt that was lying around and wrapped it around my head when the phone beside my bed rang.

I flopped onto the bed and answered, "Hello?"

"Eddie?"

"Who's this?"

"This is John, Ed's brother-in-law. Did you hear?"

"Hear what?" I asked eagerly.

"Ed died."

I paused, staring blankly into nowhere. "What? What is this, an April Fool's joke?"

"Ed died," John repeated in a serious tone.

"John, what are you talking about? Quit messing around!"

"I'm not. He died this morning."

I fell silent, not knowing what to say or think. I thought it was a nightmare that I just hadn't awakened from yet. The dark truth of what John was saying began to gradually sink into my heart. I could hear him urgently repeating, "Eddie? Eddie, you there?"

My heart, oh, God, my heart. A feeling worse than I have ever felt swept over me like a dark cloud. Time was still, and my bones suddenly weakened. My body was in incomprehensible pain, and I could not breathe.

John continued, "Eddie, are you still there?"

I could not speak. *Why?* I thought. My mind was bewildered and hazy. I needed someone to take control right then because I couldn't. I began to silently pray: *God, help me. God if you're real, wake me up, please?*

I had just enough energy to gasp one word: "Okay." Then I hung up the phone.

I raised my lifeless body and forced myself to move rapidly so I could hurry to Betty's. I struggled with my emotions, wondering what to do next, but I was a caged animal in my room with nowhere to go. I was just moving without thought, back and forth, until I swung open the bedroom door. Dad was sitting in his chair with his hat over his eyes, snoring, until I burst out of my room.

"Where you going, son? Why are you making so much noise?"

My words would not come out plainly, "E-e-Ed died! E-Ed died!" I said, quivering, choking on my own words.

"What?"

"H-h-he died this morning."

"How? God, how?" Dad struggled to sit upright on the edge of the bed, slipping his cotton hat off. "What...what happened?"

"I don't know. I-I-I don't know," I said, wiping my forehead. "I gotta go!"

I hurried to my car, almost collapsing on the way, then sped off, burning rubber. Time seemed so slow. It took forever just to get to the freeway. I got halfway there and then lost control of my car moving into oncoming traffic. I had to regain control to get back into my lane.

I hit the dashboard with a fist and slammed my steering wheel with both hands, shouting in anger, "Why, God? You're supposed to watch him, take care of him! How could you leave him?" I helplessly beat my hand in the air. The car swerved into the middle lane as other drivers watched me.

"Oh, God, no! No! No!" I yelled in torment, wiping the tears with my sweaty, red, pained hands.

Finally arriving at Betty's, I screeched to the curb, swung my car door open, and ran out, not even closing my door. I ran up a few steps and hurried to the apartment door.

Betty's oldest daughter, Anita, answered, sobbing, "Eddie!" It was as if she was relieved that an extended part of her little brother was finally there. I walked into the small, two-bedroom apartment that was filled with pain, tears, and suffering. Betty's eyes were bloodshot, her face saturated with tears. She hugged me tightly and wouldn't let me go, just as I would not release her. We finally parted, and Betty sat on the sofa, gently wiping her face with a used cluster of crumpled tissues.

I looked over at Cathy, John, and Anita. "How? What happened?"

"He was hit by a truck between three and five thirty this morning," Anita said. "I don't understand how this could happen."

I asked, compassionately and at the same time trying to control my own emotions, "Where? Who was he with?"

Anita grabbed some tissue and wiped the moisture from her nose. "He was with an Army acquaintance in West Linn."

"Who told you?" I asked, sitting beside Betty, holding her trembling hand.

Anita said, "A sheriff came by this morning and told Mom."

"Where's this person who was with him? What did he have to say?"

"Nobody knows," she said. "He hasn't called or anything. I've only met him once—Ed never thought he was a good person and said he couldn't trust him."

I said, "He's the only one who knows what happened, and he hasn't even called?"

"Yes," Anita confirmed. "We're waiting for a phone call from the coroner to identify the body."

"So we really don't know if the body's Ed's?"

"Not for sure," she said. "I don't feel right, Eddie."

I exhaled with a hint of hope.

We waited for hours until the phone rang. Anita quickly grabbed it from the dining table. "Yes, okay, okay. And where do I need to go? Okay. Thank you." She hung up and said, "They want us to come down and identify the body."

"I'll come with you," I volunteered.

"I want to also," Cathy said, grabbing her coat.

Shortly after, the coroner called again. Anita answered, "Yes, yes, o-okay…yes. Are you certain?" Then she brought her heavy, weighted shoulders over the table and the Niagara Falls of pain began to flow from her eyes.

I wanted so badly to go into remission from this unexpected cancer that hovered over us, but then Anita lifted herself up and faintly said, "Coroner said that it wasn't necessary to come down." She started talking of funeral arrangements.

I stayed there waiting for more answers, but time made it worse, and my will to stay had taken its toll. I had to go somewhere to cope with my feelings and confusion. The truth is, I wanted to kill the man who'd murdered my brother. I embraced Betty and said, "I need to go think, Betty."

She gently placed her hand over my cheek. "You go, Eddie, and do what you need to do."

I hurried out the door and saw that I had left my driver's door open. I eased into the car and paused, thinking about where to go, and then headed for Macleay Park. I walked to a bench under a wooden shelter, huddling into a fetal position, and cried.

The next morning, I could hear the birds chirping and the wind blowing through the tree leaves. I slipped my shoes off and felt the dew, damp and cold against my bare feet. *Where am I to go?* I thought. *What am I to do?* Nothing on this earth could have comforted my grief or prepared me for this moment. Then the hope of seeing Hazel gave me reason to live.

I calmly walked to my car and headed for home, feeling the breeze brush against my hair. Nothing I drove past seemed real: the stores, people, parks, cars, animals—nothing. It seemed like yesterday never existed.

When I got home, I eased to the chipped curb and gradually parked the car, turned the ignition key, and just sat there listening to a song. Finally, I realized how exhausted my body felt from lack of sleep. I was going in and out of darkness with no mental or physical strength. I eased my body to the edge of the car seat and paused with my feet on the curb. I stood up and shut the car door, unaware of any group chattering or car noise from behind me and walked toward my front door. I unlocked the front door and carefully pushed it open. There was Dad sitting in his big chair with a Bible.

"Eddie, how do you feel, son?"

I choked up a little. "Not good, Dad. I feel like dying."

"Eddie, sit down," Dad continued in a loving way. "Eddie. Ed is very much alive. Alive in the years you've had with him, alive in the years you've got to know him. He will always be the brother your mother would love as much as she did you and Joseph. Of all the letdowns and sorrow you've faced, the one thing you can look forward to is seeing your brother again."

"I'm not even sure what happened. Our life together as best friends and everything we've done, all the talks we've had, it…it all seems like a blur. I feel like someone ripped my heart out of my chest and now half of me is gone," I said, wiping more tears from my eyes.

"Eddie, I know this feeling because I went through it when your mother died. Like someone had ripped my heart out—not just for a day, week, or month, but every day of my life. Life can be taken in the blink of an eye. That's why you enjoy the people you love and never take them for granted. Eddie, your future is with Hazel now. Live it for her. Call her."

Later that night, I drove aimlessly through Portland's dimly lit neighborhoods with no place in mind. I wanted someone to take away this pain, to carry it far away and bring back my brother. I wanted to hold him in my arms and embrace his love—to rewind to a time when innocence was ignorant of pain.

I suddenly felt driven to the Mt. Scott Funeral Home, where I knew Ed's body was. When I parked, I waited, trying to reason why I'd come this far. I thought, *What would Ed do?* I stepped out and walked aimlessly for several minutes.

My heart was pumping fast, though my body felt paralyzed. I managed a few steps toward the funeral home. Then a thought cried within me, *Do I want to see him this way, or to remember the way he was?*

If it were me lying in there, Ed would be banging on the door demanding to see my soulless body. I stepped up and knocked. No one answered, so I knocked harder until I saw a man. He cautiously walked halfway down some stairs, glancing over to see who it was.

He unlatched the door and respectfully asked, "Yes? Can I help you?"

I was choked, as if my tongue would not allow me to speak. "Um, is…is my brother here?"

"Your brother? Is there someone here you know?" the man asked in a soft-spoken voice.

I swallowed saliva that had built up in my mouth and faintly replied, "Yeah. His name is, Ed. Ed Jerome." I wiped my eyes with the palm of my hand.

"Just a minute, please."

I was about to sneak in when the man came back and asked, "I don't see you on the paperwork as next of kin. Are you a family member?"

I began to breathe heavily and confirmed, "He's my brother!"

The man said, "I'm really, really sorry, but you have to be a family member or get permission from the family to see him."

"Can't I just see him?"

"I'm sorry. Really, I am. But your friend is in no shape to be viewed at this point, and we need to obtain authorization from the family."

I felt a sudden rage and wanted to force myself through him. Instead, I brought my head down and quietly walked away, hearing the deadbolt lock behind me. He watched me walk back to my car before he went upstairs. I glanced at the doors to the funeral home, unsure what to do now.

***

A couple days later, we went to go see Ed in his casket before the funeral later that week. I got into my car with Hazel and began to drive. Butler, Jimmy, and Joey followed in Butler's new Blazer 4x4. The closer we got to the funeral home, the more distressed I felt.

Hazel put her hand on my leg to comfort me. When we got to the parking lot, my body became weak. Every breath was difficult, every muscle hard to move as she helped me up the stairs and into the funeral home. Slowly, I entered this faintly lit room, noticing Jimmy slip his dark sunglasses over his eyes.

An older man dressed in a black suit guided us to where Ed lay still in his casket. Betty, Anita, Cathy, and John sat in some chairs against the wall. I knew Betty hadn't stopped crying since Ed's passing. Her body looked the same as mine felt: broken.

I slowly approached Ed's casket, then stopped partway there. After a moment, I walked farther and gazed in. My eyes froze and my hands rested still upon the edge of the casket. I could not move my head. *What is happening?* I thought.

I moved closer to Ed's barely smiling face and felt my body slowly pull toward the ground, but my will to stand and see him would not give way. I stared and stared and stared, trying to say something meaningful to Ed, but no sound would come out. Moisture crept from my nose and saliva from my mouth when I quietly uttered, "Why?" I wept silently, falling into a deep, aching abyss. Then my knees buckled to the ground, and in a loud voice, I cried out, "Nooo!"

I was sure people outside the building could hear. I stood up and draped my arms like an umbrella over my brother's body to protect him. The casket swayed from my unstable weight as I fell apart.

I could feel Hazel's hand rest upon my shoulder. Betty set her hand on my other shoulder. I slowly rose as hot tears coated my face to the point that I could not see clearly. I looked in the casket once again, pieces of my life dropping onto his pressed suit.

I lightly touched his forehead, feeling the makeup on the tips of my fingers and staring at his unblinking eyes. "I love you, I love you…"

On April 4, Ed's closest friends stayed the night at my house. I couldn't sleep, so I went into the living room. Dad was sitting in his chair reading and looked as if he were crying. On his rickety, dusty desk, Mom's pictures lived beside the same tape recorder he'd use to play their favorite song, "Memories."

"Dad," I said quietly, rubbing my eyes.

"Hey, son. How do you feel?"

"Tired, real tired."

"Eddie, come 'ere. Sit beside me."

I grabbed a metal milk crate from the corner of the living room and pulled it close. Dad lay his hand over mine and said, "When your mother passed, a part of me also left. I felt I had nothing to live for, not even for the rest of my family. And when Ed left us, another part of me died. We all loved Ed very much, and we'll all miss him. But we have to go on in hope because if this short life is all we have to live for, then there's no sense in living."

I began to cry. "It just hurts, Dad."

"I know. When someone we love so much passes away, we feel as if we can't go on or we've been cheated in life. We wake up every morning and face the ridicule and hurt the world puts on us, so coming home to see our loved ones is what we look forward to.

"Parents don't expect their children to go before their time. Always remember that all these things will pass."

I hugged him and kissed his cheek. "I love you, Dad."

"I love you too. Now go get some rest."

The next morning was the funeral. Gerard helped Dad get into his wheelchair as they left out the side door down and the wheelchair ramp. Hazel and I took my car, and everyone else got into Butler's Blazer. We could hear Yoko whining and barking as we drove away.

Hazel sensed my pain and gently lay her hand on my leg. As we neared the funeral home, I was afraid not enough people would show. Gerard opened the trunk of his car, grabbed Dad's wheelchair, and pushed it around the passenger side. The rest of us proceeded to the funeral home.

On occasion, I would pray quietly. Hazel stood close as more people entered the funeral home. I didn't know where Betty was, and I worried for her deeply.

People were seating themselves inside the chapel. Before it started, I approached the reverend to show him a cassette tape with "He Ain't Heavy, He's My Brother" by the Hollies. "Could you play this song after the funeral?"

"What is it?" the reverend asked solemnly.

"It's our song."

"Son, I really don't think it's a good idea. This is a difficult time for all of us, and we would like to make it as smooth as possible."

I looked at him somewhat disturbed and confused that he would deny my request and then sat with the other pallbearers. The reverend stood in front of the crowd and recited a eulogy about Ed. It was strange sitting there listening to this man talk about someone he knew nothing about.

After his template eulogy, he called on me to read a passage. I stood from my chair and looked around as I approached the pulpit. I couldn't believe my eyes—there were more people in the chapel than seats available. I proceeded toward the front of the chapel, Ed's open casket behind me.

I looked up at everyone and mentally thanked God for filling the place. I noticed Dad in the back of the chapel wiping his nose with his handkerchief and weeping. Betty was sitting behind a black, transparent curtain to my left. I pulled open a scroll, my hands shaking as I proceeded to read from it:

Jesus said, "Lazarus, our friend has gone to rest." I
say, Jerome my brother has gone to rest. So, when
the time comes, he will bring back my brother.
God says he will wipe out every tear from our
eyes, and death will be no more, the former things
have passed away. There will be a happier Ed
when I see him. I believe this, and I will miss him
until that day. I love you, Ed. I love you so much.

I looked behind me at the casket and stood there with this small glimpse of hope that he might rise, just like Lazarus did.

Afterward, a friend of Ed's from high school spoke about the sailing trip he went on with Ed, and then he sang a song. After a couple more eulogies, everyone lined up to see Ed's body one last time. The song "Sailing" by Christopher Cross played over the speakers as tears, sadness, and disbelief showed on faces of those who walked by Ed's casket.

Gerard had moved Dad closer, but Dad would not look in. He called me over. "Eddie, put this in his coffin." He handed me all these medals he got from fighting in the Korean War, including his Bronze Star. I laid them across Ed's motionless chest and rested my hand on his stomach. Andrew put his hand on my shoulder and then reached around and put a can of Copenhagen under Ed's jacket.

After everyone was done seeing him, the funeral director closed the casket and the pallbearers—Andrew, Tom, Butler, Ed's cousin Allen, Jimmy and I—assembled around the casket. We picked it up while a patrolman at the exit stood erect, tapped his heels, and saluted Ed's body as we proceeded outside, laying it gently inside the hearse.

Hazel held my hand as she led me to my car. We followed the hearse to the Willamette National Cemetery. I looked into my rearview mirror and saw the long line of cars behind me as we entered the cemetery through tall, gated pillars and continued up a hill. The cars parked along the nicely cut, green lawn.

Uniformed men held rifles not far from where Ed's casket lay inside a small, single-tier gazebo. We walked to the gazebo and Betty, Anita, Cathy, Ed's dad, and some of Betty's other relatives sat near the casket. It was the first time I had ever seen Buzz sober. In the gathered crowd, people I didn't know were everywhere, including an older man with a cowboy hat and a parrot on his shoulder. I thought, *Ed made friends with everyone he touched.*

Then the uniformed men fired several shots into the air. Afterward, an officer presented Betty with the United States flag and a last salute. A trumpet played "Taps" as we rested white carnations on the closed casket. Betty paused at the casket, lightly touching it as her weak, anguished body shed more tears over her son.

After the funeral, Ed's closest friends met at Tom's house to celebrate his life. It was strange knowing that Wallace Park would never be the same. I have a picture of that day and all of us standing on the driveway, happy to be together one last time. We were proud to be a part of Ed's life. I knew that, from that day on, Ed's spirit would reside in us and at Wallace Park.

Months after Ed's passing, I landed a new job at the Nike screen print department in Beaverton. Betty obtained a lawyer and tried to bring the man who killed Ed to justice, but the lawyer was a crook, profiting off her emotions and ripping her off for every last cent. Ed's death drained her mentally, physically, and financially. Eventually, she gave up the fight for answers and justice.

We all grieved Ed's loss differently. Andrew would drive to the cemetery and set near his gravesite a forty-ounce bottle of St. Ides. Betty grieved through the poems she wrote. One of them I found dear to my heart and still read to this day:

He consumed drugs & alcohol
got in his vehicle & drove away,
not far off, you were jogging
as you did at the start of every day.
A sad & stressed officer stood at my door,
my heart stopped,
I knew you wouldn't be coming home anymore.
The despair was so profound,
only the help of God got us through,

268

denial came, and a charade of
not believing this could be true.
You were so young,
so many plans ahead,
so much left undone.
He robbed you of your life;
he robbed me of my only son.
This man,
who thought he was having fun.
You left a lot of beautiful memories
that are in my heart to stay,
I love you my son
and I always will,
and miss you more than words can say.
Merry Christmas my angel,
I'll see you again someday.

***

It had been several months since Ed's death, and I had dealt with a lot of uncertainty about my life, but what I was certain of now was I wanted to marry Hazel. At the time, she was visiting her extended family in Peru. It was an opportunity for me to go to the Lloyd Center Mall and search for an engagement ring. I walked into a Wiesfield Jewelers and bargained with the salesman for a 14-karat gold band with a diamond solitaire I put on layaway.

After a month of waiting for Hazel to return, I showed up at the Portland airport to finally see her. I'd lost about eight pounds and wore my Levi's, a long-sleeved baby-blue shirt, loafers, and a new style haircut. When I saw her walk down the corridor, she was as flawless and beautiful as before she left.

"Hazel," I called as we happily rushed toward each other.

"Wow! You look great, and I look awful," she said, trying to brush her hair with her fingers.

"You don't look awful. You look beautiful!"

"No, I don't. I didn't even comb my hair and haven't taken a shower. The flight was an exhausting sixteen hours."

I held her hand. "You look fine to me." I had focused so much on Hazel that I had forgotten about Gladys and Doyle and said to them, "How was Peru?"

"Oh, Eddie, it was nice," Gladys answered in a euphoric tone. "I love my country, but I am glad to be home. You would love the markets with fresh fruits and vegetables there."

"You and Hazel are gonna have to go to Peru someday," Doyle added. "It's a beautiful country, especially seeing Machu Picchu."

I replied, "Yeah, I'd like to go one of these days."

Doyle began to speak about how beautiful the real Inca Trail and Urubamba River were, but even though I heard him speak, my thoughts were only about Hazel. It was like a wonderful dream to see her walk beside me, like she belonged to me.

A couple days later, I took her to Washington Park. It was evening, and we walked along the landscaped paths and sat on a nearby bench.

I said, "Hazel?"

"Yeah."

"Um, I love you very much and, well, you've been with me through thick and thin, and I can't see myself going through the rest of my life without you."

Hazel's eyes were focused deep into mine.

I gently held her hand and continued, "I was wondering if you'd like to marry me?"

"Yes," she replied happily. "Yes."

"'Yes,' you said?"

"Yes," she repeated softly, gently embracing me in her arms. "I love you, Eddie. I've always loved you."

***

On November 30, 1990, Doyle and Gladys joined us as we rushed down to a justice of the peace in Vancouver, Washington, deciding to later have a real wedding in March. We stayed at my dad's in North Portland until we saved enough money to move out.

One night while Hazel was sleeping, I walked into the living room and sat beside Dad. "What kind of jobs did Mom have?"

Dad waved his hands in the air and theatrically stated, "She worked in factories that paid little money, sweat shops. She worked hard. I tried to work extra hours so she didn't have to, but sometimes it wasn't easy. Once she worked in this garment factory center on Broadway in New York before you were born. She was making nothing for money, and her boss was robbing her till I figured out her paycheck wasn't right. I went back there and told him, 'Hey, man, you're robbing her. We gotta go to the National Labor Relations Board now.' The boss said, 'Relax. Relax. I'll give her the money we owe.' I said, "Yeah, don't do it again, man.' You see, Mom thought she was ignorant."

Dad paused, and I heard the ticking sound of his alarm clock and his breathing come through. "But do you know how smart you have to be to speak and write Spanish? And then be able to speak some English? Mom was smarter than I was. She was articulate like Hazel. That means she had brains! Mommy loved you guys. She would've liked Hazel too. God, she was always cleaning the house. By the time I got her into bed, even I was tired from just watching her clean. There was nights, man, I was

271

really wanting your mom, and she would say, 'Nope, first the house.'"

I laughed. "What about Mom's father? How was he?"

"He used to beat her!" Dad said angrily. "That was the kind of man he was. I don't know why. And he used to bring all kinds of women to live in his house."

"I thought he was married?"

"Mommy's real mother was Maria, your grandmother. He left Maria and brought in other women. I stood between them one day, and I was gonna beat his brains in. But your mother said, 'Please, Albert, don't do it.' But I told him, 'Man, you hit her again, I hear her scream, if there's any mark on her, I will beat you to death!'"

"You really told him that?"

"Oh yeah. I was ready to kill him! That was the woman I loved."

I chuckled. "And what'd he say?"

"He never touched her again. He hated me. He tried getting your mother not to marry me. But do you know, years later before he died, he said, 'I'm glad you married my daughter. You've been a good husband to her.' It was crazy! It took him over twenty years to realize I really loved his daughter. He thought I just wanted to sleep with her and leave her."

"Who is he to judge, bringing all those women in?" I said. "That's crazy."

"But still," Dad continued, "that was his way."

"What about her uncles?"

"I didn't know this about her uncle, but before your mom and me got married, she sat me down and said, 'Albert, would it make a difference if I wasn't a virgin?' I said, 'No, I'm in love with you! I would not have any life without you. My goodness! I'm not a virgin, *Santa*. I slept with every pig from here to Korea.'"

"Did you?" I asked, surprised.

"No, but at the time I figured the lie was better than the truth," he joked. "Anyway, I told her how much I loved her and it didn't matter. Then she told me how her uncle raped her when she was seven years old, and then we cried.

I remember we went to a dance by the East River Drive. "Your mother loved to dance to her music. Boy, she could dance. She made them hips move real beautifully, like a work of art. That woman knew how to move. The other guys in the neighborhood used to ask me, 'Hey, Al, let's go look for some *chiquitas*.' I'd say, hey, are you crazy! I got a wife at home who gets me more aroused than anything out in the street.

"I remember there were times when your mom looked at me and I would say, 'No, honey, I'm too tired right now,' but she had me goin', boy, twenty minutes working me over and she had me in the saddle. God, I loved that woman! That's why you'll never find another like the one you have, Eddie. You'll never find another Hazel."

"What about your career? I mean—"

"My career was work!" Dad stated dramatically. "That was my career—work!"

I laughed so hard when he said that.

"I worked twenty hours a day and did everything. Shoveled shit and coal, drove a cab or truck—I did everything. Your old man worked! What career? I had no education. That's why I tell you to learn as much as you can now. The one thing people will never be able to take away from you is your mind, Eddie. Don't you want to give Hazel a better life?"

"I do, Dad."

"Then do it," he said. "And when you're done with finding your career, you can give me a grandchild."

"No way. We ain't havin' no kids."

"Oh, you think so? Wait till that clock of hers starts ticking, then come back to me and say you're not gonna have any kids."

Chapter 27

Wedding Day Jitters

March 23, 1991, was our wedding day at Metzger Park Hall in Tigard, Oregon. I picked up Joey at the Greyhound station downtown. His bus came in late from San Jose, California, so when we got back to the house, I took a quick shower and practically threw my tuxedo on.

I was so nervous that, for the first time since I was a kid, I didn't know how to tie a tie. "Joey," I called. "Help me with this."

"Okay, hold on."

"No, now! I'm gonna be late, man."

He worked his fingers through my tie, saying, "Just think, five minutes of *I do* for a lifetime of *yes, honey*."

"I can't believe I'm getting married."

"How do you feel?" Joey asked.

"Feels pretty weird, especially knowing it's Hazel. I never would've thought."

"Yeah, man, she's gonna be telling you to do the dishes, clean the laundry. Your bachelor days are over. It's gonna be house arrest!"

"No, it won't. This is a good thing, Joe. Don't you ever think about settling down? You can't just keep jumping from one love to another. Besides, there are all kinds of diseases out there, man. I knew Hazel was the one. Why else would we have seen each other at Wallace Park that day?"

"But I like my freedom!"

I set my hand on Joey's shoulder. "How do you know there's no freedom in marriage?" I said. "It's just a different kind of freedom, Joe. It unshackled me from a sadness I had been feeling a long time. You'll see. You'll get married someday."

"No, I won't."

I chuckled and nodded. "Yeah, you will!"

We got into to my car and sped off, weaving in and out of traffic, trying to get to the wedding on time.

Joey urged, "You better slow down if you wanna get there at all."

I took a few deep breaths and had to stop at a gas station to ask an attendant where Metzger Park Hall was. When we got there, I rushed out of my car and into the building, noticing the guests scattered inside the hall.

"Hey, Eddie! Where've you been?" Michael asked. "We're all waiting for you."

"Joey's bus came in late."

"Well, you're lucky. Hazel's not ready."

I walked into the auditorium searching for Ed's picture. I'd asked Hazel's parents to dedicate a table to him, and I finally spotted it. His photo was framed with the passage

There is a friend who sticks closer than a brother.

Also on the table were flower arrangements and photo albums of Hazel and me when we were kids. Betty was sitting in the crowd, so I made my way to her. "Hi, Mom. I'm glad to see you here."

"My sweet son, I wouldn't miss this for the world."

"Did you see Ed's photo on the table?"

"Yes, that's the sweetest thing you could ever do. I'm so proud of you, Eddie."

"I love you very much, Mom."

"I love you too, sweetie."

I worked my way over to Dad. "How you doing?"

He said, "Give me a hug."

I did and then asked, "So whatta you think of everything?"

"Hey, man, it looks great! Doyle and Gladys did a great job decorating this place."

"Yeah, I think so too."

"Now, if only Joey could get married," he said. "Hey, look over there."

"Where?"

"Over there on the table by the cake," he said, pointing at a large bottle of Martini & Rossi champagne. "That's what I wanna taste, the good stuff."

"Sure, Dad. When we open it, I'll make sure you get some," I said, giving him another hug.

"Okay, don't forget." He looked up and gave me a proud smile.

"I won't, Dad." Then I added sarcastically, "I like your haircut." Dad sometimes cut his own hair, but this time it looked like he'd cut it with a blender.

The wedding was about to begin, and everyone sat down. I stood by the judge and anxiously waited for my soon-to-be wife to walk down the aisle.

The "Wedding March" started, and I suddenly saw Hazel's beauty move toward me. She looked as pure as the dress she gracefully wore. I couldn't take my eyes off her and wished time could stand still. Her white dress and Peruvian skin shone as if she had been sent down just for me. It was confirmation of how close true love had been all this time. I began to think how fortunate I was and understood what Dad meant when he'd said, "You'll never find another like her."

277

Hazel's nephew carried the rings on a small, white silk pillow. Hazel and I faced each other, and the judge went through the traditional wedding speech.

"Do you, Hazel, take Eddie to be your husband, in sickness or health, for richer or poorer, till death do you part?"

"I do."

He looked to me. "And you, Eddie. Do you take Hazel to be your wife, in sickness or health, for richer or poorer, till death do you part?"

"Absolutely."

"You may kiss the bride."

I gently lifted the veil over her head and kissed her softly. The judge had us face the crowd and announced, "Everyone, meet Edward and Hazel Regory."

The crowd clapped as we walked back up the aisle. The reception started, and the photographer took pictures of us almost everywhere we went. Hazel's uncle, who later started Big Kahuna's BBQ in North Portland, laid out a spread fit for gods, but I don't remember eating a thing.

Around midnight, I held Hazel's hand in mine, and we proceeded to walk out the front entrance. Michael called, "What are you doin', bozo? You're supposed to carry the bride out the door!"

I was so excited about getting married, I'd forgotten to carry her. "Oh, shoot! I'm sorry, babe." I took her hand in mine and briskly walked her back in. I kissed her once and said, "I'll do it right this time!" I picked her up and carried her out the doors.

"Aren't I heavy?" Hazel asked.

"No, this is great for the arms. I think," I said, mimicking a line from *Rocky*.

I carried her to the car as some of the guests and family followed. There was a large, yellow cardboard sign on the inside of the back window and big letters that read:

Just Married! Balloons and strings were strung to several cans dangling off the license plate.

I carefully set Hazel down and opened the passenger door. She was slipping into her seat when Doyle rushed out and said, "Eddie?"

"Yeah?"

"Here, take this Visa card and go to a nice hotel."

"Are you sure?"

"Yeah, you guys have a good time."

"Thanks, Doyle. I really appreciate it!"

As poor as I was, I was glad for the card—otherwise we would've gone back home. We drove to the Embassy Suites Hotel in Tigard and got a nice room with champagne. We walked down the hallway to our room, and as I opened the door, someone yelled from two floors up, "You gotta carry her in!"

Hazel smiled.

It was all so new to me, and I felt like a heel for screwing it up. I carried her in and yelled up to the guy, "Yo, thanks!"

"No problem. I forgot on my wedding night too," he replied, as his friends laughed.

The next morning we had a continental breakfast and left for Seaside and an oceanfront cabin for our honeymoon. I'd wanted to take her to Hawaii, but I couldn't afford it.

Chapter 28

Final Lessons

I was now twenty-eight years old, and Hazel and I lived off of Murray Road in Beaverton in the Reflections at Summer Creek apartment complex. Dad still relied on us to take care of him, so it was a big change for him when we left. He also had heart problems and often took medicine for it.

One night I got a call from a lady named Susan, a friend of the family and Dad's current caretaker.

"Eddie, something's wrong with your dad."

"Whatta you mean?"

"That's what I'm trying to tell you. He's had a heart attack."

"Did you call the ambulance?"

"I did," she said. "The paramedics are here."

"I'll be there right away!" I yelled, hanging up the phone. "Hazel! My dad had a heart attack. We gotta go!"

When we got within two blocks, I noticed flashing lights everywhere. We parked the car and saw a van bigger than an ambulance with my dad in it. He was slightly incoherent as he gazed at me through a window.

"Hey! Can I go with him?" I asked a paramedic.

"Are you a family member?"

"I'm his son."

"Well, we don't quite have enough room, but you can follow us."

"Okay. Is he okay?"

"At this point, we're not sure. You'll be informed when we get him to the hospital."

The paramedic closed the doors, and the van quickly drove away. I felt compelled to do something that would help Dad remember me if he were to die on the way to the hospital. I started to dance in the street, making a funny face at him. He smiled, which gave me some uncertain assurance that everything would be okay. We followed the van to the emergency center at Emanuel Medical Center in Northeast Portland. Gerard, Joey, Michael, and Anna showed up later. They put Dad in a room, and after hours of waiting, the doctor finally came out.

"Hi, are you his family?"

"Yes, we're his sons," Gerard answered, quickly rising from his chair.

"Your father is stable for now, but we'd like to keep him here for a few nights." He escorted us to Dad, not far from the waiting room.

"Hey, Dad," I said, happy to see him. "How you feel?"

"Oh, I feel okay."

"Man, you put a big scare in me."

The family hugged him.

A nurse came in and said, "Hello, Mr. Regory. We're going to take you to your room now."

Dad looked up at the nurse and asked, "Have you seen that movie *The Doctor*?"

She smiled. "No, I can't say that I have."

"Man, that was a good movie," Dad said. "I think every doctor should see it."

The rest of us grinned. I was hungry, so I left to find a vending machine. When I passed the nurses' station,

I overheard a receptionist say to another, "Did you see that guy in the wheelchair? He was huge."

I turned to see who it was and noticed that she was also very fat. I really wanted to insult her, but I remembered I'd promised I would never make fun of people like they did to Dad.

Days passed, and Dad was not getting better. They transferred him to another room. It was eleven a.m. when Hazel and I arrived at the hospital and saw him sitting up on the bed with IVs attached to his arm.

I kissed him on the cheek and asked, "How you feeling, Dad?"

"I feel okay," he replied with a wheeze.

I sat in a chair close to his bed and looked out the window to the parking lot below. "Nice view."

"Yeah, it's okay."

I glanced over to the IVs, which were putting iron into his body. "Is that helping any?"

"Oh, yeah, man. It's a lot better."

"Dad, you need to eat better when you get out of here."

"I know, son," he sighed. "I'm my own worst enemy."

I reached my hand over to his and quietly said, "Dad, you've made your mistakes, but I love you very much. I love you for being there when I needed you the most."

He brought his head down and, in a soft-spoken voice, said, "I'm so embarrassed."

"Why?"

"'Cause I peed myself."

I said, with a funny expression, "Now you went too far, Dad. Whatta you expect me to do with that? Don't be embarrassed."

Dad paused. "You've grown to be a fine young man. I miss your mother."

"I miss her too."

"Joey's new girlfriend, Risa, is great, isn't she?"

"Yeah, She'll be real good for Joey if he ever marries her."

"Whatever happens, Eddie, help your sister out. Ever since your mom died, she was never the same. Take care of her, son. Please."

"I will, Dad."

I walked to the chalkboard and started drawing my favorite cartoon, a mouse with a Sombrero hat.

"My son the artist."

"I'm no artist."

"Oh, yes you are," Hazel said confidently. "You're my talented husband."

The doctor came in. "How is everyone today?"

"Good, doctor," Dad replied.

"Well, I don't mean to rush you off, but your father could use some rest."

"Okay, doc," I said. "Dad, do you need me to wash your clothes?"

"Over there on the floor."

I hugged and kissed him and tried to memorize his scent and facial features so I wouldn't forget. "I love you, Dad."

Dad said, "Hazel, you've been great to Eddie. Thank you."

She said, hugging him, "We'll come back later."

Hazel respected my dad because he treated her intelligently and "like a queen," she would say. He was very much like a father to her. The doctor brought us a bag to put my dad's soiled clothes in.

"Thank you, doctor."

In my heart, I was thanking him for treating Dad like a human being. Joey stayed in the waiting room while

I drove back to Dad's house. There were blankets on the floor caked with cornstarch, and the house was a mess.

Hazel raged, "I can't believe it. Susan came in to take care of him and didn't even clean this house. God, that pisses me off!"

"I know, babe. I know. Let's just get this cleaned up, and I'll take his clothes to the Laundromat."

I washed all of his blankets, underwear, and soiled pants. When I got back, Hazel was outside mowing the lawn. She knew Dad loved a cut lawn.

When we got back to his hospital room, I said, "Dad, we washed your clothes and cleaned the house. Oh, yeah, and I mowed the lawn."

"*You* mowed the lawn?" Hazel said, surprised. "Yeah, right."

Dad said, "He's jiving me, ain't he?"

"Yeah, he's jiving," Hazel replied.

Dad felt tired, so I hugged him and said, "I'll let you get some sleep."

We later headed to my place, and Joey, Risa, and her five-year-old son, Tyler, came along. I put in a movie to try to get our minds off Dad, but by looking at everyone, it was obvious that's all we could think about.

On Sunday, April 10, 1994, at about eleven a.m., Hazel and I went back to the hospital's waiting room, where we saw Gerard. He had just relieved Michael from being there all night.

"Good, you guys are here."

"How's Dad?" I asked.

"He's resting now. He always needs to know someone is here for him, but I need to go back to work."

We walked into his room. It seemed like Dad was doing better—or maybe I was in denial that these were his last days. He saw me and began to get into his joking mood I've loved all my life.

"Hey, guys. Did you have me a grandchild yet?"

"No, Dad, not today. How do you feel?"

"I feel okay. I'm sick of all the blood they keep squeezing outta me. You'd think they were selling it or something."

"Now you know how I felt when I was in the hospital," I said. "It sucked!"

"Whatta you guys doing today?" Dad said. "Why don't you go out and have a good time?"

"Whatta you mean?" I said. "We're gonna be here all day."

"You don't need to be here. Go out and have fun. I'll be okay."

"I don't think so, Dad."

Hazel said, "We like being here with you, Al."

"I'm just a boring, fat, old man."

We talked and joked, and eventually I left for a walk through the hospital. For hours I aimlessly paced the hallways, waiting and praying for a miracle.

At about four thirty, I walked in to see Dad again, and this time he was breathing hard in his sleep. I saw Joey walking my way.

"Joey, Hazel and I are going home. You're gonna stay here all night, right?"

"Yeah, I am bro. You go home."

When we got home, I couldn't eat or sleep. I thought about my dad's scent, the blue cotton hat he rarely took off, and all the funny times we'd had together—how his melodramatic personality was always humorous to everyone who knew and loved him.

The following Monday, I had about four hours' sleep and went to work. All I wanted was to be with Dad. I couldn't focus on my job while I was waiting for an update call from the hospital. I got sick of waiting and called the hospital's waiting room.

"Joe, is Dad okay?"

"Yeah, he's still breathing hard, though."

"You must be tired, bro."

"Yeah, I am, but Gerard should be here."

"Well, I'm gonna be there after work." I was happy everything was still okay.

At eleven thirty, I called again.

"Hello?" Michael answered with a deep, firm voice.

"Hey, Mike. How's Dad doing?"

"Eddie, get down here!"

"Why?"

"Dad died!"

My heart was at a total stop. It was the same stop I'd felt when Ed passed.

"When?"

"Just get down here."

"I'm leaving now!" I said, hanging up the phone.

I couldn't think straight and quickly walked toward the exit. I saw my manager in passing and said, "I'm leaving."

I peeled out of the parking lot and raced through a stop sign. I began to feel the same daze I'd felt when Ed died. Unaware of my surroundings, I began to think, *Eddie, calm down. Just be calm. If you wreck this car, you'll never see Dad. Relax, Eddie, relax.*

I finally crossed the Fremont Bridge, took the Kerby Avenue exit, and screeched into the hospital parking lot. I rushed out of the car and started to feel dizzy, but I sprinted toward the entrance of the hospital, my legs feeling heavier and heavier until I could no longer run.

I wanted to cry, but tears wouldn't come. After nervously stepping out of the elevator, I saw Susan crying. Joey was trying to comfort her when he motioned me to Dad's room.

When I pulled open the curtain, every bone in my body was weak from the pain in my heart. I froze, unable to tear my eyes away from Dad's partially opened mouth and still, obese body.

That's when I cried, silently. I wanted to be strong because, even at the end, that's the way Dad would have wanted it. I cleared my throat, softly laid my hand on his forehead, and quietly said, "Now you're in peace, Dad. Now you'll be with Mom."

There was a sense of tranquility in the room, and Dad really did look like he was sleeping. I wiped the tears from my face and walked out of the room, trying not to feel angry, but it was all I knew how to feel.

I walked slowly into the lobby, pressing my head against the window and staring down at the people and cars. I tried to remember all the good things Dad had shared with me, but for some reason, I couldn't. What I did remember was the spirit he once shared: love, joy, peace, long suffering, kindness, goodness, and faith. It was all I had left in me to keep it together.

Dad was to be put to rest at the same place as Ed was. We parked along the grassy hill, walked a few feet, and saw a forklift elevate the casket off the back bed of a truck then lower it into a huge cement box.

Naomi, Michael's daughter, asked, "How's Papa gonna breathe?"

I wanted to pick her up and hold her tight in my arms. Dad's death was unbearable for me, and I couldn't imagine what she was going through.

Michael hugged Naomi and said, "Papa's just sleeping right now."

The next day, Joey and I removed all of Dad's belongings from the house. I perused his stuff and found a tape by the empty milk jug he used to urinate in because it was difficult for him to go to the bathroom. I played the tape and heard Dad's last words to his family.

When you hear this, I will be gone. But I wanna leave something behind for you guys. I never could give you the wealthy things Mom wanted to give ya—the nicer things in life. I failed you all—Mom never failed you. But I do love you guys!

Michael, you've grown to be a fine man. You're doing a good job. Continue serving and loving God. And continue being honest to your wife. To bend when it hurts, bend some more. Love your children. Do what you can for them. Promise them nothing, 'cause promises can be broken. Take care of them; lead them so they have a safe life.

Gerard, we always called you the peacemaker. You were the one Mom called on to make peace between the family. She loved you like she loved all of you. I'm sorry I couldn't bury her right. I know that hurt you. I don't know what happened to me then. I didn't want it to come out that way. I was so confused; I didn't know. Please forgive me.

Anna, my daughter, my only daughter. I've always loved you. How I always wanted to hold you and hug you and listen to what was hurting you inside. I don't know, I guess I'll never find out. But I hope you can settle it between God and yourself.

Eddie, you're married now, and you've got a wife to take care of. You've gotta bend too, Eddie, you've gotta love. It's love you gotta give, not gifts; that's nice, but you've gotta love, you've gotta bend. Talk to her gently. She's precious! She's a gift from God to you. You'll never get another one in your lifetime. You're good in the heart, Eddie. You have a lot of kindness and a lot of dreams, and I know someday you'll make it because I've always believed in you.

Joey, you make me proud! And I know it's none of my doing. I'm proud of you, Joey. I'm proud of all my children. You've grown to love God, and God looks into the heart—there's where it counts.

Rachael and Naomi, I want to leave this. Maybe you won't remember your grandfather when you grow older, but I love you two, and I know you'll grow up to be fine women, because your mother and father are fine. You may not be foolish in your ways, for there'll be much wisdom given to you two from your family and from God.

As for me, I've tried to be the best I could and to be the kind of father my family wanted. I never fought real hard. I never even tried. I wanted to die so much because I missed your mother. I loved her very much. I've made my mistakes 'cause I was young and foolish and stupid. I was meant to be alone so I couldn't hurt people. It seemed like all the ones I love seem to have hurt. I'm sorry, fellas! I'm sorry for not being the way you guys wanted me to be.

But never forget this: I do love you all and prayed for you constantly. If we're fortunate, we will see each other again, and that'll be a joyous time. Because like God said, "There will be no more pain, no more crying, no more mourning, and no more suffering." Jesus never spoke a lie. That was the truth. So I don't know when or how long it will take, but I believe in all my heart that we will see each other again. I don't know what else to tell you guys. You guys help one another and love one another to the very end of time.

So where I am, well, maybe we'll see each other as long as we believe. Goodbye, all of you, and may God bless all of you.

One day I sat down to watch *Rocky* and thought about all the Apollo Creeds I'd fought in my life. At the end of the fight, I became a champion. I won because I gained a family and a best friend who loved me unconditionally—and the life I realized I was meant to have. I will no longer strive into the wind to find what isn't there. Instead, I've learned to keep what I have and to be thankful for each day. I want my tomorrow to be with those I love, and I continue my journey as the same giant to my daughter as my father was once to me. Life has new meaning now and so do the riches that come with it. It just took me a long time to see it.

Never, ever forget that the only time you were poor
is when you didn't know how rich you were.
—*Albert Regory*

A Note from the Author

I will always remember the voice of my mother's prayers for a better place to live. We found that place when we moved to Portland, Oregon. There were times when I felt I couldn't finish this memoir, as I hoped to bring out the lives of those who played a significant role in my life. I try to live life to the fullest, to appreciate it, and to be thankful that every day I wake is another day I get to enjoy with my family.

I hope you enjoy this book. But most of all, I thank you for your support in achieving my dream to be a writer. Thanks for reading.

Edmond Jerome

Hey Ed,

I just wanted you to know that you were right; that day we met at Couch Park did happen for a reason. I'm now married to Hazel and I named my son after you. He's awesome. He has my nose and Hazel's eyes. You would really love him. He's everything a father could want in a son and more. And Eliana my daughter, she always asks about you. She's also a gem. Every night I fall asleep I think of you. Until the next time we ride our bikes, play with ferrets, throw footballs at Wallace Park or go jogging through the Portland streets, I'll catch up with you later, bro.

Love,

Your brother, Eddie